In a most engaging narrative style, Pro modern educators and the developmer personal, cultural, and historical perspe... .... ideas to those of Fethullah Gülen, a highly influential educator of today who draws on an entirely different tradition.

Open-minded, yet with strong commitments of his own, Gage ably transcends cultural barriers to compare Gülen and educators of the western 'canon.' The result is to reduce the potential for alienation between practitioners of different traditions and to increase the likelihood of fruitful cooperation.

Tom Gage's balanced, well-structured, and immensely readable account comprises a thorough scholarly contribution to culture, education, community service, and resources for global understanding and peaceful coexistence.

— Muhammed Cetin, PhD is the author of
*The Gülen Movement: Civic Service without Borders and
Hizmet: Questions and Answers on the Hizmet Movement*

This sweeping work reminds us of the achievements of the West's great educational thinkers and connects them to Gülen's ideas and accomplishments that have arisen in the east and have spread throughout the world.

— Dr Paul M. Rogers
George Mason University

In an extraordinarily rich and ambitious work, Professor Tom Gage compares, and at times contrasts, the educational theories of Fethullah Gülen, the Turkish Sufi scholar and theologian, to those of a spate of modern educational theorists, among them Jean Piaget, Marie Montesori, John Dewey, Benjamin Bloom, Alexander Maslow, Kurt Hahn, Lem Vgotsky, Albert Bandura, and James Moffett.

Gülen, chosen in 2013 by Time magazine as one of the most influential leaders in the world, believes that parents and teachers should serve as role models of ethical principles and spiritual values. Gülen's influence has been profound: His followers have founded non-denominational schools in 140 countries, including the United States, in which students are implicitly taught moderation, cooperation, and moral values.

One can find no better introduction to the educational beliefs of Fethullah Gülen and no better review of the theories of modern educational theorists than Gülen's Dialogue and Education Caravanserai.

 —Dr. Edmund J. Farrell
  Professor Emeritus of English Education
  The University of Texas at Austin

Gülen's
Dialogue on Education

To Ammerah,
    Dear Friend, I so
look forward to another
SKYPE.
        Best,
        Tom Gage
        10/21/13

Gülen's Dialogue on Education

A Caravanserai of Ideas

Tom Gage, PhD

Gülen's Dialogue on Education:
A Caravanserai of Ideas
© 2014 Tom Gage
Cune Press, Seattle 2014
First Edition
2 4 6 8 9 7 5 3

Hardback ISBN 978-1-61457-072-1 $34.95
Paperback ISBN 978-1-61457-073-8 $21.95
eBook ISBN 978-1-61457-074-5 $9.99

Library of Congress Cataloging-in-Publication Data

Gage, Tom.
Gülen's dialogue on education: a caravanserai of ideas / Tom Gage, PhD.
pages cm.
Includes bibliographical references and index.
ISBN 978-1-61457-072-1 (hardback : alk. paper) -- ISBN 978-1-61457-073-8
(pbk. : alk. paper)
1. Gülen, Fethullah. 2. Education--Philosophy. I. Title.

LB880.G762G34 2013
370.1--dc23

2013025682

Select titles in the Bridge Between the Cultures Series:
Syria - A Decade of Lost Chances
Repression and Revolution from Damascus Spring to Arab Spring - by Carsten Wieland

The Ottoman Mosaic: Exploring Models for Peace by Re-exploring the Past
by Kemal Karpat and Yetkin Yıldırım

Steel & Silk: Men and Women Who Shaped Syria 1900 - 2000 - by Sami Moubayed

A Pen of Damascus Steel: The Political Cartoons of an Arab Master - by Ali Farzat

The Road from Damascus: A Journey Through Syria - by Scott C. Davis

www.cunepress.com | www.cunepress.info

Contents

Preface 8

Introduction: From Averroes to Voltaire and Kant to Gülen:
Exchanges in a Caravanserai of Ideas 12

1 Pragmatism: Gülen Viewed from Dewey's Century 19

2 Pedagogy, Explicit & Implicit:
  Montessori and Gülen Methodologies 31

3 Research: Gülen's Ideas on
  Schooling in the Vygotskian Tradition 42

4 Outdoor Education as a Third Space:
  Compatibility of Gülen and Hahn 55

5 Genetic Epistemology:
  Jean Piaget & Fethullah Gülen* 67

6 Domains of Knowledge: Gülen and Benjamin Bloom 80

7 Bandura and Gülen:
  Social Modeling, Cognition, and Self-Efficacy 93

8 Holism: Gülen and Moffett's Universe of Discourse 106

9 Culture and Social Contextualism 119

10 Conclusion 130

Endnotes 138

Index 167

*Co-authored with Laura Rose

Preface

THE AUTHOR AIMS TO PROVIDE new information for interested readers about how Mr. Gülen's wisdom is congruent with well-known education philosophers, researchers, and pedagogues. Before discussing *Gülen's Dialogue on Education: a Caravanserai of Ideas*, I should acquaint the reader with my experiences in education and with Turkey. After my sophomore year at Berkeley, I stopped out a year to travel in 1957. Unlike schooling, hitchhiking requires improvisation. Until the car stops, you don't know for sure where you are going. I often changed intended destinations: rather than Paris, I'd wind up in Toulouse; instead of Naples, a Korean correspondent corrected my inquiry outside Rome, "No, I go Seoul, Korea." That's how in 1959 I found myself on the Syrian/Iraq border, as my ride had decided to ship his VW and fly home from Beirut. I'd spent close to six months in the Middle East, traversing Turkey and eventually returning to Europe by way of Egypt. A quarter century later in a troubled year, 1983-1984, I taught in Syria, a Fulbright Scholar in American Studies at University of Aleppo, close to the Syrian-Turkish border.

Berkeley in 1957 was auspicious. I had the honor of hearing on campus and then meeting Martin Luther King, Jr. Later that year, I met, through a job working at San Francisco's Bohemian Club, former Ambassador to Brazil, James Kemper, an acquaintance that latter led to a scholarship and career opportunities. The two meetings shaped my future, like a ride on the autostrata. Finishing my BA, I passed up a CEO-training position as assistant to the president of Kemper Insurance in Chicago in order to teach at an inner-city school in my hometown Oakland, California. My travels, meeting the leader of the Civil Rights movement, and JFK's "Ask not what your country can do for you; ask instead what you can do for your country" influenced my choice of rides over this journey of a half-century, which fittingly led me to meeting a King-like figure in Mr. Gülen. Reading words of encouragement to pursue service rather than to "follow the money" attuned with thoughts from the 1950s and 1960s.

During the last half century, I continued to way fare around the world, including long sojourns in Turkey and the Eastern Mediterranean—lands, peoples, and cultures that I deeply love. As a tourist, lecturer, and scholar in Turkey, I have met many people and enjoyed hospitality during periods of disruption and growth. While in Ankara in 1959, I witnessed the return of Prime Minister Adnan Menderes, who ironically had avoided death from an airplane crash departing Gatwick only to be hanged a few years later by the generals. I was in Istanbul in 1980 when for the third time since becoming a Republic the military expunged a democratically elected government. From 1985 until his death, I was a friend of Çelik Gülersoy, Director of Turin Kubulu, the one most responsible for the earliest restorations of Ottoman splendor and gentrification of Istanbul. The family of a retired judge befriended my wife and me with the use of their villa for several summers in Bodrum. We met representatives of various political and ideological positions—imams, doctors, academics, former military personal, and a princess. Yet, only in 2007 at a conference in Austin, Texas, did I first learn of Fethullah Gülen and the Hizmet Movement. In none of my trips have I been a guest of any of the *Hizmet*-sponsored tours of Anatolia, education excursions so kindly arranged for many Americans to visit that wonderful land.

My academic credentials are not in Middle Eastern studies nor am I hopefully what Edward Said coined "an Orientalist."[1] As world events increasingly captured the attention of a media that misinforms about a world and people I love, I created and taught many courses at Humboldt State University that I felt needed inclusion in curriculum. A hitchhiker, I'm a *de facto* scholar. With three degrees from Berkeley, I've never majored in English, yet rapidly earned by deed the rank of full professor in that department; I'm what Gülen calls an "*aksiyon insan*"—that is someone who actualizes their ethos.

I have participated as speaker and/or facilitator at several Gülen conferences, held at the University of Erasmus in Rotterdam, The University of Texas, Louisiana State University, the University of Southern California, Santa Clara University, the University of Houston, Temple University and the Peace Islands Institute, co-sponsored with Yale, Baruch College, and Quinnipiac University. The subjects of these papers include rhetorical theory, Rumi, and methodologies to advance cross-cultural fluency among students around the world to foster mutual understanding and good will. For a number of years, I have chaired the Youth Platform of the Gülen Institute, Houston, Texas. In 2012 thirty-seven secondary school authors with chaperones, winners from sixty-five nations and twelve US states assembled in Washington DC to receive awards and certificates of merit from Congresspersons and ambassadorial representatives at the Rayburn Building. The funding for this, plus a day trip to the UN in New York, came from donations of Turkish Americans and others moved by the words and inspiration of Fethullah Gülen.

I am not a Muslim, though two of my sons-in-law are, and my three grandsons are half-Arab. I have enjoyed the company of many Muslims over my career, Sunni and Shia, Alevi and Alewi. Martin Luther King, Jr. and Fethullah Gülen book-ended my career. I am impelled to do what

I can for my county to better understand a part of a world and a religion that since after 9/11 its citizens so gravely misunderstand and view as monolithic. As the World's superpower, the US cannot afford such lazy Manichean categories of good guys and bad guys; if it does, its tenure will be brief compared to that of the British Empire. Winston Churchill observed during World War II that it governed the world's most populated Muslim state as it had since Queen Victoria. The United States lacks such a heritage, and that lack plays into the hands of both al-Qaeda and Western bigots chanting class of cultures nonsense. Those in the U.S., who ignore the Gülen Movement, imperil world peace to the joy of fanatics.

Hoja Effendi is a Muslim humanist, a scholar of Sufism. Though Humanism is a term coined only in the last two hundred years, it frames an intellectual heritage that posits a philosophy predicated upon the conviction that people can improve themselves by establishing belief systems that venerate reason, tolerance, and openness to dialogue.[2] This role is not unlike that of Maimonides who, during the Middle Ages, resolved tensions in *Guide for the Perplexed* between law and reality for Judaism. Of late, humanism has been narrowly associated with atheism, but since its heritage dates back to Pico Della Mirandola, it has always been grounded in religion and classical authors, most of those Greek works that reached Pico, were translated and commented upon by Islamic scholars of the Maghreb and al-Andalusia. Perhaps, Pico today would be shocked that a fellow traveler of humanism is a Turkish Sufi, but Pico would be more resonant with F. Gülen's faith convictions than he would be with the atheism of Jean Paul Sartre.

Gülen's philosophy derives from an earlier palimpsest of humanism, ignored largely by the Eurocentric academy, a humanism deriving from multiculturalism of the dhimma or millet, which afforded tolerant communities with grounding in reading the Book. With the fall of Constantinople, the Gutenberg press imprinted European paranoia with the moniker, the "Terrible Turk." Later, with Europe emerging out of millennium of torpor, the West for the next half millennium embedded mental "structures of reference and of aesthetic" that vilified this Other, the Turk and Islam.[3] Today, in our global village, Muslim intellectuals like Gülen have helped us demythologize such provincialisms so that we can acknowledge our debt to the Middle East, to a heritage that accounts an influence nearly equaling that of Rome.

This book would never have come about had it not been for the San Francisco's Rock Rose Institute, which held a conference in 2007, at which I met Dr Yetkin Yıldırım. Dr Yıldırım prompted me to engage in this project and tirelessly assisted me in completing the project. I am no less appreciative of Dr Y. Alp Aslandoğan, President of Interfaith Dialogue Institute, who foremost guided this project to fruition. I am also deeply appreciative of Ms Janet Crane, whose editing I have often relied upon, and to Laura Rose for her scholarship on Jean Piaget. I am indebted to Dr Bruce Novak, scholar of Dewey and author of *Literacy and Wisdom: "Being the Book" and "Being the Change*.[4] Equally, I am beholden to Dr James Davis, University of Northern Iowa, career friend, who, as the leader with the longest tenure as a director in National Writing Project network provided depth and crucial insights into how transactionalism bridges with Gülen's vision. Thanks, too, to Kevin Miller, Jr., instructor in several Gülen-inspired schools in Central and Southeast Asia, for his help on Maria Montessori. My good friend and publisher Scott C. Davis has been outstanding as a colleague. I also thank my comrade Miles Myers, former Executive Secretary of the National Council of Teachers of English, with whom I began teaching in 1961. And to even older friends, I thank John and Cynthia McGuinn, whose love and substantial support of Gülen-related projects enabled international students to participate in the 2012 Your Platform in Washington DC. But above all, my wife Anita, whose tireless support accounts for so much of my achievement: thank you.

Authoring *Gülen's Dialogue on Education* entailed the services of a number of other Turkish scholars, Dr Sait Yavus, Dr Ozer Ozgur, Dr Adam, and Dr Kurt Erkan, to name a few. Our efforts to explain how writings of F. Gülen resonate with foundational theorists of education have required fair use of copyrighted materials to advance knowledge for the public. Every effort has been expended to attribute sources of information. If in the fluidity and plasticity of digital utterances, some information of others appears unattributed, the author apologizes. To write is to forward knowledge that since before Aristotle describes and explains how the world ticks; in recent centuries these expressions have become grounded in property rights. Law understandably should protect these. Yet, even more recently, digitization and the waning of the idea, or ideal of the creative genius, has tested denotations of originality, as drop-and-drag, copy-and-paste supersede inkwell and quill pen. We compose from a heteroglossic fog. The subjects of originality and copyright warrants exploring Steven Johnson's appeal for reform and recognition of peer-to-peer resourcefulness in his *Future Perfect: The Case for Progress in a Networked Age*.[5]

From Averroes to Voltaire and Kant to Gülen

A Caravanserai of Ideas

Introduction

Viewing the *Otogar* on the Asian side of the Bosporus, one can imagine beneath its present activities an ancient Turkish caravanserai. Here is a palimpsest of history where merchants converge, as they have converged since Homer, to await arrival of Europe-bound ferries. This caravanserai has been transformed beyond immediate recognition by modernity and celerity. Busses, cars, vendors, and pedestrians await, some out of the rain munching on sesame-encrusted *simits*, others thumbing through newspapers, still others helping the crippled traverse barriers of this temporary sanctuary, a refuge that in its past offered shelter, rest, sustenance, and community before the next stage of life's journey.

Now, from a satellite in Space, view Earth:

A doctor performing free cardiac surgery in Kenya.

An architect designing a school building for refugee children in Darfur.

A woman organizing community efforts to provide aid to Haitian victims of the earthquake.

A student from humble background becoming world champion in the International Physics Olympiad.

An educator teaching in perilous conditions in Afghanistan.

A plumbing manufacturer from South East Turkey financing a school in Cambodia.

An entrepreneur committing resources and time to support

a conference in Holland at which scholars of many countries deliver papers on violence and peaceful reconciliation.

A newly built school in Southeast Turkey north of the Iraq border with teachers instructing Kurdish youths, some of whose older siblings recruited by terrorist groups.

A poor student from rural Black Sea, who arrived in Istanbul lacking academic skills, receiving assistance that helped him to transition into university, and who is now completing his PhD in American literature.

The informed space traveler would know that M. Fethullah Gülen inspired these social, cultural, charitable, and educational activities, the latter of which is the subject of this book.

Fethullah Gülen

Yes, Gülen over the last four decades has inspired people to actualize the objectives portrayed in these vistas of a *Hizmet* caravanserai. First in Turkey and then throughout the world, dedicated people have chosen not to pursue the highest paying jobs but to address needs and then to secure funding from the business community and philanthropists for projects to address those needs. This combination of will and funding serve many of the older functions of a caravanserai, shelter, sanctuary, safety, and sociability during life's transit. Turks and those from countries beyond Anatolia hearing and reading the words of this intellectual have become committed as aksiyon insanları to benefit today's global commonweal.

The word *Hizmet* translates in English as "service." Both Dr Helen Rose Ebaugh[1] and Dr Muhammed Çetin[2] have enumerated a range of enterprises from radio stations to cooperatives, disaster relief organizations, health therapy, banking, and building construction, all recipients of the wisdom of this Turkish mentor to help, care for, shelter, inform, reconcile, finance, and educate in the spirit of caravanserai. It is likely that because of these activities an international survey in 2008 ranked Gülen the world's number one living intellectual and in 2013 *Time* included him as one of a hundred most influential persons alive.[3][4]

In his seventies, this philosophical theologian, influenced by Sufism, has spent much of his career encouraging the establishment of new schools and reformation of education in Turkey to become more responsive to and integrated with local communities. Dr B. Jill Carroll situates Gülen in the humanistic tradition by juxtaposing his thoughts on education, freedom, responsibility, the ideal human, inherent human value, and moral dignity with those of Confucius, Plato, Kant, Sartre, and Mill.[5] Some critics fear that education and curriculum inspired by a Muslim might advance religion but such assertions have been soundly refuted (Solberg, 2005).[6] Others have found that these schools worldwide, though inspired by an imam, are neither Islamic nor religious: "Instead, they are secular private schools inspected by state authorities and sponsored by parents and entrepreneurs. They follow secular, state-prescribed curriculum and internationally recognized programs."[7][8]

During the early decades of the Turkish Republic, religion was severely restricted in a nation whose vast majority were Muslims, with Orthodox, Jewish, and Christian Arab minorities.[9] For all sectarian groups, the Kemalists, following Ataturk, centralized an education bureaucracy in Ankara, where governance, certification, accreditation, licensing, and teacher training emanated from the Capital. At first private religious schools were forbidden. The state, rather than the local community, extended its authority, in loco status, with schools having no autonomy or local authority to influence curriculum or hiring teachers. Separate from education, the state governed religion, appointing imams and determining where mosques were constructed, a secular policy deriving from Jacobin France of 19th Century called laicism (lay control). This is quite unlike the policy and practice of division of church and state in the US. In recent years Turkish education has moved away from Francophone hierarchy toward the US traditional model.[10]

Gülen's influence is clearly evident in the evolving status of and respect for education and teachers in Turkey. As in America, teaching had not been as respected as most white-collar vocations, and, therefore, few of Turkey's superior students had selected education for careers. In the wake of Gülen's discourses, however, an increased number of students today have become or are aspiring to be educators, and the career choice has greatly risen in prestige.[11] So popular are Gülen's editorials, sermons, and essays that a palpable increase of college students choosing teaching as a career has effected demographics. The increase of applicants into teacher preparation and education training programs in Turkey has resulted in a rise of admission standards that reaches levels of qualifications demanded of engineering schools and nearly of medical schools.[12]

In the last two decades in Turkey, nondenominational, private Gülen-inspired schools have become an option for Turkish parents. The curriculum of these, as elsewhere in over 200 countries, conforms to the nation's criteria and credentialing requirements. Gülen-inspired schools must operate within the policies of state guidelines, whether they are in Australia, the US, the Philippines, or Kosovo, another nation composed of a vast majority of Muslims, though whose educational governance is strictly laical.[13]

Gülen emphasizes the need for a holistic model of education and on the crucial role that education can play in serving humanity and working toward intercultural dialogue and world peace. Gülen sees the lack of moral guidance as a critical weakness of curriculums in many contemporary schools. To address this shortcoming, he believes that teachers should be role models for their students, giving "due importance to all aspects of a person's mind, spirit, and self."[14] This does not mean eschewing academic learning; quite the contrary, teachers at Gülen-inspired schools are encouraged to integrate disciplines with ethical behavior by teaching the former while modeling the latter. Gülen shares with many educators the belief that schools have put too much emphasis on testable knowledge, leaving little time for moral guidance and other increasingly neglected aspects of an education.

Gülen's ideal learning environment consists of groups of students in classrooms, in which teachers and students are able to foster close relationships. Such relationships will help students to participate actively and to think critically through dialogue by creating healthy discussions of ideas. To ensure that tolerance and diversity of thought is present in classrooms, Gülen proposes that schools enroll students from varied cultural and economic backgrounds, for such a variety of voices, after democratic give and take, facilitates collaboration for working with all toward common goals and, ultimately, world peace. In Bosnia, both Serbian and Croatian children attend with predominantly Muslim children in Gülen-inspired schools to work side by side in classrooms, a policy fulfilled elsewhere like the Philippine and Turkish School of Tolerance in war torn Mindanao.[15]

Gülen has observed that students from homes where parents promote learning and take responsibility for the education of their children are far more likely to succeed than students whose parents leave that responsibility entirely to educators. He encourages parents to create a healthy home environment by modeling and encouraging positive behavior and pursuit of knowledge. Gülen often has asserted "although knowledge is a value in itself, the purpose of learning is to make knowledge a guide in life.[16-18] [19] Teachers who have read Gülen or are teaching among others inspired by his insight at schools provide curricular lessons relevant to the lives of their students.[20]

Gülen believes that in addition to students' learning cognitively from curriculums, they must become passionate and enthusiastic—a word etymologically signifying spirituality. Along with knowledge these two attributes are equally important components of a child and adolescent's development into responsible adulthood. Gülen advances, "Humans are creatures composed not only of a body and a mind, or feelings and a spirit; rather, we are harmonious compositions of all these elements. Each of us is a body writhing in a network of needs; but this is not all, we also posses a mind that has more subtle and vital needs than the body, and each of us is driven by anxieties . . ."[21]

The subject of the initial chapter, John Dewey amplifies the aforesaid insights:

> Impulse is needed to arouse thought, incite reflection and enliven belief. But only thought notes obstructions, invents tools, conceives aims, directs technique . . .. Thought is born as the twin of impulse

in every moment of impeded habit. But unless it is nurtured, it speedily dies, and habit and instinct continue their civil warfare. There is instinctive wisdom in the tendency of the young to ignore the limitations of the environment. Only thus can they discover their own power and learn the differences in different kinds of environing limitations. But this discovery when once made marks the birth of intelligence; and with its birth comes the responsibility of the mature to observe, to recall, to forecast. Every moral life has its radical ism; but this radical factor does not find its full expression in direct action but in the courage of intelligence to go deeper than either tradition or immediate impulse goes.[22]

Gülen, like Dewey, envisioned every human as a whole composed of dynamic tensions—of impulse, instincts, and thought accreting from unconscious toward consciousness that amount over the years as reasoned wisdom. Relatedly, yaqin, a crucial thesis of Gülen's, is addressed in chapters that follow, specifically those devoted to Dewey (Chapter 1), Montessori (Chapter 2), and Bloom (Chapter 7). Gülen believes the levels of observation, experience, and certitude should be fostered and facilitated by family and schools. A balanced approach will prepare students to lead a commendable life and contribute positively to society.[23] Therefore, students should be exposed to ethical dilemmas in classrooms, and they should also be able to put their developing moral standards to practice in interactions with their school community.[24] The emphasis that Gülen places on educating the whole person stems from his belief that "a community's well-being depends on idealism and morality, as well as on being able to attain sufficiently adequate scientific and technological knowledge and skills."[25] Yet communities have histories that differ in every nation.

In contrast to the Republic of Turkey as cited above, Americans traditionally have assigned the responsibility to govern schools in local community boards. The Latin phrase in loco parentis embodies a principle that the parents of children accept the school as proxy. As the US is a comparatively religious nation, the First Amendment to the Constitution protects not only the freedom of assembly and the freedom to practice a religion of one's choice in every community, but implicitly the Amendment protects freedom from having religion imposed upon a person by any community. Secularism, as practiced by local control in the US, has not condoned ostracizing religion nor approved of imposing the majority religion upon students. By contrast, France and the Republic of Turkey of the past endorse a very different concept of secularism, a strict laical policy that subordinates religion to the State, a State that appoints heads of sectarian communities.

In nations that host Gülen-inspired schools, there can be private, secular, tuition-funded schools and public schools governed under the auspices of boards of trustees.[26] There are fewer than a half dozen private schools in the US but more than a hundred public schools that benefit from the service of dedicated teachers, some of whom have read and are inspired by Gülen's theories. These services range from tutoring, to offering special classes in language or mathematics, to innovative schools that realize the goals and objectives of the community and the State.

Gülen has attained prominence by composing essays, delivering lectures, consulting, and writing editorials. His remarks pertaining to education are embedded in rhetorical genres of sermons or inspirational essays, cultural genres appropriated for specific audiences and occasions and not necessarily to those in search of concrete objectives for curriculum or pedagogy. Gülen has not addressed himself specifically to pedagogy and curriculum but generally to a holistic approach to life, of which education is an inseparable component. His words serve as inspirational guides to educators who, subsequently, educate in elementary, secondary, and higher education. But no one "teaches Gülen."

Gülen and International Foundations of Modern Education

This volume explores the educational philosophies, research, and pedagogies of the some of the most prominent twentieth century educators and practitioners of the West, who in turn have been influenced by three millennia of global interaction. Each chapter relates ideas on education to those of Gülen from Anatolia, a global crossroad. The subjects of each chapter are the following: the American John Dewey (Chapter 1), the Italian Maria Montessori (Chapter 2), the Russian Lev Vygotsky (Chapter 3), the German Kurt Hahn (Chapter 4), the Swiss Jean Piaget (Chapter 5), the Canadian Albert Bandura (Chapter 6), also from America Benjamin Bloom (Chapter 7) and James Moffett (Chapter 8), and a number of international scholars associated with social constructionism (Chapter 9). Cumulatively, these chapters blend with the thoughts of this Turkish scholar in exploring how children learn and how educators, schools, and curriculum can best facilitate their education.

The ongoing research on children's intellectual and emotional development throughout the last century has resulted in a rich and vigorous dialogue on how education can best serve the economically and culturally diverse student populations of the early twenty-first century. The comparisons of convictions and findings in this volume will provide readers with insights not only into current educational research but also into the *Hizmet* Movement and its ongoing growth and influence on education around the world.

These thinkers, by and large, concur with Gülen on how to provide pre-college level students with meaningful education. They believe in the power of education to help shape young men and women into compassionate, thoughtful, and productive members of society. They believe that methods reflecting the best ways to interest, include, and develop children should be promoted in classroom practices and lessons. They recognize the need for a holistic educational model that includes physical activity and a moral component.

The discussions of this volume aim to inform those unfamiliar with Gülen's work how his writing intersects with Western foundational scholarship. This scholarship and research have constituted, and constitutes, the grounds for pre-service teacher training institutions and of in-service staff development in Western countries. Gülen's thoughts on education in English are dispersed among the following titles: M. Fethullah Gülen: Essays-Perspectives-Opinions, Sufism, Pearls of Wisdom, and Toward a Global Civilization of Love and Tolerance. In the title chapter of his book of essays The Statue of Our Souls, Gülen identifies as sculptors of a better world parents, educators, business leaders, and community leaders. He believes that all persons are born with the potential and capacity to develop and, in the case of some, to reach a level of being builders of that better world. Those achieving this state have acquired competencies through study, obtained by personal will and by family guidance, and by a culture that complements personal will and family with its education system.

The reader residing in this caravanserai of ideas enters into a dialogue on how the general thoughts of Gülen dovetail with the thoughts of those foundational thinkers whose comparison warrant inclusion in this collection of essays. The foundational philosophers share with Gülen lofty themes, some have tested hypotheses derived from theory to produced research findings, others have published works of pedagogy and still others have dealt with curriculum and taught in schools. From Aristotle to Wittgenstein, many of the aforementioned, like Gülen, began as classroom teachers and acquired pragmatics and wisdom.

1
Pragmatism
Gülen Viewed from Dewey's Century

JOHN DEWEY IS CONSIDERED to be America's lone systemic philosopher and an important contributor to Western thought. During the most influential period of his work, the progressive era of the early twentieth century, Dewey advocated applying logical, scientific methods to the education of the whole child. Deweyan Progressive Education clashed with what might be called academic curriculum, or Greek and Roman based-classicism of the trivium and quadrivium. It was only near the end of Dewey's long life and career that he embraced the need to supplement logically based, free social inquiry for informed citizens with attention to feelings, aestheticism, and what might be deemed spirituality. It is during this final period and after subsequent developments by his students that his influence has commonalities with the philosophy and pedagogy of Fethullah Gülen.

Dewey, Gülen & a Wisdom Revolution

The great pleasure of Dewey's youth was hiking in the wilds of Vermont with his brothers Davis and Charles, a pleasure he returned to throughout his life at his retreats in the Adirondack Mountains and on the coast of Nova Scotia. He stayed in Burlington to attend the University of Vermont, later writing that the most influential experience of his college years was his reading of Coleridge's *Aids to Reflection*. Coleridge presented reason as the principal aid to conscience: "He that speaks against his own reason, speaks against his own conscience: and therefore it is certain, no man serves God with a good conscience, who serves him against his reason."[1] One can only imagine the powerful effect these words had on a very young man who had suffered for years under the watchful eyes of a stern but loving family. For the first time, Dewey had in Coleridge the voice of a real conscience.

After graduating from the University of Vermont and being unable to find suitable work nearby, Dewey found himself teaching high school in Pennsylvania. One night, while reading Wordsworth's poetry, he had a metaphysical experience that definitively changed who he was. Toward the end of his life, he described this epiphany to his student Max Eastman as a sudden certainty about his "spiritual sincerity." This issue of belief had plagued him since he was a late adolescent, in spite of the self-examination he had learned from Coleridge. In Dewey's words to Eastman: "I've never had any doubts since then, or any beliefs. To me, faith means not worrying.[2]

Shortly after this experience, he wrote his first philosophical article, "The Metaphysical Assumptions of Materialism," the publication of which he credits for his acceptance into the newly founded graduate program in philosophy at Johns Hopkins University.[3] At Hopkins where he thrived, the Hegelian scholar George Sylvester Morris influenced Dewey. Morris' influence imbued Dewey's thought with the activist component that characterized his motives for the rest of his life—a distinctly American, by the bootstraps, version of German Idealism: "A spirit is not made; it is self-made. It realizes itself . . . . The true and perfect being of man is dependent on his doing . . . . By his own self-conscious, self-determining, purposeful activity, [an individual] must redeem and realize the divine possibility that exists within him."[4]

Dewey's awakening brings him close to the observations of Fethullah Gülen, for whom "all matters related to faith . . . can be demonstrated by reason."[5] For Dewey, conscience and reason can only exit in harmony, Gülen echoes this sentiment in his own writings:

> Come and make our spirits meet the bright light of the
> mind and hearts with the immensity of logic and
> reasoning; save us from alienation with our own selves.[6]

Where Dewey refers to divine possibility, Gülen adheres to the possibility of fulfilling the potential of perfection implicit in God's design for every human. Gülen would argue, "We are not composed only of body and mind. Each of us has a spirit that needs satisfaction, without which we cannot find true happiness and perfection."[7] Gülen believes in "the continuous striving to be rid of all kinds of bad maxims and evil conduct and acquiring virtues."[8] For him, achieving the rank of human (*insan-i kamil*) is primarily the responsibility of the individual.

Dewey and His Impact

John Dewey became the most influential educational theorist of the twentieth century, and, perhaps, the most important and influential academic philosopher the United States has produced. Dewey joins Plato and Rousseau as the three most prominent Western philosophers whose thought can be said to center on educational issues. Yet Dewey's legacy in educational theory and practice is complex and remains controversial.

Dewey's ideal of "progressive" education was inclusive and non-elitist, emphasizing the practical, emotional, and social aspects of education. These progressive ideals rejected practices like intelligence testing and cost-benefit analysis in education that prioritized testing. From the 1920s until the 1950s, Dewey's ideas were quite influential, although they never fully upended the prevailing educational models that centered on uniformity and standardization. One of Dewey's most prominent critics was Robert Maynard Hutchins, president of the University of Chicago. In the 1930s Hutchins engaged in a series of infamous, vitriolic debates with Dewey in the pages of *Social Frontier*. Hutchins, a purist, criticized Deweyan education as catering to societal needs rather than strict educational goals. Hutchins believed in giving students a standard intellectual framework based on the classics.

Hutchins abhorred open classrooms, vocationally oriented and cooperative learning, and non-graded assessment of the student-centered activities, all of which were associated with Deweyan methods. With the advent of the Cold War and the race for scientific and military supremacy over the USSR, Dewey's philosophy was essentially ignored. Subsequently, instructional methods and curriculum in the U.S. became even more rigid, elitist, and distributive.[9] In 1958, for example, the political thinker Hannah Arendt called the Progressive Education movement that Dewey spawned "an astounding hodgepodge of sense and nonsense.[10] In recent years, standardized curricula often mandated by the state and answering the public's demand for accountability, have intensified the rigidity of much of the education in the US. Yet, at the same time, many of Dewey's ideas and practices have also enjoyed a spontaneous resurgence in classrooms and schools around the nation. Late in life, Dewey lamented the misinterpretation of his philosophy as "anti-intellectual." He saw no contradiction between his advocacy of experiential education and intellectual growth and achievement.

Gülen couldn't agree more with Dewey on this point. Against the increasing standardization of education, Gülen emphasizes that moral instruction must always complement scientific thinking. In fact, many of these negative reactions to Dewey are symptomatic of the modern problem, as Gülen understands it: "At the root of the modern education crisis lies the fragmentation of the once-harmonious heart and mind connection in education and scientific thinking." Gülen suggests instead that the true role of education is to "redefine the natural and inherent relationship between humanity, the cosmos, and God."[11]

Longitudinal research has demonstrated that students who matriculated through secondary schools whose curriculum was based upon Dewey's theory and pedagogy exhibited equal, and in some areas greater, intellectual development, and they led more fulfilled lives than their peers. During the 1930s, the Dewey-inspired Progressive Education Association (PEA) launched one of the most extensive, longitudinal assessments of effects on student learning in history, *The 8-Year Study*.[12] After negotiating with admission offices of universities and colleges across the United States, the PEA was able to establish control and experimental populations of high school graduates from around the country. At thirty-sites in Colorado, California, Ohio, and other States, students from Deweyan high schools were admitted to higher education regardless of cumulative records that documented having fulfilled requirements necessary for college. After four years in higher education, these students' performances were compared with the performance of randomly selected students admitted after succeeding in college preparation curriculums at traditional schools. On no index of achievement did students from college-prep schools outperform students educated in Dewey curriculums. In fact, many of the Dewey students outperformed the traditional students. Numerous publications of research, the Progressive Education Association in 1943, The Faculty of University School, 1948, publications of the Class of 1938, reported these findings, including *Thirty Schools Tell Their Story*,[13] *The Philosophy and Purposes of the University School*,[14] and *We're we Guinea Pigs.*[15]

Furthermore, Willis studied two decades later a surviving population from The Ohio State University of 1943 "guinea pigs."[16] They were compared with their traditionally educated peers, and then again, with a randomly selected population of students with IQs of over 135 and above from the Terman Study.[17] The "guinea pigs" from the Dewey Schools performed equal to both populations and performed better on several incidences. They had lower incidences of negative behavior, such as criminality, alcoholism, and divorce. They had a greater range of success in other measures such as breadth in reading of books and magazines. Beyond subscribing to *Time* and *Newsweek*, the "guinea pigs" subscribed to a greater range of periodicals, such as *National Review* and *The Nation*. Even some sixty years later, another investigator sought out those still living among the Ohio "guinea pigs" and found that they had lived enriched, intellectual, and happy lives, apparently beyond the mean of the control group.[18]

These findings would not surprise Gülen, who believes that education plays the primary role in achieving the values that make a person a virtuous human being. According to him, education embraces the whole of life and plays an important role in spreading harmony, balance, discipline, and order throughout individual and social life. He writes, "Right decisions depend on having a sound mind and on sound thinking. As science and knowledge illuminate and develop one's mind, those deprived of science and knowledge cannot reach right decisions and are always exposed to deception and misguidance."[19]

In a society seemingly polarized by religious and ethnic intolerance, and by political ideology, illiteracy, moral laxity, and spiritual emptiness, it is vital for today's public, especially educators, to recognize all that is beneficial in Dewey's thought and educational practice.

In his later years, Dewey more thoroughly developed his naturalistic philosophy, exalting the exhilarating power of art and feeling over the rationality of science and technology. Beginning with the publication of *Experience and Nature*,[20] continuing with *Art As Experience*,[21] and culminating with *Knowing and the Known*,[22] Dewey moved from placing his faith in intelligent social interaction to an understanding that this was secondary to the power of aesthetic transaction, which is how art evokes emotions. Moreover, Dewey came to believe that aesthetic interactions with others and the natural world, as distinct from the pragmatic, intelligent problem solving associated with a scientific world-view, were central to both authentic democratic education and to authentic democracy. Gülen shares with Dewey this value of aesthetic experiences. He affirms, "by means of art, humanity sets sail for the outer limits of the Earth and sky and reaches feelings beyond time and space."[23] Gülen's primary evidence for such claims is the record of early Islamic civilizations. "Islam cannot be opposed to aesthetics, art, beauty, and the expression of beauty," he insists. For if this were so, the "the magnificent Islamic civilization that flourished in the first five centuries of Islam would never have occurred."[24]

Dewey's later development seems both to have taken him beyond the narrow optimism of his most influential work on education and to have advanced him into what can be understood as a fertile connection with ethical progressive thinkers such as Gabriel Marcel, Albert Schweitzer, Paul Ricoeur, Martin Buber,[25] and, I would add, Fethullah Gülen. All of these philosophers converge around an alternate education tradition, what might be called a Wisdom Revolution, which redeems the world from the dehumanizing misuse of the Scientific Industrial, and Information revolutions of the last several centuries.

Chicago & Columbia: Marrying Philosophy and Education

In 1894, Dewey arrived in Chicago to assume the Chair of the Department of Philosophy, Psychology, and Education. He was greatly influenced by the democratic community there, created by the activist Jane Addams at her Hull House settlement. The following year he started the Laboratory School at the University of Chicago. This school, popularly known as "The Dewey School," established his name as foremost in the world as an educational philosopher. He first envisioned the mission of the school and its teaching methods in a letter he wrote to his wife Alice just a few months after their arrival in Chicago:

> I sometimes think I will drop teaching philosophy directly, and teach it via pedagogy. When you think of the thousands and thousands of young 'uns who are practically being ruined negatively if not positively in the Chicago schools year after year, it is enough to make you go out and howl on the street corners like the Salvation Army. There is an image of a school growing up in my mind all the time; a school where some actual and literal constructive activity shall be the centre and source of the whole thing, and from which the work should be always growing out in two directions—one the social bearings of that constructive industry, the other the contact with

nature which supplies it with its materials. I can see, theoretically, how the carpentry etc. involved in building a model house should be the centre of a social training on one side, and a scientific on the other, all held within the grasp of a positive concrete physical habit of eye and hand . . . . The school is the one form of social life which is abstracted and under control—which is directly experimental, and if philosophy is ever to be an experimental science, the construction of a school is its starting point.[26]

The establishment and operation of The Dewey Lab School embodied Dewey's philosophical project in education. Its success rapidly gripped the imagination of the educational and social worlds in a way that is unrivaled today. Dewey's core pedagogic philosophy can be summarized by a few phrases from his writings: "Learning from experience"[27] "Education is a process of living and not a preparation for future living"[28] "The true centre . . . of school subjects is not science, nor literature, nor history, nor geography, but the child's own social activities"[29] "When the school introduces and trains each child of society into membership within such a little community, saturating him with the spirit of service, and providing him with the instruments of effective self-direction, we shall have the deepest and best guarantee of a larger society which is worthy, lovely, and harmonious." The successive themes of Dewey's own development —the recognition of the inappropriateness of imposing adult consciousness on growing children, the importance of instilling inner direction, the competence to link one experience to another in a coherent chain, the fusion of philosophical idealism and empirical science, and the conviction that the institution of democratic progressive education would ensure the social progress of humanity—were all united in a coherent vision that embodied the latent redemptive possibilities within the diversity and discord of the modern world. The final three paragraphs of "My Pedagogic Creed" in particular continued to inspire generations of teachers to work towards the fulfillment of this vision:

I believe... that the teacher is engaged, not simply in the training of individuals, but in the formation of the proper social life.
I believe that every teacher should realize the dignity of his calling; that he is a social servant set apart for the maintenance of the proper social order and the securing of the right social growth.
I believe that in this way the teacher always is the prophet of the true God and the usherer in of the true kingdom of God.[30]

Fethullah Gülen holds remarkably similar beliefs regarding the definition of learning and the role of effective instruction. He has stated that "Most people can be teachers, but the number of educators is severely limited,"[31] by which he means that the task of educating youth involves much more than simply relaying information. For Gülen, the Prophet Muhammad personified the perfect educator: the Prophet "led by example and it is through his behavior and good deeds that he taught his family and companions the virtues of Islam.[32]

Just as Dewey expresses in his "Pedagogic Creed," Gülen too views educators as integral and lasting figures in the development of individuals, purporting that "real teachers sow the pure seed and preserve it. They occupy themselves with what is good and wholesome, and lead and guide children in life and whatever events they encounter."[33] However, for both Dewey and Gülen, student transformation does not happen overnight. A deep and meaningful educational process requires patience if the seed of knowledge is expected to have a chance to sprout into a brighter future for the student. Such a goal is not simple, for "educating people is the most sacred, but also the most difficult, task in life."[34] In addition to setting a good personal example, teachers should be patient enough to obtain their desired result. They should know their students very well and address their intellects and their hearts, spirits, and feelings. "The best way to educate people is to show special concern for every individual, not forgetting that each individual is a different 'world.'"[35] To Gülen, a true educator "is one who has the ability to assist the students' personalities to emerge, who fosters thought and reflection, who builds character and enables the student to interiorize qualities of self-discipline, tolerance, and a sense of mission." An educator must derive his sense of motivation from the persistent desire to serve society and the future of humankind. For, according to Gülen, "The main duty and purpose of human life is to seek understanding. The effort of doing so, known as education, is a perfecting process through which we earn, in the spiritual, intellectual, and physical dimensions of our beings the rank appointed to us as the perfect pattern of creation."[36] Furthermore, "Those who want to secure their future should apply as much energy to raising their children as they devote to other problems," for children are the future, and therefore "whatever is spent for raising a young generation elevates them to the rank of humanity. Such people will be like an inexhaustible source of income."[37]

After controversy over the administration of The Lab School, Dewey resigned and accepted a position at Columbia where he remained until he retired from teaching in 1930. In addition to his contributions to the related fields of psychology, ethics, and philosophy itself, which Dewey famously defined as "the theory of education as a deliberately conducted practice," his writings form a mighty testament to the metaphysical power inherent in good educational practice; they encompass theory, practice, polemics, religion, journalism, and a host of other disciplines.[38] This account grounds those writings on education as a fixed place in the educational canon.

Dewey wrote his first significant essay on education, "Interest in Relation to Training of the Will," the year after he arrived in Chicago.

The paper establishes the connection between the individual (or personal), with the community (or social), a theme that preoccupied him, in various permutations for the remainder of his life.[39] Shortly thereafter in1897, he wrote "My Pedagogic Creed." It became his first bona fide classic and has been and is still being read by many educators in the US.

Dewey's first book on education, *The School and Society*, was compiled in 1899 from a series of lectures he gave to parents and interested others at the Laboratory School.[40] In this work Dewey described how pedagogy fosters learning by means of the methods that teachers use in instruction that elicit from students empirical and scientific discoveries. The book awakened the world beyond the professional education community to the epochal importance of what Dewey had accomplished at the Lab School. This volume helped establish Dewey as one of the world's most recognized intellectuals, a status he occupied until his death fifty-three years later.

A summation of Dewey's entire philosophy, entitled *Democracy and Education,* was published just a year after the appearance of *Schools for Tomorrow*.[41] Dewey saw personal growth and social interaction as the two linked goals of democratic education. When teachers pursue these aims deliberately and intelligently the result is the creation of an environment that advances the universal interests of humanity more effectively than any laws or electoral procedures could.

Breakdown and Gradual Reformulation of Dewey's Faith in America, Democracy & Education

Between 1918 and 1938, the global community lived through the aftermath of World War I, the build-up to another worldwide conflict, and a great economic depression. Although Dewey had been something of a warmonger in regards the U.S. involvement in World War I, he soon came to regret his endorsements.[42]

In 1919, Dewey and other notable American intellectuals formed in the New School in New York, a free progressive school for adults, where students themselves could participate in the direction of the curriculum and could engage in open inquiry without fear of censorship. That same year, Dewey left America and became a global educator. For a short period Japan was experiencing an interest in internationalism and a willingness to experiment with Western education. There, Dewey met with liberal educators and gave lectures on his educational philosophy. But he ultimately judged his visit to be a failure. He traveled to China from Japan at the invitation of President Sun Yat-Sen where he remained for nearly two years, lecturing and teaching at universities.[43] When Sun Yat-Sen died, a civil war ensued that brought Dewey's work to a close. Then in 1924, Dewey was invited by Kemal Ataturk to become educational adviser to

Ismail Hakki Tonguç in the newly established Republic of Turkey. Under Dewey's aegis, the government launched a literacy campaign and a massive reorganization of the school system. The new plan included village institutes that ultimately evolved into teacher training programs. Several years later he visited the University of Mexico and then, with a contingent of educators, went to the USSR in 1928.

After his return to the US, Dewey turned his attention to issues tangential to education. He began to theorize about sensitivity and feeling rather than of reason. These reflections on aesthetics would occupy much of Dewey's later work. This work most clearly converges with that of Fethullah Gülen, who champions art as a "spirit of progress and one of the most important means of developing emotions."[44] Evidence of this shift can be seen in his 1927 essay, "The Public and Its Problems." Here Dewey argued that only when free social inquiry has been wedded to full and emotional communication will democracy become a mode, not just of effective social interaction, but also of full, deep co-existence, capable of effectively and continually generating a more and more energetic love of life.

Transaction and Reverence: Reading Dewey and Gülen

Dewey's thinking evolved from interactive transactionalism toward a promise of transactional pragmatism that resonates with the philosophy of Gülen. Dewey, the instrumental pragmatist of *Democracy and Education*, wrote in 1916 "books are to be read and employed as tools, no different from any other." By *Art As Experience*, written in 1934, he advocated a very different idea: "In the end, works of art are the only media of unhindered communication between man and man that can occur in a world full of gulfs and walls that limit community of experience."[45] Dewey never directly elaborated on how art as communication should be employed educationally. Gülen identifies art as the eighth attribute of those who benefit from wisdom education: "Human beings . . . responsible for constructing their world of faith and thought, either by establishing pathways from their own essence to the depths of existence or by taking various crosscuts from existence and assessing them within their essence."[46]

Yet, Gülen cautions: "However, due to certain considerations at present, I will say, 'Some circles are not ready yet to set out on such a journey within our criteria, leave it to sometime in the future.'" So, both Dewey and Gülen, so soundly grounded in science education, seem to be at a loss when describing art education. Perhaps the future to which Gülen alludes may have been anticipated in the work of Dewey's student Louise Rosenblatt and is being realized in the work of Bruce Novak and Jeff Wilhelm, who authored *Literacy and Wisdom: "Being the Book" and "Being the Change.* This 2012 publication shows how the intimate, transactionally communicative world of art is expanded and deepened through artful teaching.[47] Rosenblatt differentiated two concepts that seem to exemplify Dewey's shift from 1916 to 1934 and may fulfill as sound pedagogy what Gülen anticipates: efferent and aesthetic learning. Students who learn efferently carry away and put into action what they learn. Students who learn aesthetically are affected by what they learn with the effect of character development. The teacher who elicits efferent responses from students anticipates the results of their reading. This is sound when it insures practical applications to everyday needs and success on tests or in taking action in matters of pressing demands but not for teaching literature and art. In contrast to efferent reading and viewing, the teacher who elicits from students aesthetic responses anticipates the students experiencing heighten evocative, metaphysical, and moral feelings and clarifications. A teacher's stance in fostering aesthetic reading must assume a role of trusted adult not the role of examiner or assessor of the correct responses. This teacher in a role as trusted adult elicits very gently the students' aesthetic responses to creativity and discovery.

Ever beholden to Dewey's late vision, Rosenblatt challenged educators to "consider the text as an even more general medium of communication among readers [in a democratic fellowship]." The late writings of Dewey led to an education centered on aesthetics, as fleshed out by Rosenblatt, and from here we can discern an affinity to Gülen's opinion that teachers should feature stories as powerful vehicles for learning. Gülen provides perspectives here, as he recommends teaching stories that model positive examples. Like Dewey, Gülen acknowledges the power of aesthetic response. He cautions that teaching must not be preachy, which may coincide with what Rosenblatt refers to as misapplying the efferent stance, which is least effective when teaching humanistic subjects in contrast to the sciences. Story for Gülen is meant to be inspirational; for Rosenblatt, the reader attunes with the voice behind the print to become that voice, a transaction that generates virtual experiences from which readers learn moral balance, crystallize belief systems, and refine judgments about behavior. For example, while reading *Huckleberry Finn,* the reader comprehends the irony of Huck's judgments, but more important is that the student both recognizes friends in the community as avatars of Huck and recognizes Huck in the looking glass, this latter constituting Rosenblatt's "live-through evocation."

The transactional process, inclusive of aesthetics and metaphysics, must become part of public practice and experience, as the economy of commodities and information has penetrated and dominated nearly every nook and cranny of our globally interactive but transactionally impoverished world. The teacher who assumes an aesthetic stance refrains from imposing her experience or spirituality upon students but rather aims to elicit in students their heightened subjective experiences.

> Accepting an account of someone else's reading or experience of a poem is analogous to seeking nourishment through having someone else eat your dinner for you and recite the menu. The summary of a biology text, the rephrasing of the technical language of a law, may serve but only the relationship between the reader and the actual text, his attending to and synthesizing his own responses to the particular words in the particular order, can produce the poem for him.[48]

The transformative fellowship created by artful teaching and the trans-actional aesthetic experience between individuals and works of art, be it literature or an essay about biology by Loren Eiseley, becomes the foundation for bestowing this heightened learning in the larger classroom of democratic life. Ultimately, an emerging wisdom movement, inspired by Gülen, by John Dewey, by Louise Rosenblatt, or by James Moffett (see Chapter 8) among others offers benefits of an education that embraces the heightened feelings of metaphysics and reason.

The movement to restore wisdom to education implied in late Dewey promises three changes. First, education would no longer center on the commodity of knowledge; that is, the transmission of established facts and job training skills only but on the generation of new life through authentic, meaningful aesthetic transactions and the acquisition of wisdom. Re-centering education in this way would lead to a restoration of wisdom in education. Gülen expresses a similar belief when he states, "True philosophy is only a spiritual and mental trial that appears when God arouses us to seek wisdom."[49] That is, only through the pursuit of wisdom as opposed to the pursuit of facts, do we truly become educated and find ourselves on the path toward human perfection.

Second, democratic education requires a refocus on personal studies that would fulfill Dewey's late recognition that "individuals who are democratic in thought and action are the sole final warrant for the existence and endurance of democratic institutions."[50] This curriculum would center, in addition to science education, on human language, artistic expression of cross-cultural fluencies, and character development in addition to science education.

Third, a curriculum centered on the humanities and on civic and community engagement generates a democratic population ready and willing to be a functional citizenry for voluntary cooperative undertakings, which Dewey saw as a natural development from the generation of individuals who are democratic in thought and action. Dewey in *The Public and Its Problems* predicted a public wedding of free social inquiry with "full and moving communication."[51]

Fortunately, fulfilling Dewey's vision does not require reinventing educational institutions and practices from the ground up. Wisdom-centered education based on the individual was, to a large extent, the human norm until the Western Enlightenment in the 18th Century, when it was replaced with the transmission of scientific knowledge and technological manipulation of the natural world. Wisdom, in any society, had been derived from particular cultural inheritances and interactions with the local environment and renewed in each generation time-out-of-mind.

The central educational question of our time becomes how to integrate the powerful, long-established wisdom-centered forms of education within the existing global systems of knowledge-based education. This requires changing the overall paradigm from one in which knowledge may lead to wisdom to one in which wisdom becomes the guide overseeing the acquisition of knowledge. To some extent, the failure of Deweyan education to achieve this integration in the works for which he is best known, resulted in criticism of him by those enamored of humanistic, secular liberal education.

These reflections in many ways resonate with Gülen's convictions and many of those teaching whom Gülen has influenced. Their words inspire practices and education models around the world that combine rigorous science and mathematics curriculums with the moral development necessary for democratic societies. He, among a number of others, advances an ideal, democratic educational systems that "will fuse religious and scientific knowledge together with morality and spirituality, to produce genuinely enlighten people with hearts illumined by religious sciences and spiritual minds illuminated with positive sciences."

2
Pedagogy, Explicit & Implicit
Montessori and Gülen Methodologies

THE CAREER AND INFLUENCE of the Italian educational theorist Maria Montessori compares to that of Fethullah Gülen in originality of theory, impact on pedagogy, and inspiration behind the worldwide establishment of schools.[1] The "Montessori Method" and "Gülen-inspired schools" are phrases heard among the world's education establishments. The former connoting early childhood pedagogy: the latter, the manifestation of schools now operating in the Philippines, Viet Nam, Turkey, the United States, and South Africa to name just a few of over one hundred nations. In the chapter that follows, the reader will encounter a discussion of Maria Montessori's methods, her sensitivity to environment, and her child-centeredness—all characteristics that have become associated with her name, as is the case with Fethullah Gülen.

"The Most Interesting Woman in Europe"
Maria Montessori (1870-1952) was an innovative Italian educator, educational practitioner, developmental theorist, and developmental psychologist.[2] She engaged in a vast array of interests and academic pursuits and received a diverse, well-rounded education.[3] She began her secondary education at a technical school in 1883 and upon completion of that program in 1890, she enrolled in college at a time when it was still rare for women to attend universities. For a two-year preliminary course, Montessori earned a diploma in the natural sciences,[4] and in 1896 she became the first woman to earn a degree in medicine from the University of Rome Sapienza.[5] She is the first female doctor in Italian medical history. As a psychiatrist, she began her career and later branched out into the world of educational philosophy.[6]

Initially, Montessori worked with sick and mentally disabled children. She became a founding member of the "Lega nazionale per la cura e l'educazione dei fanciulli deficienti" (National League for the Care and Education of Mentally Deficient Children) in 1899 and also established many Casa dei bambini (Children's Houses). She was known for her oratory skills, often giving public lectures to promote her causes and speaking on topics that ranged from medicine to feminism to educational theory. She held her first teacher training session in 1909 at the Franchetti estate in Villa Montesca. The phenomenal success of this course ultimately led her to offer nearly one hundred similar courses all over the world.[7] In 1912 she published her first book, the acclaimed and influential *The*

Montessori Method: Scientific Pedagogy as Applied to Child Education in the Children's Houses, which brought her worldwide recognition. Since then, her voluminous writings have been translated into many languages and disseminated throughout the world.

The *New York Tribune* in 1917 referred to Montessori as "the most interesting woman in Europe." Her eloquence and charisma made her one of the most intriguing personalities of her time and contributed to her renown. Montessori was a spiritual woman and for her, education took on a quasi-religious status. "Reflection and meditation played an important part both in her personal life and in her educational program."[8] Julia Fox lauds Montessori as someone "continually striving toward self-perfection, towards the realization of [her] essential nature."[9] A Roman Catholic Montessori Guild was established just before her death in 1952.[10]

Basic Ideas and Theories

Montessori elaborated and revised her theories over the course of fifty years, combining education and psychology into a philosophy sometimes referred to as what Hornberger called "psycho-pedagogy."[11] Her educational psychology focused on the importance of understanding, and she fully recognized and utilized the successive stages of development in children. She coined the phrase "absorbent mind" to describe a child's development from birth to the age of six—a period when the child unconsciously absorbs information from his or her surroundings. She described "sensitive periods" as particular phases during maturation when children are especially receptive to new ideas and exhibit a heightened sense of creativity and eagerness to learn. Montessori believed strongly in the freedom of each child to choose his or her own activities and to work at an individualized pace. However, she emphasized that this unique pacing does not necessarily lead to disorder, unstructured activity, or freedom from parents and teachers. Rather, as Montessori described it as "the utmost freedom for self-development and self-realization compatible with service to society."[12]

"For Montessori," Mary Alice Hornberger explains, "the intellectual development of the child takes place in successive stages, with each stage providing the foundation for the next stage."[13] She identifies three crucial periods of child development when the child's heightened sensitivity provides the great accessibility to learn:

Stage I – From birth to age six. This stage is divided into two sub-stages, birth to age three and age three to age six.
Stage II – Ages six through twelve.
Stage III – Ages twelve through eighteen.[14]

Montessori described a child in the first three years of life as an "unconscious creator," assimilating information from the environment easily and without conscious effort. This phase has also been referred to as the "psycho embryonic" stage, in which a child develops various unrelated skills, such as language and control of physical movement. From about age four the child becomes a "conscious worker," developing and fine-tuning the functions that were acquired unconsciously during the first three years. During this second sub-stage, the child becomes self-aware and capable of introspection and reflection.[15]

During the child's first six years, he or she begins to learn about and exhibit mastery of skills relating to orchestration, images, motor development, language, writing, reading, detail and small objects, and refinement of senses. For Montessori, intuition about morality and socialization occur in the two later stages, between the ages of six and eighteen.[16]

Montessori called the transition between stages I and II a "veritable metamorphosis." Learning becomes more of a voluntary action, in contrast to the unconscious and spontaneous learning of the earliest years of life.[17] In stage I, a child works with the concrete and material, whereas in stage II, he or she begins to process and comprehend abstractions, hence the initial development of a sense of morality and conscience occurs during these years. This is also when the child emerges from his or her "closed environment," the home, to enter more varied, comprehensive environments that offers new opportunities for exploration and growth. This "open environment" includes the child's neighborhood and community with the expanded social interactions and exchanges they offer." A child now begins to ask and answer questions of "how" and "why." She or he discovers cause and effect relationships and acquires the ability to classify and to generalize from part to whole, a trait that Montessori referred to as the onset of "imagination."[18]

Stage III, the stage to which Montessori devotes less attention, is the sensitive period for socialization and the process of developing a positive self-image. In these years, the adolescent learns to become self-sufficient and forms a sense of his or her own place in society. Pre-school and primary students have been the subjects of Montessori education over the years, with some implementation at higher levels. The schools are usually private, though in many cases educators familiar with Montessori's methods have implemented them in public elementary education. Additionally, many Peace Corps Volunteers opening up schools abroad draw from the efficacies of Montessori theory and methods.[19]

Morality and Spirituality

Morality and spirituality were an integral part of Montessori's writings and teachings about childhood development and education. She believed that children form their concepts of morality through social interactions in both closed and open environments—at school, at home, in the community, and in the neighborhood. "The structured environment provides the necessary means for spiritual growth, just as the material environment provides food and air for the development of the body."[20] "It is through interaction with this environment that the individual is molded and brought to perfection."[21]

Montessori and Gülen employ similar rhetorical utterances when they speak of combining "theoretical and methodological concepts with the mystical.[22] Montessori found no contradiction between the practice of precise experimentation and observation in the scientific tradition, and the belief that "faith, hope and trust to be the most effective means of teaching children independence and self-confidence."[23] Gülen echoes similar themes in his writing, saying that "everything learned from rearing and teaching should be directed towards exploring the subtle unifying interaction between the inner world and the meta-world.[24] Reflection and meditation held an integral place in Montessori's personal life and in her educational program, a program, which she believed, could not exist without faith. "It is in vain," she wrote, "that one explains or demonstrates a fact, even if it is an extraordinary one, if there is no faith; the realization of truth is not made possible by evidence but by an act of faith."[25] Gülen's educational theory is remarkably similar, integrating scientific curriculum with the modeling and practicing of moral values. He too places great value on self-reflection, which he describes as "the heart's lamp, the spirit's food, and the spirit of knowledge."[26] Self-criticism is also fundamental to the acquisition of true human values and nourishing self-improvement and faith.

Montessori's work with sick and mentally disabled children in the Casa dei Bambini inspired the educator Babini to hail her as an "apostle of a religion who reached out to humanity through the preaching of science."[27] For Montessori, according to Cossetino, culture is, "bounded, ritualized, and driven by a cosmology that links practical means to moral and spiritual ends."[28] For Montessori mental health and progress are equally dependent on "mental and spiritual growth. Gülen's educational theory blends academics with moral values. His educational vision is to fulfill students' academic and spiritual needs, producing intellectually and morally sound individuals who will be competent and well-adjusted members of society.[29]

Fox praises Montessori as someone "continually striving toward self-perfection, toward realization of [her] essential nature.[30] Gülen, too, seeks self-perfection and believes this should be one of the goals of education. He describes education as "a perfecting process through which we earn, in the spiritual, intellectual, and physical dimensions of our beings, the rank appointed to us in the perfect pattern of creation."[31] Only when we have achieved such perfection, says Gülen, do we become complete human beings and valuable members of society. One must keep in mind that in the case of Montessori and Gülen, schools for young children are private schools that for many parents complement what children might learn in public schools should the parents wish to enroll them. However, though methodologies like story telling or exploratory learning are sound techniques used by public school teachers, those teachers are not teaching the religious convictions of faith of either Montessori or of Gülen.

Dialogue, Peace & Holistic Education

Early on, Montessori schools were recognized for their effectiveness in employing a child-centered, prepared environment that allows children to work at their own pace with a high degree of independence. The development of such independence required classroom linguistic activities such as dialogue and discussion. After observing a Montessori classroom, Gazza expressed her amazement at the diverse groups of students and teachers "working together to foster independence, self-motivation, concentration, cooperation, and individual success, all within a peaceful and productive environment."[32] A Montessori education is also concerned with "linking healthy human development to social harmony and world peace." These educational ideals converge neatly with those of Gülen. Foremost among his educational priorities are dialogue and tolerance, along with an appropriate educational environment that contributes to human progress. Both Montessori and Gülen believe a comprehensive education is a key means for bettering the individual and society as a whole.

Montessori's model that includes teaching preparation entails distinct characteristics that warrant calling her educational vision holistic. She placed value on the development of the child's total personality, which consists of "character, sentiment, mind, knowledge, and actions."[33] The Montessori Method is based on an underlying principle of respect for the child. This holistic approach to student and teacher education parallels Gülen's perspective on teaching that holds that students must be encouraged to grow and to learn both intellectually and spiritually: that is, as both students in academia and as human beings. Gülen also mentions the importance of respecting children, treating them as complete human beings and taking care not to underestimate or undervalue them.

Being honest and establishing trust among a child, its parents, and teachers are integral to the Montessori method. Children's questions ought to be answered in a concise and truthful manner. There are times for play and times for exploration. Careless observation of children learning might elicit that what is going on is chaos. Montessori warns parents not to mistake whimsy for randomness; often children obsessed with fantasy are learning creativity. She distinguishes unproductive play as a "fugue," "a kind of flight, or taking refuge" from reality. Such behavior can be a sign of a distracted child whose attentions ought to be redirected."[34] She explains that "a flight into play or into a world of fancy often conceals an energy that has been divided" that should sometimes be discouraged but other times commended as imagination and intuition that leads to growth. Gülen stresses similar beliefs underscoring that adults need to be honest with children and respectful of them but not permit them excitement that leads to intense obsession, "if we want our children to be courageous. Instead, parents should instill in their children a love of truth, a desire for knowledge, and "a firm faith which will enable them to face up to any kind of difficulty."[35]

The Role of Teachers

In a Montessori classroom, it is the "teacher's charge to embody education as an aid to life."[36] A Montessori teacher "is aware of her importance as a role model and should utilize grace, courtesy, fairness and consistency" in her actions and interactions with the students."[37] One Montessori trainer commented that being an effective teacher is "just like being an actor" in that "you have to *be* the actor; you can't just memorize the lines." Gülen makes a similar point when he distinguishes between a teacher who simply disseminates knowledge and an educator who must do more than simply know the lines.

Montessori believed that during a child's early years of development, imitation is a key component of education. "The capacity to imitate," Hornberger explains, "is a process that stimulates intellectual growth, and as the child becomes more agile, it assumes a more active form."[38] According to Montessori, once a child reaches a certain age, he or she begins to imitate adult actions "not because someone has told him to do so, but because of a deep inner need that he feels.[39]

Perhaps this natural impulse to imitate is why Gülen stresses the importance of modeling moral values as key aspect of education rather than preaching moral values. As it has been noted, teachers in Gülen-inspired schools set examples for students by being flexible and behaving comfortably when coexisting with all people regardless of their class, ethnic, cultural or religious affiliation. Teaching by example is an integral part of the educational model that teachers influenced by Gülen follow. For him it is in this way that students gain strong moral values by avoiding these habits and corruptions with the help of guidance and education given at the schools."

What the child perceives becomes stimuli for subsequent behavior for which it assumes authorship. Montessori gives examples of children imitating their parents in daily activities and imitating the activities of peers.[40]

This propensity to imitate is a helpful educational tool for both Montessori and Gülen, the latter who believes that when adults serve as positive role models, they foster the intellectual and spiritual growth of children. But Gülen does not limit this imitation to the student-teacher relationship. Instead, as Montessori also suggests, a student's home is just as much a learning environment as their school. So, as the school provides curriculum that is embedded with information and knowledge with teachers modeling virtuous behavior, it is the home that nests assurances of safety, sanctuary, and quality environment. It is for this reason that Gülen-inspired schools around the world find it so important to work closely with their students' families.

Classes in Montessori schools consist of mixed-age groups allowing children to learn from one another, emulate one another, and practice working together collaboratively. In Gülen's writings, he also advocates for multi-age classes and activities that are designed to promote good behavior, morals, and work ethics through the encouragement of peers and the examples set by older children. Montessori's and Gülen both share this preference for multi-age arrangements with theory and pedagogy of John Dewey (see Chapter 1).

Preparing Children for the Future

Montessori believed that "the 'true child' was living proof of the ongoing process of creation, of rebirth and renewal," thus education and preparation for life contain within it a loftier significance." "Teachers..." Montessori writes, "help the great work that is being done."[41] They have an important role to play in "the unfolding of the human soul and to the rising of a New [Human] who will not be a victim of events, but will have the clarity of vision to direct and shape the future of human society." For Montessori, "The children have been vested with unknown powers that could lead the way to a better future. If a genuine renewal is to be sought . . . then the development of [human] potential must be the task of education."[42] There is a remarkable convergence between her educational beliefs and those of Gülen. Both see education as a moral and spiritual mission intended to benefit all of society and to determine its direction. In Gülen's thought "A child has the same meaning for humanity's continuation as a seed for a forest's for it to continue to grow and multiply." Because today's youth will be tomorrow's leaders, it is essential that parents, teachers, and society provide them with a sound education of both reasoning and moral behavior. "Any people," he writes, "who want to secure their future should apply as much energy to raising their children as they devote to other issues."[43]

Educators should share these goals for education with parents who complement learning in school with learning at home. Accordingly, Montessori encouraged mothers to teach their offspring of their future roles in society. Gülen speaks in almost identical terms when he asserts "It is fundamental for a nation's existence and stability that mothers be brought up and educated to be good educators for their children."[44]

Montessori suggests that during adolescence, developmental stage III, the young people should participate in activities outside the family because "Through practical experiences, the adolescent becomes aware of his [or her] social responsibilities and his [or her] forthcoming role in society."[45] Montessori believed that the end goal of education should be to prepare mature citizens. This purpose is achieved through what she termed "socialization," a process fostered in various stages through interactions at home, at school, in youth organizations (e.g. cub scouts, camp, music or sports groups, etc.), and any other social experiences the adolescent participates in throughout his or her development. Socialization is also facilitated by imitation.

The Impressionable Nature of Children

Montessori pointed out the incidental or unintentional impact parents and teachers can have on children, simply through their everyday actions and behaviors when in the presence of children. She explains:

> The education of children must be conducted in a balanced manner from the beginning; otherwise, the first impressions will produce distorted or biased forms of understanding, expectations and behaviors which are then perpetuated. The first impressions are not only permanently engraved in the children's minds; developmental structures also develop as a result of them, patterns according to which all subsequent experiences are dealt with and assimilated.[46]

Parents, teachers, and other adults play the role of mentor and role models at all times but particularly during a child's earliest years, before the child acquires discretion. Gülen therefore warns adults against exhibiting negative behavior in front of their children, even if they think the children are too young to understand the context of an argument or conflict. He compares this negative behavior to a poisonous seed, which, once planted in the child's mind, will to sprout and be difficult to eradicate.

In Montessori's developmental psychology, the child adjusts to their setting. In the earliest stage, the child's perceptions stimulate development. But "once [social] patterns have become established within [a child], they remain as fixed characters, just like his mother tongue [language]."[47] To Gülen, "[children's] souls are as bright as mirrors and as quick to record as cameras."[48] This adaptability may be a helpful educational tool, but parents and teachers must be aware of their children's propensity to assimilate any behaviors or actions that they observe in their environments.

Comparison to Fethullah Gülen

According to her son, Maria Montessori wanted above all to answer the question, "What influence did the physical environment, on the one side, and the human society on the other, have on this [development of a person from birth to maturity]?"[49] She was searching for the answer to the nature-nurture dichotomy that has preoccupied psychologists and educators for many years. Her son further wrote, "Montessori's experiences...showed that children of all races, in the most varied cultural environments, even [less complex] ones, arrived at the same knowledge more or less at the same age." This indicates that all children develop the same awareness's and abilities and therefore have the same intellectual and social potential when provided the appropriate educational environment. Gülen's educational theory is built upon the similar presupposition that human beings of all cultures and backgrounds share more similarities than differences. Enhancing and realizing a child's potential require providing a supportive academic environment that focuses on those similarities.

A precursor of Piaget (see Chapter 5), Montessori believed that the mental organism is a dynamic whole, the structure of which is transformed by active experience with its surroundings. Environment plays a major role in the process of maturation. As reviewed above, Montessori believed that a child's intellectual development takes place in successive stages, with each stage providing the foundation for the next stage. The universality of mental development that Montessori observed resonates with Gülen's concept of *yaqin*, drawn from Sufism, which will be more fully discussed in Chapter 6. The similarities of Gülen from Turkey and Montessori from Italy warrant a summation of these two of educational innovators. Their theories and pedagogies are practiced in private schools and emulated by teachers in public schools. Their theories and administrative management have influenced practices around the world. However, the institutionalization of the two is quite different. During her lifetime, Montessori launched the American Montessori Internationale in 1929, responsible today for organizing meetings at local and international conferences. It publishes *Communications*, a magazine and website that voices the official mission of the international organization, hosts workshops, and generates instructional materials, publishes and disseminates approved documents, and coordinates the courses for teachers in Montessori schools. And since 1960, the American Montessori Society has instituted a number of aims related but different from the Internationale. The Society provides school visitations to Montessori sites. It has secured accreditation as The

Montessori Accreditation Council for Teacher Education, which received Federal recognition from the US secretary of Education. It is also designated as the umbrella-accrediting agency that oversees nearly a hundred courses to prepare teachers. It also publishes its own missile *The Montessori Life*. Since 1985, it has sponsored Teacher Research initiatives so that practitioners can assess the effectiveness of their practices as revealed in the performance of children.

Organizationally, the Gülen-inspired schools have no central superintending governance. Centrifugally, the schools appear initially in local areas. Networking for community funding and fusing the standards of the predominant community, these schools provide educational programs that in time demonstrate superior educational results. These results centripetally attract more candidates from the larger community. Over time this results in a shift of a majority of students of Turkish heritage to a majority from the dominant culture, an evolution best described by research from Australia.[50] Similar research in school demographics is needed for the US.

Montessori's main objective in education was to launch youth into productive lives as leaders in society. Some of those learners who have become famous adults include Google founders Larry Page and Serge Brin, who provide examples that validate the Montessori model.[51] Gülen similarly believes that environments of school and home play crucial roles in the intellectual and personal development of children. To provide positive academic environments, Montessori established her "Casa dei bambini" (Children's Houses). Both Montessori and Gülen believe that providing children with a salubrious learning environment is the essential first step toward making education more effective and of higher quality. In a Northern California Montessori school, children participate in Montessori pedagogy that aims to heighten children's curiosity and use of senses to understand objects in their world. Materials include *realia*, manipulatives that children can feel and smell in order to create their own knowledge. A well-known methodology involves blindfolding children so that they rely on their sense of touch to identify unidentified objects in paper bags. Such activities aim to develop and refine vocabulary and to sharpen discrimination and classification. Teachers tell or read stories to children that afford discussion, and the parents of the children look to the local education with expectations that the teachers have a good understanding of educational theory. Recently, a parent from a California town withdrew her children from the private Montessori school because the parent, well read in Montessori theory, felt that the teacher was too influenced by nearby public schools and the climate of accountability. The teacher appeared to push children too early to read. The parent contended that though her daughter knew the alphabet, she felt that the little girl did not want to read yet, and the teacher was pressing her to read prematurely.[51]

The basis for Montessori's educational program, now referred to as the "Montessori pedagogical script," is a handbook of diagrams, notes, and paradigms compiled by each Montessori teacher during his or her training session. One component of this script is the always-present triangle of teacher-student-environment interactions. In several of his essays, Gülen discusses a different but related triangle, that of teacher, student, and parent; for him it is the teacher's task to provide an academic environment that will most effectively cultivate intellectual and spiritual growth, while it is the parents' role to strive for the same at home.

Montessori education connotes privately funded pre-school and primary education, while schools inspired by Gülen, both private and public, may be elementary schools, secondary schools, or colleges. In Gülen-inspired schools the curriculum emphasizes science and math in addition to other requirements, but there appears to be no approved teaching methodology. Since these schools are relatively new, there is little research of their teaching methodology, as the instruction derives from bottom up rather than top down

3
Research

A Look at Congruence of Gülen's Ideas on Schooling in the Vygotskian Tradition

L EV VYGOTSKY IS PERHAPS the most influential theorist whose insights emanated radially in an array of disciplines including psychology, sociology, anthropology, and education during the last century. Vygotsky principal work was as a Soviet experimental psychologist. His empirical studies are seminal landmarks for scholars not only in learning theory but also in linguistics, cognition, and philosophy. Fethullah Gülen shares with Vygotsky an understanding about the unique and differentiating role of a child's sociocultural environment as the source of development, language, thought, and moral behavior.

Lev Vygotsky: Theories + Comparison to Fethullah Gülen

Lev Semyonovich Vygotsky was a Russian psychologist born in 1896 to a wealthy Jewish family in Orsha, a city in what is now Belarus. When he was still young, the family moved to Gomel. Vygotsky had a strong sense of both his Jewish and Russian heritage. His childhood readings of the *Talmud* and the *Torah* considerably influenced his perspective on life and his approach to his studies. In school he studied literature and was particularly taken by Shakespeare's plays in translation. Vygotsky first majored in medicine at college but received his degree in law. After graduation he taught literature and philosophy for seven years in Gomel, at the same time serving as head of a psychology laboratory at the Teacher Training Institute there. Vygotsky took a position at the Psychological Institute of Moscow in 1926, where he and his wife lived in a basement as newlyweds. The following year, he finished a doctoral dissertation in psychology at Moscow State University. It was a field in which he was largely self-taught. Over the next fourteen years he researched, wrote voluminously, and functioned as the leader for a group of Marxist intellectuals.

Vygotsky lived and wrote in the aftermath of the 1917 Bolshevik Revolution, a time of great social turmoil, intellectual ferment, with all of the problems associated with class struggle, class hatred, and political terrorism. Although he joined the Party, Vygotsky was in time criticized by it. Stalin banned his writings and theories and just before Vygotsky's death in 1934, he was even threatened with excommunication that could have meant Siberian exile. For this reason, it was not until after Stalin's death in the early 1950s that Vygotsky's ideas became known and eventually quite influential not only in the Soviet Union but in the West after 1960. Even today, many of his papers have yet to be translated.

In the early 1930s Vygotsky's writings and research alarmed the Soviet ideologues in his field; they were adherents to a school of strict behaviorism and opposed any inferences about the mind beyond observable physical manifestations. If it quacked like a duck, it was a duck and that utterance came not from genetic determinism but from imitating those around it. They considered Vygotsky to be a mentalist, a negative denotation that suggested that thought did not derive from society. Vygotsky persevered despite both political oppression and the chronic tuberculosis, which, in 1934, cut short both his work and life at the young age of thirty-seven years. His students, however, never forgot his genius and began publishing and discussing his work during the post-Stalin thaw of the 1950s.

As his works gained visibility and influence in the USSR, they also came to the attention of American scholars. In 1962 MIT Press first published a widely circulated collection of essays, titled *Thought and Language* in English.[1] *The Psychology of Art,* which included some of his earliest essays as well as his thoughts on Shakespeare's *Hamlet,* was published in 1971. In 1978 another compilation of translated essays, lecture notes, and student papers was published as *Mind in Society: The Development of Higher Psychological Processes.*[2] *Thought and Language* was then in 1986 revised, with Alex Kosulin as co-author.[3] This edition included expanded versions of essays that had appeared earlier in truncated form. The remarkable impact of Vygotsky's work deeply influenced not only psychology but also fields like linguistics, education, literature, and anthropology, an impact that prompted a foremost scholar of rhetoric to declare him the "Mozart of Psychology."[4]

Theories

Vygotsky investigated children's development to explain the relationship between language and thought. Secondarily but relatedly, he examined the connection between generalization and communication. One of his crucial insights revealed how a child negotiates word meaning, beginning with listening, then utters isolated words to itself as egocentric speech, and finally internalizing them as thoughts. For Vygotsky this increasing sophistication in word usage and meaning indicated the maturation of intelligence. Through his research Vygotsky explored the previously unexamined, or incorrectly investigated, interrelationship between thought and language. Word meanings, he argued, are present in both thought and speech and therefore provide for a synthesis of the two, which leads to verbal thought.

Vygotsky formulated a child's developmental progression from the initial hearing and listening of a parent's public speech all the way to written thought as follows: hearing the speech of parents, making utterances, egocentric speech, inner speech, wordless thinking, and written thought. More important than this sequence, he reasoned, is how at each phase, through the use of words and language, the mind functions dialectically to advance the person's cognitive development.

Early, the child silently listens, internalizing sounds and then words. Then she will parrot what is heard from others—simple utterances often starting with a single word—usually in the presence of a parent or audience. In the next stage, "egocentric speech," a child intuitively tries out initial verbalization. Egocentric speech appears to be performed to the self but in fact is performed for a public, generally a parent. If these others fail to acknowledge or depart from the room he or she will cease speaking.[5] Vygotsky demonstrated that soon after this stage, inner speech first occurs, which remains a handmaiden to thought throughout one's lifetime.

Vygotsky makes important structural distinctions between inner speech, external speech, and writing, in that the first develops out of the next by internal acquisition, and the last is learned. The structure of inner speech is much more succinct than normal speech; it eliminates pronouns and subjects but manifests mostly predicates, yet it does have its own structure, grammar and function in a kind of dialogic.[6] Eventually, with schooling, thought is written out as sustained monologue, with acceptable conventions of the individual's language community. Functionally, the utterances are directed to self or to others, with different audiences requiring varying degrees of formality defined by society. Developmentally, each stage evolves predictably by genetic hardwiring inherent in the human species. To sum up function, structure, and development, this ongoing dialectic engages as three strands of reasoning—of structure, of function, and of evolutionary aspects of speech—all being woven together and interacting in egocentric speech, inner speech, writing, and thought.

Vygotsky believed that thought is a socio-cultural product or, as Au summarizes it, "the individual is the social and the social is the individual, and social structures impact the cognitive structures of the individual."[7] To explain how teaching influences this dialectic between language and thought, Vygotsky introduced the concept of the Zone of Proximal Development (ZPD) as a way of describing and understanding a child's potential for cognitive development. He explained that every child has an Actual Level of Development (ALD), which is what she can already do on her own. The ZPD is the distance between a child's ALD and what she is able to accomplish with guidance. A teacher, other adult, or more capable peer provides this guidance. Vygotsky's pedagogical hypothesis is that if a child is able to perform a task with assistance, she will later be able to complete the same task independently. Thus, the ZPD diagrams a promising of scaffolding, with constant shifting upwardly of conscious understanding as the child progresses cognitively. The ZPD also defines the relationship between instruction and development. Vygotsky's research challenged the commonly used measurements of child development.

> Most of the psychological investigations concerned with school learning measured the level of mental development of the child by making him solve certain standardized problems. The problems he was able to solve by himself were supposed to indicate the level of his mental development at the particular time ... Having found that the mental age of two children was, let us say eight, we gave each of them harder problems than he could manage on his own and provided slight assistance ... We discovered that one child could, in cooperation, solve problems designed for twelve year olds, while the other could not go beyond problems intended for nine year olds. The discrepancy between a child's mental age [indicated by the static test] and the level he reaches in solving problems with assistance is the zone of his proximal development.[8]

Vygotsky did not view education as a transmission of facts and knowledge but as a collaborative process in which both teacher and student learn from interaction. At the time, this was a progressive view. Today, scholars herald Vygotsky as foundational though school practices have yet to adequately institutionalize his genius. With the current cost-cutting fad for distanced learning over computers, the future for children's learning anticipates the dismal past.

One aspect of Vygotsky's work, particularly relevant here, is his view on ethics and moral education. For him "the foundation of moral feelings [must] be sought in the instinctive sense of sympathy for another person, in social instincts...."[9] Moral behavior, like thought, is a product of the sociocultural environment. For Vygotsky, "moral behavior is a form of behavior which is amenable to education through the social environment in exactly the same way as is everything else." Educators therefore have the responsibility to make morality an integral part of education, modeled through their social and cultural behavior and learned by the student from experience, through externalizing that which is observed. Teachers should be careful not to engage in preaching moral values, or what Vygotsky called sermonizing.[10] His perspective on moral education is consistent with that of Gülen's, though Vygotsky's scope is usually not considered to include as holistic a realm of human development. Vygotsky has much in common with the scope and practices of Dewey, Montessori, and Moffett, covered in other chapters.

To explain the role of social interaction in cognitive development, Vygotsky wrote that "Every function in the child's cultural development appears twice: first, on the social level, and later, on the individual level;

first, between people (interpsychological) and then inside the child (intra-psychological). This dualism applies equally to voluntary attention, to logical memory, and to the formation of concepts. All the higher functions originate as actual relationships between individuals."[11]

Vygotsky studied how a child's development was guided by the culture and by interpersonal communication. He observed how mental functions developed through interactions with significant people in their lives, particularly parents. Learning and development occur in society and are shaped by cultural contexts. How a child constructs knowledge and derives meaning is highly affected by social interactions of speech patterns, written language, and symbolic representation.

Empirical Studies that Relate to Learning

Behaviorism was first assaulted in the West by Noam Chomsky's publication of *Syntactic Structures* and later in the MIT linguist's review of B. F. Skinner's model of operant behaviorism.[12] [13] Skinner and other American behaviorists, like the Soviet ideologues of the 1930s, considered the brain a "black box" about which one could only measure overt behaviors, not infer what goes on in the mind. Chomsky argued that this model provided only a descriptively adequate theory of language and its use. Chomsky's cognitive model provided an explanatorily adequate theory of how word sequences lead to sentences and a formal grammar in any language. Chomsky, thirty years after Vygotsky, was probing inside the black box into mental operations that would change our understanding of mind, thought, and language. Of the three domains of language, that is meaning, syntax, and sound, Chomsky's focus was on syntax, or the linguist's preferred term grammar. The child's grammatical lattice supersedes the other two in importance, that is semantics and sound, whether phonics or phonemes. Children acquire the domain of syntax or grammar; it is not taught. Chomsky explained how language nests in the hardwiring of mind, a thesis that implies a refinement away from the semantic and sociocultural components emphasized by the Russian. Vygotsky's work, which came to the attention of the West around the time of Chomsky's breakthrough, concurred essentially with Chomsky's naturalistic and dialectic core. Concomitantly, neuroscience, linguistics, cognitivism, and education theory have been evolving since to braid orthodoxies of naturing nurture and nurturing nature that feed heated debates on campuses around the world.

From the 1960s on, Vygotsky's insights into thought launched empirical studies that influenced and bolstered a developmental model of education, particularly applicable for the elementary and secondary teachers to comprehend but not as pedagogy, for the grammar is inherent in the student (usage, or the conventions, is another subject). Then, late in the twentieth century, his theories caught the attention of many whose work further influenced scholarship in higher education. Scholars in different fields inferred from these advances very differently about learning, language, and society, with some launching competing counter movements, especially the dominate one today social constructionism (see Chapter 9).

Along with Chomsky, Jean Piaget, the Swiss genetic epistemologist (see Chapter 5), was central in promoting developmentalism, the movement that followed behaviorism as the dominant paradigm in language theory. Vygotsky, coincidentally, had written an introduction to the Russian edition of an early work by Piaget. Developmentalism posits that the brain of the learner evolved through predetermined stages, each of which limited accessibility of what a student might potentially learn. The insights contained therein inspired and redirected Western scholars, notably the pedagogue James Moffett in the United States and the researcher James Britton in the United Kingdom, who ratified and extended Piaget's and Vygotsky's models (see Chapter 8).[14] They also led Britton and Applebee to test the reliability and validity of Vygotskian hypotheses, demonstrating how findings derived from theory can influence pedagogy in benefiting student learning. Further empirical studies established the validity and power of developmental theory in education, including rules that governed and explained the growth of syntax and internalization in children from the age of five to ten.[15]

A child's developmental stage determines potential accessibility. The hardwiring of the brain requires development before certain sophisticated acts of language can be performed. This conforms to Vygotsky's vision of the internalizing process of speech, egocentric speech, inner speech, and thought. Both Loban, the University of California at Berkeley, and Britton, the London Schools Council, conducted longitudinal assessments of language development. In 1953 Loban began a 13-year study of the oral and written language development of youth by assessing a cohort of 338 kindergarteners through to high school graduation.[16] His findings, which included analysis of frequency of language units and complexity of syntax, corroborated Chomsky's and Vygotsky's hypotheses. At about the same time Britton investigated the development of student writing abilities in five different subjects commonly taught at forty-two schools in England and Wales, at levels equivalent in the United States to grades seven, nine, eleven, and the first year of college.[17] Congruent with Vygotsky, Britton found the act of writing to be an active intervention that grows or expands thought. His conclusion is that we learn by writing not just use writing to report on prior learning. This is a major finding for pedagogy in the teaching of science, history, geography, language arts, and religious education, the subjects required in British schools.

Extending implications from Vygotsky (see Moffett, Chapter 8), Britton differentiated discourse into factors of writing: first, the subject of discourse, that is, what you are writing about, and second, the audiences, for whom you are writing. These variables foster and enhance learning that results from expression in speech or writing as three types: 1. as transactions to inform of real worldly affairs, 2. as utterances to find meaning as pencil meets paper, and 3. as artifacts of crafted stories or poems. Britton argued that the greatest growth and most promising discoveries in learning occur when the writer, under certain conditions, is expressing to discover what he or she thinks.

Concerning audience, the second factor, there are seven sequenced from the author spatially and temporally; and with each interaction, these audiences influence growth, fluency, and maturity of discourse: 1. Self, 2. Peers, 3. Teacher, and 4. Public. The third, the teacher instantiates four different roles, the last of which bear important links to Gülen. These four over-lapping teacher/audience roles include the examiner who checks for what is correct, the dialogist eliciting further elaboration or checking for clarity, the teacher learning new knowledge from the student, and the teacher as trusted adult. Gülen emphasizes how parents at home foster learning that will seamlessly transition to schools where teachers assume the role of trusted adult. Both philosophers hope that the influence of educator/audience as trusted adult sustains beyond into secondary schools and colleges, though Britton's findings reveal this role of trusted adult wanes at the onset of testing for knowledge.

Each of these distinct audiences requires the student writer to alter his or her stance, or adjust to how to convey information, each shift is sometimes limiting, sometimes inaugurating. The study showed that in school subjects teachers use student writing differently, in terms of both audience and purpose. In required classes, especially the higher up in grades for geography, history, science, English language arts, and religious education, teachers overwhelmingly functioned as examiners and limit using student writing for learning. Sometimes, in religious studies and English classes, roles vary frequently. This variation fostered and enhanced what Vygotsky called inner speech and verbal thought.

The study found that students who were writing to express something to trusted adults developed significantly greater competence in writing and wrote more abstractly at the highest levels of Bloom's categories of ratiocination (see Capture 6). In fact, among the five school curriculums in British classrooms, the optimal levels of thought that were evidenced in writing exercises in English and religious studies classes were never evidenced in student writing in geography or history classes; yet such high levels were the purported objectives of these teachers.[18] Britton extrapolated from his findings about adolescents what Vygotsky asserts about how society transacts in thought development.

Applebee, one of Britton's students from the United States, plumbed the third domain of Britton's model, the use of writing. Following Vygotsky,[19] Applebee focused on how children from ages two to eighteen narrate.[20] He found children's stories emerge developmentally in patterns that follow what Vygotsky discovered generally about the phases of children internalizing concepts non-consciously (1986 Chapter 5). A child's story formation is key to his or her learning, and this explains why art and narrative are central to human development of thought and social integration, a parallel to what Gülen's claims. Story is a species-specific human attribute that provides a social tool for adaptation. Boyd has written on the adaptive role of story: "Fiction's appeal to our appetite for rich patterns of social information engages our attention from infant pretend play to adulthood. Because it embraces us again and again to immerse ourselves in story, it helps us over time to rehearse and refine our apprehension of events."[21]

Applebee found that children's story form evolved from centering plot to chaining episodes, a progression that resulted in evolving stages of non-conscious concept of story.[22] This observation paralleled nearly exactly what Vygotsky's research revealed and bears directly upon a central theme of Gülen's writings.[23]

Applebee, with Langer, further explored the Vygotskian concept of the zone of proximal development (ZPD). They analyzed how students learned from the instruction of eighteen secondary teachers in disciplines around the San Francisco-Bay Area, all of whom had participated in summer institutes of the National Writing Project. During follow-up of two years of instruction, the researchers studied how teachers had students use writing, that is writing as a source of diagnosis, writing for accessing consolidated information, and writing for probing new insights and fostering deep thinking. Applebee and Langer articulated a model for structuring a scaffolding pedagogy, a term that Vygotsky did not use but that was later coined by Bruner. Scaffolding refers to helpful support given to a student by an adult, or more advanced peer, to enable the learning of new concepts and skills. Subsequently, the child recognizes the concept or can utilize the skill on his or her own. They identified distinct features of this learning model as advances in ZPL: ownership, appropriateness, support, collaboration and internationalization.[24]

Concerning concept formation, Vygotsky posited two categories that are descriptive of thought development: scientific (abstract) and non-conscious, the formation of each interacting dialectically to advance the thought through stages.[25] For example, a young student will recognize a trite or vague definition of democracy, the depth of which is signaled by parroting or fillers as answers like "You know what I mean," but the same student will be hard pressed to write out a descriptive definition of democracy. Non-conscious concepts like "brother" or how to tie one's shoe are personal and habitual and differ from abstract scientific concepts, which are learned. Yet, non-conscious concepts are even more difficult for the student to articulate. Initially the concept of "brother" may be voiced as "Bobby" but non-verbalized because the child only registers a sense of the word. The word "brother" or even the brother's name will evoke a host of unuttered associations or agglutinated word-units and feelings. To paraphrase Vygotsky, word meaning is but a stone in the edifice of sense.[26]

In the classroom the learned scientific concept interacts with the student's non-conscious social relationships with peers and teacher. For a student to acquire the abstract, scientific concept requires focused thinking, which enables her to comprehend explicitly in speech, or in writing, what she implicitly, though non-consciously, knows. Vygotsky approved of teaching formal grammar because the pedagogy achieves just this understanding of what intuitively any native speaker conceptualizes non-consciously. The student best internalizes both scientific comprehension of non-conscious concepts and the conscious learning of scientific concepts required by school through a dialectic of trial and error, while engaging in an array of school activities, inside and outside the classroom (See Chapter 4 on Kurt Hahn).

These findings led us to a hypothesis of two different paths in the development of two different forms of reasoning. In the case of scientific thinking, the primary role is played by initial verbal definitions [democracy], which being applied systemically, gradually [encompasses], concrete phenomena. The development of spontaneous concepts [brother] knows no systematicity and [proceeds] from the phenomena upward toward generalization.[27]

While both Piaget (see Chapter 5) and Vygotsky viewed a child's cognitive development as gradual and defined it according to stages, Vygotsky's crucial contribution was his recognition that increases in the complexity and sophistication of human thought derived from the individual's social interaction. This emphasis on social influence characterizes Vygotsky's position in the nurture/nature debate.

Vygotsky plotted stages and phases of concept development networked by chaining and centering formation in the realization of understating.[28] Applebee, mentioned above, later identified this pattern of stages and phases emerging in plot structures of children's narratives including heaps (groups of words), chained incidents, primitive complexes, centered action, and well-formed story.[29] Applebee's findings demonstrate Vygotsky's general theory of how children formulate concepts that bear directly on how Gülen promotes the use of story in the education of students.

Comparison to Fethullah Gülen

Vygotsky was well read in the arts, literature, philosophy, and experimental sciences. This breadth of learning contributed to the wide and diverse influence that his work has achieved among academicians and practitioners around the world. He is, however, best known for his cultural-historical psychology and its relevance to education. This model holds that "all human forms of mental activity are of social origin; the individual absorbs them from outside, from his cultural surroundings," then internalizes them to produce thought.[30] Gülen's educational theory expounds on the immense impact of culture and environment on a child's development. Because children nonconsiously absorb from their environment, their mental and emotional development are greatly influenced by the behavior and characteristics of those around them. Acknowledging that a child's socio-cultural environment plays a role in their education, Gülen extrapolates the responsibility of educators and parents: "Our homes should always reflect the atmosphere of a temple and an educational unit at the same time; in this way we can satisfy our children's spirituality, their hearts and souls, this we can save them from being slaves of their material desires."[31]

He ultimately holds parents accountable for the education of their children. "Children can receive a good education at home only if there is a wholesome family life. . . . Peace, happiness, and security at home derive from the mutual accord between the spouses in thought, morals, and belief. . . . Children's mischief and impudence reflect the atmosphere in which they are being raised. A chaotic or abusive family life reflects upon the child's spirit, and therefore upon society.[32]

Vygotsky posited how important is social cognition that results from interactions with parents, other adults, more competent peers, and surrounding culture as key factors in a child's intellectual development. "What children cannot do on their own but can do with the help of an adult constitutes the zone of proximal development (ZPD)."[33] Vygotsky therefore concluded that education must be developmental (i.e. Must focus on the ZPD), and that what frames a child's ZPD today will eventually become his Actual Level of Development (ALD). He viewed education within the context of communication and collaboration among the participants in the process." Gülen's educational approach emphasizes similar collaboration between child and adult, child and older siblings and acquaintances, and student and educator as crucibles for developmental progress. Because children learn in all cultural contexts, parents should be concerned about not only the school and the home but also the entire external environment to which their children are exposed.[34] Gülen writes: "The future of every individual is closely related to the impressions and influences experienced during childhood and youth. If children and young people are brought up in a climate where their enthusiasm is stimulated with higher feelings, the will have vigorous minds and display good morals and virtues."[35]

Vygotsky differed with Gülen on the matter of knowledge acquisition. Where Gülen envisioned knowledge to be a cumulative, Vygotsky envisioned it as a result of a dialectical process. He used the terms "spontaneous non-conscious concepts," which are acquired and "scientific concepts," which are learned, whereas Gülen refers to "knowledge without means" and knowledge that is obtained through some means, such as the teacher. In Sufism the term *yaqin*, which translates as "certainty," is divided into three levels, a discussion that is most elaborately explored in our discussion of Benjamin Bloom (see Chapter 7). Until then, briefly, there are three levels, factual knowledge, direct observation, and direct experience, which make up the concept of *yaqin*. Gülen provides for *yaqin* the maxim, "exerting strenuous effort to arrive at certainty."[36]

Vygotsky discussed a means for interpreting Nature, mechanisms that encompass imagination, reason, and intuitive knowledge. Imagination involves developing in the mind an idea about the existence of something external. Intellect, a cultural mental form, is a rational process of working with the information acquired by the imagination to understand its essence. Finally, intuitive knowledge is the level at which one is able to understand the existence of that which was originally an idea formed by the imagination. What Vygotsky termed scientific concepts, he believed could only be attained "through an extraordinary effort of [one's] own thought."[37]

Both Vygotsky and Gülen considered the acquisition of knowledge (or certainty) to be a complex, internal process.[38] In Vygotsky's cognitive development perspective, thought is formed through a dialectical process of internalization. For Gülen, *yaqin* is "obtained only by those who have an innate capability to progress and develop inwardly."[39]

Conclusion

In *Mind in Society,* Vygotsky advanced that mental development includes thought, language, and the process of reasoning through social interactions with others who impart cultural knowledge.[40] Adults, through their activities, their behavior and their speech, transmit knowledge of the cultural heritage to their children. Gülen in his "Language and Thought" asserted:

> Language is one of the fundamental components of a culture. The cognitive, intellectual and scientific reserves and riches of a nation can develop and be transmitted only by means of a language rich and powerful enough to

embrace this heritage as a whole... The more richly and colorfully a nation can speak [and write], the more they can think; the more they can think, the broader and richer is the span their speech can reach . . . The relationship between language and thought comprises cognitive and intellectual reflections on existence and events, transforming these reflections into sources of information, and becoming productive [in their community] while forming links between the cosmos and our knowledge.[41]

Collaboration and leadership are central to Vygotsky's approach to learning and development. Gülen discusses the importance of cooperating with members of other cultural or religious backgrounds in order to work toward common goals and world peace. He encourages parents and teachers to model leadership, working alongside children, because he believes that "until we help our young people through education, they are captives of [those negative influences in] their environment.[42]

Gülen promotes an education that is developmentally appropriate for the child. He cautions parents and teachers to assess correctly the levels of development and monitor the accompanying signs relevant to these levels. The more knowledgeable, experienced person overseeing the child can change the level of assistance; in other words, they can scaffold the child's learning to the next level. Aslandoğan has discussed how Gülen's understanding of levels of development compares to Vygotsky's notions of zone of proximal development" and continuous adjustment.[42] Both Vygotsky and Gülen emphasize that the teacher must be able to evaluate the level of development of each student individually and instruct accordingly. "... It is not so important to teach a certain quantity of factual information as it is to inculcate the ability to acquire such knowledge and to make use of it."[43]

For both Vygotsky and Gülen morals are integral to a holistic education. Teachers should model moral values and imperatives so that such behavior becomes an integrated part of students' daily lives. Vygotsky specified that "morality has to constitute an inseparable part of education as a whole at its very roots, and he is acting morally who does not notice that he is acting morally." He also went on to explain why explicitly teaching morals is futile, describing these sets of jussives, as only words in a child's mind, bearing no relation to actions or behaviors, a disjunctive stance he compares to an idle motor. In Vygotsky's terms, such explicit teaching of morals would be teaching scientific concepts; Gülen aims at children acquiring moral behavior non-consciously. Vygotsky also believed that one's propensity for moral or immoral behavior is not biologically predetermined but rather issues "from social factors that guide and adapt this behavior to the conditions of existence in the particular environment in which the child has to live."[44] Gülen takes a similar position, believing that morals are transferred to children through their daily social interactions and that "a child's mischief and impudence arises from the atmosphere in which he or she has been reared."[45] According to Vygotsky, "moral behavior must become the individual's true nature and be enacted freely and effortlessly" and this can be made possible through the kind of moral education (teaching by example), which Gülen prescribes.[46]

4
Outdoor Education as a Third Space
Compatibility of Gülen and Hahn

BEYOND THE HOME AND SCHOOL, other sources constitute educational potential, called by some a third space for the development of children, the tenets of which predate the modern period. Solon, the Athenian lawgiver, recommended curriculum only of swimming and reading. In the early 20th century Kurt Hahn advanced transformative pedagogy beyond classroom into a third space that complements home and school. With the onset of television and now computers, the need to attend to physical fitness and mental acuities should be major components in a student's education. Obesity endangers growing children, often plaguing them with diabetes and other debilitating ailments that erode cognitive learning and a happy life. Hahn created schools and launched outdoor programs in Germany and the United Kingdom on a more limited scale than Gülen.[1]

Education Adventurer

Born in Berlin in 1886, Kurt Hahn was the second of four sons in a Jewish family. As a teenager, Hahn took a trip that shaped his values and view of the world and made clear his life's goals.[2] A walking tour of the Dolomite Alps forever engrained in Hahn a reverence for nature and a conviction that a healthy mind comes hand in hand with a healthy body.

Hahn attended a traditional German secondary school, but upon graduating in 1904 he left for Oxford, England, to study Classics. In Greek literature, he was taken by the wisdom of Plato, the heroism of Homer, and the simplicity of Solon the Lawgiver.[3] He returned to Germany to attend a number of universities but never earned a degree. Hahn found institutions unpleasant, unnecessarily rigid, lacking in eliciting mutual respect, compassion and understanding.

When World War I commenced, Hahn was in England but found himself judged an enemy of his newly adopted home, so he returned to Germany. There, he was considered an expert in British culture and language, so during the War, Hahn served the German Foreign Office and later the Supreme Command.[4] Despite his contribution to the war effort, Hahn remained an outspoken advocate of peace negotiation with the Allies to end a war he hated. Yet, he, like the American philosopher William James, acknowledged that warfare developed uncanny and remarkable virtues like camaraderie, physical stamina, and loyalty. This paradox led to James' famous credo "moral equivalent to war," a challenge Hahn answered with,

"Nothing but goodwill between nations and classes can save this generation from wars and revolutions. And education can help to build this bedrock of goodwill as foundation of the society to be."[5]

During WWI, Hahn's accomplishments caught the attention of the surprisingly forward thinking Prince Max von Baden, Germany's last Imperial Chancellor. The Prince, who hired Hahn to be his personal secretary, was the first of several aristocrats to admire Hahn's ideas, along with other German princes, English lords, and today's HRH Prince Philip, Duke of Edinburgh of Great Britain.[6] With Baden's support, Hahn began writing articles that promoted tough minded idealism, political vigilance, and a renewal of the ethical traditions in German social life. Baden appointed Hahn director of Salem School to operationalize his pedagogy in what became known as the Round Square model. The site at Baden's castle near Lake Constance commenced as alternative to the stifling traditional education that he and the Prince had received as youths. During the twelve years he served as director of the school, Hahn incorporated noncompetitive physical activity, community service, and democratic forms of social cooperation in the school curriculum. While such an institution attracted children of the wealthy, Hahn insisted that spaces be reserved for less privileged children as well.[7] Later at Gordonstoun, he replicated Salem in Scotland.[8]

Hahn had been a controversial figure in a hostile, war-torn Germany. He remained a fervent opponent of the Nazi party that was expanding its popularity and power in the years between WWI and WWII. His refusal to back down from his beliefs about how society should be organized resulted in a failed assassination attempt in 1923.[9] In 1932 supporters of Hitler beat and killed a leftist activist in front of Hahn's mother. Hahn's disgust with the mob's actions, coupled with anger for Hitler's praise of the murderers, led him to take actions that would have him expelled from his homeland. Hahn sent a letter to all Salem students, alumni and staff instructing them that they must choose between Hitler and Salem. The values taught at the Salem School were not compatible with the ideology of the Third Reich. When Hitler was promoted Chief of State in 1933, he imprisoned Hahn. However, friends in Britain negotiated for his release, and he emigrated to the United Kingdom.[10] Hahn in Germany and in Britain was actively political, a stark contrast with Gülen, who refuses to be brought into affairs of state.

The English Ministry of Education tried to get Hahn to lend his experience to schools, but Hahn was wary of bureaucracy. Its rigidity reminded him of German education, so Hahn opted to move to Scotland and later Wales where the rules were less stringent. Gordonstoun, a school for boys, soon became one of the most distinguished progressive schools in the UK and later served as a model for other similar institutions around the world.

In hopes of strengthening the will of Britain's young men during World War II, the English government appealed to Hahn to establish an institution specifically for young males that led to the first Outward Bound program, which dealt with sea rescues in Wales.[11] Outward Bound Schools provided an adventure education that placed emphasis on physical fitness, much like Hilter's Youth Program.[12] But, while the Hitler Youth encouraged competition and indoctrinated young men with racial stereotypes and Aryan superiority, Outward Bound schools promoted third space education that instilled compassion through community service, democratic social interaction, and non-competitive physical activities.[13] Hitler's German dream was racist. Hahn's was multicultural, a pedagogy that celebrated diversity.

After the war Hahn was given an opportunity to realize a lifelong dream, one that would stand as his crowning achievements. The establishment of Atlantic College eventually led to the United World Colleges Program in 1962.[14] This program aimed to bring students together from all around the world to foster world citizenship and promote interconnected leadership among individuals through dialogue and peacemaking practices. Hahn provided the bases for the International Baccalaureate Program, instituted in 1968.[15] He retired to Germany for the final years of his life, dying at age 88.

Hahn's impact has been remarkable, but with aspects institutionalized here and there the average person is not aware of his influence. In the US since the 1960s, the National Outdoor Leadership School in Colorado offers courses and certification that teach educators how to include wilderness experience for youth not provided in tradition school curriculums.[16]

More than any other subjects discussed in this caravansary of educators, Hahn shares much in common with Gülen, especially geopolitics, their interest in internationalism, incomplete academic preparation, and the educational goals discussed below like developing, love, compassion and leadership.[17] Hahn's life during Hitler likely elicited the posture of a "Moral Dictator" who celebrated student's individuality, a posture that Hahn characterized in his "angry growl" to rectify social injustice, a penchant for political engagement that he sought to be realized in students.[18] Though the Third Reich cannot be compared in any way with Turkey, Gülen also lived during a period when the military overturned four democratic governments, and like Hahn, Gülen encountered persecution.[19] Yet, here is a glaring contrast in style and substance between the two in terms of social justice. Gülen never evidenced an angry growl; this humble intellectual resembles more the example of Martin Luther King.

Hahn's Educational Philosophy

During his post-secondary years, Hahn was never able to find a sense of fulfillment that he expected from higher education. Unable to find an institution that came close to Plato's ideal, Hahn took it upon himself to be its creator. Hahn's educational philosophy stems from a drive to develop a holistic curriculum that adequately trained students in all aspects of personhood and equips them to become productive and helpful members of society. Yet, when asked about that philosophy, he disclaimed being original but embodying an eclectic philosophy from others. He chided lofty intellectuals who cited a "Hahnian model."[20] Hahn was a pedagogue, who observed, supervised, and administrated teaching methods and projects. Lacking formal research, he relied on anecdotal reportage, abundant testimonies from those taught, and endorsements of the very powerful.[21] Over his career Hahn used awards for stellar achievement to publicize success. Gold and silver metals and wreaths traces back to the symbolism from Hesiod.[22] Hahn envisioned students emulating the absolutism of Achilles or the pragmatism of Odysseus.[23]

Hahn analyzed the times as plagued by incursions of technologies that led to a decaying society, an analysis akin to medicinal diagnosis. He identified deficits that contributed to diseases for which he recommended four antidotes.[24]

"Six declines of modern youth evidenced" this prognosis.[25] Youth was decaying, "their nervous strength, their stamina, their resilience, their wind, their seed, their resource and initiative, their vigilance, their patience, their faculties of care and skill."[26] The first was a decline of physical fitness. Hahn argued that modern methods of locomotion, planes, trains, and automobiles, led to lack of physical exercise and laziness. Young people no longer had to rely on their own powers of locomotion to get from point A to point B, and thus were conditioned to be adverse to physical activity. The second, a decline of initiative and enterprise, stemmed from a growing culture of voyeurism. Radio and graphic representations, like photography and movies, conditioned youth to become passive observers rather than active participants. After living life in awe of nature and the power of personal physical experience, Hahn loathed the idea of sedentary young people unknowingly missing out on all of the wonder and richness of experiences of an active and engaged lifestyle.

Hahn's third objection to the modernity addressed the decline of memory and imagination that only would have increased since mid century.[27] He observed in traditional schools an over emphasis on academic cognition, which resulted in confused restlessness and addiction to hedonism, of "quick radio ears and quick cinema eyes .. [looking] everywhere, ever impatient for a change of scene."[28] With the onset of computers and digital revolution, some modern critics assert deleterious effects on the plasticity of the maturing brain.[29] In the 1920s Hahn had observed lack of focus and decline in critical thinking, which resulted from the growing chaos of an industrialized world. Impersonal mechanization contributed to confused restlessness among young people and erosion of skills, analytical thinking. Mass production made obsolete craftsmanship.

A decline of self-discipline was Hahn's fifth deficit in modern society. With ever-present availability of stimulants and tranquilizers, individuals no longer had to endure their inner turmoil. The troubled could sate stress and painful emotions with pills that required no development of character or internalization of responsibility. Hahn was disgusted with the notion that adversity could be overcome through chemical assistance rather than through introspection and perseverance.

A sixth factor contributing to the degradation of the modern individual was a decline of compassion for animate life. Hahn argued that unseemly haste of modernity caused lack of consideration for feelings and needs of sentient life, including wild life. Celerity resulted in a kind of self-induced autism, a retreat into the self barricading from others, which often elicited aggression and cruelty modeled after film violence. Children reared in such a world lacked exposure to brotherhood, community, and the richness of experiences in helping others.[30] The speed of a living overload with sensory information results in near elimination of time available for quiet introspection, a recommendation central to that of Gülen as well as James Moffett (see Chapter 8).

After decades, many critics argue that Hahn's declines have precipitated exponentially, that students lacking palliatives like communing with Nature are more likely to suffer attention deficit disorders and obesity and have greater frequency of bullying and suicide.[31] Today Richard Louv carries Hahn's torch by publishing insightful criticism of how modernity is detrimental to child development.[32] Third space experiences in and with Nature edify, spiritually uplift, and are formative in the developing autonomy.

Gülen's educational theory operates with many of these hypotheses. For Gülen, "good morals and sound conscience, and good manners and virtues, are like a currency universally acceptable . . . which [are] not affected by changes in the values of other means of exchange." He argues that while technology promises ease and efficiency, it also alienates us from our true human inheritance: virtue. Gülen only opposes science when it comes at the expense of our humanity. On the other hand, those provided with virtue are "like merchants with the highest credit who can do business wherever they want."[33]

Having identified six deficits of character that jeopardized youth, Hahn enumerated palliatives: "The Four Antidotes." These are to be institutionalized in school and third space curriculums as remedies. Physical fitness training is his first antidote.[34] Non-competitive physical activity countered decline in fitness, initiative and self-discipline. By setting fitness goals and accomplishing daunting physical tasks, youths are able to internalize habitual behaviors. Regardless of hardship, a regimen of pursuing achievement and fulfilling goals without others coddling or dictating rules enable youth to experiencing fulfillment.

Hahn believed in leaving urban settings for expeditions out to sea or into wilderness, hiking in the mountains and backpacking where youth must rely upon them to endure and prevail. This self-reliance was the second antidote to modern deficits. Anderson likens Hahn's goal of students realizing their autonomy to Alexander Maslow's theories of self-realization or actualization.[35] Engaging in long, challenging tasks of endurance, which might entail risks, provided a cure for declining discipline and introspection. Experiencing firsthand the beauty and power of Nature instilled in young people a reverence for the outdoors while teaching how to overcome insurmountable tasks.

Hahn's third antidote came in the form of hands-on projects, a goal shared with Gülen.[36] Students at Hahn's schools were required to study a craft like blacksmithing, cobbling, or sewing.[37] Crafts provide a cure for decline in skill and imagination.

Hahn's fourth antidote came in the form of requiring students to serve their community, an essential recommendation of Gülen's as revealed by Hizmet. Serving as a cure for the decline of compassion, Hahn insisted that his students engage physically and mentally by contributing to their community.[38] His students volunteered for the fire brigade or participated in storms with the coast guard.[39] Such service allowed Hahn's students to experience the joy of enriching the lives of other people.[40]

The Ten Expeditionary Learning Principles

According to Hahn, a proper school instills principles that manifest in compassion, mindfulness, and contributing members of society. "Ten Expeditionary Learning Principles" undergirded the antidotes correcting the declines, principles evident in both in class and field pedagogies.

The first principle is self-discovery.[41] While Hahn's projects stood as stalwart examples of group and community action, Hahn understood that a strong sense of self and personal identity must come first before a healthy community evolves.[42] Emotional investment stems from challenging tasks that blossom in values, passions and responsibilities. Such investment results from accomplishing physically taxing endeavors that require perseverance, craftsmanship, and imagination, which gives one a sense of significance. Hahn believed that a teacher's and school administrator's primary methods should be to help students overcome their fears and allow them to discover that they can do more than they think they can. This resonates with a central tenet of Gülen's wisdom. In his words: "Those who want to reform the world must first reform themselves. If they want to lead others to a to a better world, they must purify their inner worlds of hatred, rancor, and jealousy, and adorn their outer worlds with virtue."[43]

Achieving self-discovery emerges from Hahn's second principle, cultivating heuristic ideas. First put into practice at the Salem School, Hahn believed that school pedagogy should foster curiosity about the world; teachers create learning situations that provide students with something important to think about, time to experiment, time to make sense of what was observed, and time to infer generalizations about phenomena.

However, students will not intuit wonderful ideas of succinct and valid generalizations without embracing Hahn's third principle, taking responsibility for learning. Educators need to explain to students that learning is both a personal process of discovery and a social activity, for everyone learns both individually and as part of a group. At Hahn's schools teachers and administrators cultivated democratic social assemblies, in which nearly every member of the school community was autonomous and encouraged to make his opinions heard. Hahn insisted that all decisions, following dialogue, are made collectively.

Hahn's fourth learning principle expresses the need for educators to assist and promote empathy, compassion, and caring. This need is of paramount importance to Hahn for a number of reasons. He had firsthand experience of pre-World War II Germany, a society in steady decline of compassion that led to death camps of the Third Reich. In responsible schooling students' and teachers' ideas are respected in an atmosphere of mutual trust and empathy. Students should never fear or feel ashamed of expressing opinions or asking questions. How important is this atmosphere was significantly established by the London School's Council's longitudinal study of forty-two secondary schools in England and Wales that verified Hahn's fourth principle.[44] James Britton et al found that students in five subject areas at five grades demonstrated the highest level of cognition on Bloom's scale of cognitive knowledge when they were learning from a "trusted adult" (Chapter 8 and 10).

Such nurturing environments are fostered in small learning groups led by an adult who acts as an advocate for each student. In this situation, students learn by examples set by teacher and, eventually, by older students, who serve as mentors to younger ones in a community of physical and emotional safety. Compassion fostered in Hahn's schools spill over into the neighborhoods and surroundings as students regularly engaged in community service projects.

Compassion and mutual respect in Hahn's schools did not result from coddling. For education to be effective, methods must provide students with trial and error, which benefit from success and failure. If students are going to build sufficient confidence to take risks to meet increasingly difficult challenges, they require resiliency to face the demanding world. Experiences that require perseverance in the face of hardship teach students how to turn failure and disability into opportunity. Hahn, who had learned from adversity caused by sunstroke, encouraged students to embrace hardships as a means of learning determination and patience.

Hahn's sixth pedagogical principle involved collaboration. Individual maturation and group solidarity integrate to produce friendship, trust and group action. Rather than competition, group activities are the best means to teach teamwork and cooperation. Rather than against others, Hahn encouraged competition against one's self, a competition that fosters extra effort to top previous marks. What's more, competition with one's self encourages self-discovery, promotes personal accountability, and sharpens responsibility.

Hahn promoted diversity and inclusion throughout his career, the thrust of his seventh principle for proper education. Class and ethnicity increases creativity and richness of ideas, improves problem solving, and promotes respect among students. This proto-multicultural pedagogy ran counter to other schools of the time. Hahn taught students to investigate their different cultural histories as well as those of others. Diversity of opinion and point of view in small group collaboration results in broadened understanding of issues at hand.

A direct relationship with wilderness refreshes the human spirit and teaches about seasonal cycles, an appreciation that formed Hahn's eighth principle. Communing with Nature as well as finding personal space for silence and contemplation is crucial for teachers to orchestrate for students. (See Moffett in Chapter 8). Alumni of Hahn institutions have become stewards of the earth, who influence future generations, for people whose experiences with nature have indelibility affected their character are inclined to pass on this appreciation to later generations.

People need time alone to explore their thoughts. A reverence for solitude and reflection formed Hahn's ninth principle. Without appropriate time to meditate, digest, and apply meaning to what is taught in a school, seldom will the benefits of learning have a lasting effect. In addition to allotted time for private contemplation, Hahn encouraged students to exchange their ideas, questions, conclusions and doubts with peers after substantial personal reflection.[45] Such experiences around a campfire that cannot be replicated in classrooms.

Gülen's educational philosophy is similar: "Extra-curricular and social activities such as picnics, fishing trips, excursions, field trips and other recreational programs provide time for teachers to build friendship with students outside of school time, and give them time to discuss good manners, respect, tolerance, understanding, love, helping others, and being beneficial to society." These activities enable teachers to "Personify these characteristics through their actions."[46] For "success is not only accomplishment in academic acceleration but also improvement in behavior."

While many of these principles made Hahn's educational curriculum unique, none was as defining of a Hahn school as the promotion of and commitment to compassionate service. This tenth principle was founded upon the belief that all humans are crew, not passengers on our global vessel and that serving the needs of others requires sustaining the health of the planet. Contrary to the view that people inherit the earth, Hahn implicitly suggested that humans have the earth on loan from their grandchildren.[47]

To picture a typical school week of antidotes ministering declines, undergirded by these ten principles, Anderson plotted the following[48]: excepting Saturday, nearly four hours of academics preceded lunch, with the afternoons devolved to different activities; Mondays was sited for study hall; Tuesdays, for physical education; Wednesdays, for either agriculture or construction projects – that is gardening produce or building shelters for the poor; Thursdays, other projects binding town and gown, so to speak; Fridays, for physical education. On Saturdays, students work at crafts, perhaps apprenticing with local unions, or occasional visits to museums to attend lectures, or visiting the aged or impaired.

Though worship was encouraged on Sundays, some consider Hahn's religious beliefs are not apparent in his philosophy.[49] Others cite the Judeo-Christian heritage undergirding a pedagogy that explains his Good Samaritan projects to aid the unfortunate.[50] Certainly not anti-spiritual, Hahn believed that spirituality emerged from experiences in nature.[51] As a scholar of Sufism, theology guides Gülen, "Humans do not only consist of a body and a mind. Each of us has a spirit that needs to be satisfied. Without this, we cannot find true happiness or perfection. Spiritual satisfaction is possible only through knowledge of God and belief in Him.[52]

The network of declines, antidotes, and learning pedagogies are foundational in Hahn's holistic model, which Henderson likened to a Greek Temple: the stair foundation or stylobate, pillars, and roof composed of tympanum and architrave.[53]

Transformative Education & Fethullah Gülen

Hahn's adventure education differs from either education by transmission of academic knowledge or education by transitioning knowledge advanced by Dewey or Moffett (see Chapters 1and 8 respectively): the former pedagogy is typified by teacher delivering information, the latter by teacher/student collaboration.[54] Hahn's transformative education, which can include outward bound sea ventures that risked lives in saving others, challenges litigious cultures like the US and limits the number of educators willing to engage in methods that augur the most lasting learning.

Hahn lived during, arguably, the most violent generation in history. It is remarkable that he as a citizen of Germany during the rise of Hitler had any optimism left after witnessing the horrors of two world wars. But, Hahn, like Gülen, was always able to see the best in people and the promise of youth. Both educators were raised in political environments infamous for intolerance. Hahn, a Jew converted to Christianity, endured Nazism. The post-Ataturk revolution mandated inflexible laicism, dividing state and religion, voiding diversity. Both philosophers developed reputations as outspoken supporters of inclusion and the benefits of difference. Gülen has devoted much of his life to promoting his view that "we are all limbs of the same body," and thus "we should cease this duality that violates our very union. We should clear the way to unite people . . . we should remove all ideas and feelings that pull us apart and run to embrace one another.[55]

It is not a melting pot of assimilation that Hahn and Gülen espouse, but a more risky mosaic, a community where individuals from diverse cultures live and interact in harmony, serving as examples of tolerance and goodwill. As Gülen argues, "we must remember that in a world like this, national existence can be ensured only by protecting the specific characteristics of each nation. In a unified mosaic of nations and countries, those who cannot protect their unique characteristics, 'patterns,' or 'designs' will disappear."[56] If unique characteristics of an individual's culture are allowed to slip away in the face of assimilation, then their unique perspective will be in danger of slipping away as well. Hahn observed "the boy growing up in brotherhood with foreigners cannot help but learn to care about the rights and the happiness of at least one other nation."[57] Though more risky, the more diverse an institution, the more transformative the opportunities for students to broaden their understanding of valuable cultural differences.

In Hahn's and Gülen's ideal transformational education, students develop character from manual crafts and neighborhood involvement that contribute to identifying with all of humanity, not just a hegemony, and at the same time are exposed to fundamental differences among people that can lead to tension and conflict. When basic differences are met with respect and curiosity rather than fear and close-mindedness, a peaceful and mutually beneficial community rich in diversity will follow.[58] Because "all humanity has more in common to bring people together than what would separate them," Gülen argues, "it is not difficult for students to identify those similarities while simultaneously learning to respect and value another's culture through coming to understand their unique differences.[59]

Gülen writes, "now that we live in a global village, education is the best way to serve humanity and to establish dialogue with other civilizations.[60] If young men and women are exposed to Gülen's and Hahn's learning environments, the prospect of rearing a generation of respectful, open minded, compassionate and self-motivated young people would greatly increase the potential for resolving conflict among nations and for instituting eco-justice for a planet besieged by greed, consumerism, and carelessness.[61] As Gülen writes, "In regards international relations and humanity, [it is important] to eliminate factors that separate people, such as egoism, self-interest, and discrimination based on color, race, belief, and ethnicity . . . Education can uproot these evils. Education is the most effective and common [language] for relations with others."[62]

Teaching altruism and tolerance are essential in how both Hahn and Gülen encourage character development. Gülen advocates that "a good lesson is one that does more than provide pupils with useful information or skills; it should elevate them into the presence of the unknown.[63] In doing this, a school will "quickly open the way to unveiling the meaning of things and events, thereby leading a student to wholeness of thought and contemplation.[64] In Hahn's and Gülen-inspired schools, introducing students to this "unknown" represents an important transformative means to release young minds from stifling confines of provincialism.

Discussing an ideal education, Gülen argues, like Hahn that, "crafts should be taught, beginning at least at the elementary level. A good school is not a building where only theoretical information is given, but an institution or a laboratory where students are prepared for life.[65] Many crafts from Turkish heritage have been lost like water painting, bookbinding, tile glazing, and cuisine.[66] Hahn and Gülen's commitment to acquiring manual skills exemplifies their belief that proper education should reach all corners of a student's mind, body, and spirit, for crafting artfully evokes pride of dexterity.

Concerned about the decline of personally investing in community, both Hahn and Gülen expect youths to engage in their neighborhoods as preparation for citizenship. In addition to the schools' role, Gülen insists that such transformational extension be shared with parents, for "if parents encourage their children to develop their abilities and be useful to themselves and the community, they have then given the nation a strong new pillar."[67] Increasing compassion and a capacity for service has been a primary objective of Hahn in nurturing youth in school, an objective Gülen echoes in his belief that "improving a community is possible only by elevating the young generations to the rank of humanity . . . Unless a seed composed of faith, tradition, and historical consciousness is germinated throughout the country, new evil elements will appear and grow in the place of each eradicated evil."[68]

Hahn stressed introspection and sharing self-discovery; he would no doubt support Gülen's assertion that "we were created to learn and communicate to others what we have learned."[69] Where Hahn recommended expeditions, day walks, ocean voyages, treks, and overnight backpacking, Gülen inspired educators to travel anywhere to help nations by opening schools from the Philippines to South Africa and to the Americas.

Kurt Hahn hoped to leave this world with better standards of education and thereby improve the lives of future generations in many societies around the world. Today, we can confirm that he succeeded, but within Gülen's lifetime the achievements of Hizmet are perhaps less transformative as regards to risk but more so in terms of striking results. Gülen has been an influential voice in many fields, his reputation as an educator and advocate of diverse, holistic, and service-oriented educational institutions is acknowledged globally. In the 2008 international survey of living intellectuals, Gülen ranked number one, and in 2011, one of only three honoree for peace by the three-decade old East/West Institute of New York.

5
Genetic Epistemology
Jean Piaget & Gülen*

THE PHILOSOPHER JEAN PIAGET researched the behaviors of young children to derive a theory of mind. According to Piaget, the growth of mind and the development of thought mature in distinct stages that imply how accessible a learner is to instruction and acquisition of knowledge. In the following chapter is a discussion of how this genetic epistemologist from Switzerland established a constructionist/developmentalist school that influenced education in the Western world. Many of the teachers in Gülen-inspired schools around the world use instructional methods that reveal an affinity with Piaget's theories.

Piaget in Switzerland

Born August 9, 1896, in the French-speaking portion of Switzerland where he lived his entire life, Jean Piaget exerted a seminal and lasting influence on child psychology and education. Working during the earliest years of the field of child psychology, Piaget brought a new perspective to the nature/nurture debate regarding cognitive development. This perspective intrigued him from the time of his early studies in philosophy and held his interest over his entire career: What is knowledge? How do we acquire it?

Piaget argued that nature provides a biological structure that dictates the process of a child's systematic mental development through four distinct and age-related stages. His theory and research on children resulted in his becoming the leader in the genetic and developmental viewpoint. This viewpoint posits that children learn or develop knowledge through actively making sense of experiences with their own intelligence and critical reflection. Each learner is set in motion with a predictable inborn timeline of increasingly complex ways to interact with the world to create their personal schemes of adaptation for success. Piaget saw learning as a biological process building in cognitive complexity and effectiveness through the intelligent, self-directed interaction of a person's genetic organizing structures with the real world.

Jean Piaget was born to Arthur Piaget, a professor of medieval history, and Rebecca Jackson, an intelligent, energetic mother whom Piaget himself judged to be neurotic. He credited his unstable home life as motivation for his later interest in the study of mind.[1] Piaget's mother encouraged him to study religion, which he subsequently rejected for its lack of logic. He

*This chapter is co-authored with Laura Rose.

credited his grandfather for the turning point in his intellectual pursuits, for it was his grandfather who introduced the young Piaget to the world of philosophy that exists outside of organized religion. In Piaget's words, "It made me decide to devote my life to the biological explanation of knowledge."[2] At an unusually early age Piaget demonstrated a strong penchant for science and research. He wrote his first paper at the age of ten about an albino sparrow he had encountered. Piaget began his lifetime of observation by collecting, observing, and writing about the behaviors of mollusks. Under the tutelage of the director of Nuechatel's Museum of Natural History, he published twenty scientific papers that his fellow scientists had no idea were coming from a high school student.

After earning his Doctorate in Zoology at the University of Neuchatel in 1918, Piaget spent a year in Zurich at the famous Burgholzli Psychiatric Clinic where he was introduced to the ideas of Freud, Jung and other major thinkers of the burgeoning science of psychiatry. However, he found that he preferred "the study of normality and of the workings of the intellect to that of the tricks of the unconscious."[3] His investigations contrasted with how American educational psychologists studied mind, namely John B. Watson (1878-1958), and these differences are discussed below.

In 1919, Piaget taught psychology and philosophy at the Sorbonne in Paris. In what he called a stroke of luck, he met Dr Simon in Alfred Binet's laboratory where the first intelligence testing was being developed.[4] He did not like the right-wrong format of the tests but became intrigued with patterns of wrong answers. He had found his research focus: the experimental study of the psychological processes that operated underneath logical operations.[5] He named this new field "genetic epistemology." This phrase entails the empirical study of how people *know* as a result of the hardwiring of the brain.

In 1921, an invitation to teach at the Rousseau Institute at the University of Geneva allowed Piaget great freedom to engage his students in interviewing elementary school children. There he published his first five books on child psychology, which were met with surprising public enthusiasm. Among the five was *Le Langage et la Pensée chez L'enfant*, a work that related to insights of his Russian contemporary, Lev Vygotsky, whose influence is dealt with in Chapter 3.[6][7]

From 1925 through 1929, Piaget taught philosophy at the University of Neuchatel in addition to his work at the Rousseau Institute. In 1929, he founded the International Bureau of Education, serving as its director until 1967. He is remembered for bringing women into experimental research, including his wife.

Piaget married one of his student coworkers, Valentine Chatenay in 1922, and their two daughters and a son were born between 1925 and 1931. The children became the focus of intensive observational research by both Piaget and his wife. This resulted in three more books *Origins of Intelligence in Children*, 1936 (trans 1953), *The Construction of Reality in the Child*, 1937 (trans 1954), and *Play, Dreams, Imitation in Childhood*, 1945 (trans 1951). The major benefit that Piaget saw in these case studies of infants and toddlers was the realization that the organization of reasoning systems begins well before language development. Thereafter, he always relegated language to a lesser role than action in his paradigms. He encouraged Madame Sinclair, a psycholinguist in Geneva, to study the relationship of language and cognition. Through her work with deaf children, she found operational stages progressed even without corresponding language development, and that the operational growth gave rise to language development, not the other way around.[8]

In 1936 Piaget began collaborating with other researchers, notably Alina Szeminska and Barbel Inhelder (Piaget and Szeminska 1941 an Piaget and Inhelder 1941). His colleagues offered him a rich array of new approaches, particularly setting up problems for children of various ages to solve. He soon realized that experimental situations were far richer than mere interviews, since the researcher could be present while the child was actually learning. From questioning children about their thought processes during and after the experimental tasks, Piaget developed his renowned stages of cognitive development: sensori-motor (age 1-2), preoperations (age 2-7), concrete operations (age 8-11), and formal operations (11 and above).

In 1940 Piaget was elected chair of Experimental Psychology at the University of Geneva. He became director of the psychology laboratory and the president of the Swiss Society of Psychology. He began to study the relationship between perception and intelligence and to test Gestalt's theories.[9]

Piaget was a prolific writer of sixty books and hundreds of articles, although his books were not translated into English until after World War II. His influence was soon widely felt. After the war, he became president of the Swiss Commission of UNESCO and received a number of honorary degrees. In 1955, he created the International Center for Genetic Epistemology, serving as its director throughout his lifetime. Here Piaget served as a touchstone in bringing scientists and researchers together. In 1956, Piaget created the School of Sciences at the University of Geneva. He died in Geneva on September 16, 1980 having changed the face of child psychology. There is hardly a textbook on child psychology that does not give his ideas an honored place.

Piaget's Basic Ideas

Piaget is most famously identified with four age-specific stages of cognitive development.[10] When Piaget first presented them, he thought they were more fixed than he believed in later life. Over time he found that cultural factors and elements of individual variance could make a difference of up to two or more years, but the stages always follow one another and are never skipped over. The one exception is the final stage, which he realized was only attained by a portion of the population.[11] In later life, Piaget stated that one of his greatest errors was in paying too much attention to these stages, regretting how inflexible many people mistook them to be. He called himself his own greatest revisionist, as he continued to question, experiment, and revise his ideas throughout his life.

Sensori-motor Stage (ages 0-2)

Although Piaget divides this stage into six sub-stages, it generally describes a continuum of the child's shift from exhibiting only a few limited abilities and movements, all centered on the child's own body, to the development of purposeful actions and an understanding that objects that are out of sight still exist and can be sought and found.

A great example of this is the young child's fondness for the game of peek-a-boo where, to much hilarity, the child is repeatedly reassured that the adult still exists even though temporarily out of sight. By the end of the sensori-motor stage, children can hold an image in their minds, seek and find items that are out of sight, solve simple problems such as putting a toy down to open a door, and imagine scenarios when pretending with toys.

Pre-operational Stage (ages 2-7)

This stage is marked by what Piaget calls egocentrism: a kind of autism in which a child is unable to see the world from any perspective but its own. Piaget's classic experiment illustrating this stage involved the creation of a set of three-dimensional mountains for the child to sit in front of. The researcher sits viewing the mountains from a different angle. The child is asked to draw the mountains from her own perspective and then from that of the researcher, and there is no difference in the two drawings at this stage.

The child can engage in use of symbols, such as words or gestures to symbolize things not present, such as using a walnut shell to represent a cup or a sheet of paper to be a blanket for a doll. The use of language also relates to this category of using symbols for objects and ideas.[12]

The child also begins to use what Piaget calls "half-logic." She can classify, but only one category at a time—by length or color but not both. She can look at a problem from only one of its elements, either color or shape, but not both at once. She lives in New Orleans but not in the US as well.

Another significant key to this stage is the child's lack of the concept of conservation. Piaget explains conservation as the ability to distinguish between the appearance and the reality of an object.[13] For example, when a child at this stage agrees that the amount of liquid in two identical glasses is the same, and then one of the amounts is poured into a taller, thinner glass, the child will say that the taller glass holds more. Even if the liquid is poured back into the original glass and proved to be identical, the child will say that it now holds more when it is poured back into the taller glass. The liquid in the glass seems to hold more because the glass is taller, rather than having the same volume, because it is taller yet thinner.

The child thinks that once a ball of clay is squashed flat it has more volume than the one that remains a sphere because the flattened circle looks bigger. A crooked line of sticks (/ \ / \ / \ / \) is shorter than a straight line of sticks (_ _ _ _ _ _ _ _) even though the child counts both sets as containing eight marks and the span is the same. A set of six large circles (O O O O O O) is judged to have more when compared to a set of small circles (o o o o o o) even though the child counts them both repeatedly.[14] Appearance trumps reality at the preoperational stage.

Concrete Operations Stage (ages 7-11)

Now the child can perform operations involving conservation through the mental process of reversibility, one of Piaget's earliest postulations.[15] In this stage, if the liquid in the two glasses was equal before, it is still equal even though the liquid in one has been poured into a taller container. The child can mentally reverse the pouring process. Piaget identified a great many kinds of conservation, including number, area, length, mass, weight and volume. He found that the ability of the child to understand the reality of conservation (things remain the same even though they appear to be changed) would vary. At various points during this stage, any given child may understand conservation of volume but not yet understand conservation of length, or shape, and so on.

The child at the concrete operational stage can also perform mental operations such as mental math with addition, subtraction, multiplication and division. He overcomes egocentricity and can see from perspectives other than his own. He can draw the mountains from both his own and the researcher's perspective.

The child's classification progresses in that it's perception includes that one set, such as "red blocks," can be part of a larger set, such as "square blocks of many colors," or "mammals" can include a subset of "mammals that live in water." The child can say, as Emily does in Thornton Wilder's *Our Town*, "I live in Grovers Corners, New Hampshire, United States of America, Continent of North America, Western Hemisphere, the Earth, the Solar System, the Universe, the Mind of God."

Formal Operations Stage (ages 12 and older)

This stage does not have an upper limit because not everyone reaches it. Some cultures value and develop it more than others. This stage marks the child's ability to think in the abstract and to look at problems from more than one angle, to understand metaphor, irony, illusion or double entendre. The child can now hypothesize and test a number of possible solutions mentally. The child can now think about the future, the effects of her actions on the future, and has an increased awareness of her own thinking processes. She can say, "I found myself thinking about my future and then I began to think about why I was thinking about my future, and then I began to think about why I was thinking about why I was thinking of my future."[16]

Amplification of Piaget's Work

Jean Piaget's work stands in stark contrast with contemporary work in American educational psychology. Following the 17th Century British philosopher John Locke, the newly assembled academic community in the US adhered to Locke's concept of the mind being a tabula rasa or blank slate. By the 20th Century, scholars of mind in the US established a school of thought known as Behaviorism. The Behaviorists limited investigation of psychology to overt manifestations from what they relabeled of Locke's blank slate, the "Black Box." With this constraint, the investigator of the developing child's thought processes is limited to the child's public utterances beginning with whisper and later with recognizable language as data for analysis. It limited explanation and theory only to overt manifestations of stimulus and response. John B. Watson and B. F. Skinner are most frequently attributed as the leaders of this tradition in the academic community.

By the 1960s, Piaget's theories were becoming central to the development of the genetic viewpoint that considers children to be active, intelligent participants in their own increasingly complex stages of the development of knowledge rather than being merely acted upon by outside forces. His position sets his theories in opposition to Vygotsky (Chapter 3), those associated with situated learning (Chapter 9), but with aspects of Moffett (Chapter 8) and with Fethullah Gülen.

When Piaget began his work with children, the two opposing models in the US and Europe attempted to explain how the human mind developed through either "nature" or "nurture." In the oeuvres of either Watson and of Skinner, "nurture" is the all-important factor.[17] This model saw the child essentially waiting to be reinforced into patterns of behavior by actions of the physical and social world. The opposing view of Gestalt psychology, Nativism, home of Gestalt psychology, came down on the side of nature and argued that human personality was inherited and consisted of whole systems from birth. Piaget favored the Gestalt viewpoint, but he saw himself more as a middleman, a position resonating with Gülen who concurred with Piaget's emphasizing the age appropriateness of teaching certain subjects.[18] As Gülen argues, "If a child's subconscious is open and receptive to the highest extent between ages 0 and 5, then it is worth performing whatever good actions one is capable of doing in order to set a good example for the child."[19]

Piaget proposed a genetic set of biological structures, which he called schemes, or schemata. These developed in greater complexity throughout childhood, enabling only certain types of thinking that is natural for each age range. Both Piaget and Gülen were influenced by Emanuel Kant's monumental discussion of perception. Piaget believed that through interacting with physical and social environments, each child actively developed the potential for these stages. The interactions between environment and mind result in knowledge accretions, of nurturing the mind. On this subject, Gülen has written, "Individuals that make up a nation influence, or are influenced by, each other to a certain extent. Thus, influences from the immediate or remote environment as well as customs and traditions play a certain role in the education of children."[20] Piaget believed that behaviorism explained how some schemata constructed theories of reinforcement, of which he asserted them of "making good things last.[21] This dualism of nature and nurture began to answer Piaget's central question What is knowledge?

Piaget actively opposed the idea that knowledge consists merely of a collection of memories, facts, and ideas. For him it is defined as a set of Kantian schemes of apperception, perception, reasoning and logic that develop over time through the interaction of the developing biological capacities of the child with its environment. The schemata, then, is a set of skills that a child develops to enable effective interactions with certain objects or experiences. Piaget postulated that the motivation for the child to work at developing these structures, or in other words to learn, is that they are seeking equilibrium, an ideal state of balance between themselves and their environment, which will provide them with an effective internal model for dealing with their world.

Piaget proposed that as children encounter ever-widening experiences, they develop systems of knowledge by a process that Piaget called adaptation. Adaptation occurs through two organizational factors, assimilation and accommodation. Assimilation is the process whereby children find a way to fit their new experiences into current understanding or schemata of how things work. For example, an infant might inadvertently insert its thumb into its mouth and find that to be pleasant. The child will repeat this action as patterns of circular motions. He or she has now developed a schema that tells him: putting things into your mouth results in a pleasant sensation. He may then put other things into his mouth, such as a small rattle. This does not feel the same as the thumb and the infant must adjust his mouth and his sucking response in some new ways, but the old schema does fit this new experience. It just takes a bit of assimilation, or alteration of the old, reliable schema. Another case might be a child who learns that the four-legged animal in his home is called a dog. When he sees a cow, a horse, or a cat, he calls these dogs as well. He has assimilated new objects into his old schema.

Adaptation is the process that comes into play when the old schema does not fit with the new experience and thus must be altered to work effectively with this new object. For instance, the child may find that some object, such as the satin edge of a blanket, feels better on his cheek than in his mouth. He has adapted by forming a new internal schema to fit the new reality that some things are nice to rub against his cheek. In the case of identifying dogs, he can now learn what cues define a horse, a cow or a cat, and will then have multiple schemata for four-legged animals.

Another area of interest for Piaget was the development of moral reasoning. This interest resonates with a paramount interest of Fethullah Gülen. Foremost among Gülen many publications is the mission of education to foster in the maturing child and adolescent an ethical and moral understanding. Gülen has written, "During the early years of school, the child should be endowed first with linguistic capabilities, ideals, morality, and good character, and then, building upon them, with social identity."[22] Gülen envisioned parents and schools coordinating and synchronizing efforts.[23] In light of what Piaget found about the four developmental stages of cognition, both are agents for establishing congruence of children's ethical understandings with the following:

- Pre-moral (age 0-4): the child has no sense of right and wrong or awareness of rules.
- Conventional (age 4-7): the child comprehends rules as fixed and part of a punishment and reward system.
- Autonomous (age 7 and above): the child begins to have a sense of justice and the ability to consider the consequences of moral decisions. A forbidden act can be performed in a cause for greater good.

One of Piaget's experimental methods is similar what Gülen's proposes in teaching, which has been cited frequently is other chapters of this book. Piaget's approach to uncovering these moral stages in children was to tell them a simple story about a person facing a moral dilemma and then asking the child what is the right action to take and why it is right. He then recorded these answers and grouped them according to patterns of underlying rules. Patterns cluster cases of children having no ideas about right and wrong, of children with a sense of the consequences for breaking immutable rules, and of children developing a kind of moral relativity, which indicated an awareness of judging the intentions of the individual. These patterns are age-based and sequential.

Piaget's work in this field influenced many who later explored the subject of values and moral development, such as Lawrence Kohlberg.[24] Before his death, this Harvard researcher drew insights from Piaget's stages of cognitive formation to posit a theory of development of moral reasoning.[25] At stages parallel with cognitive acquisition, Kohlberg theorized levels of adjudication that revealed moral development, which he published in *The Philosophy of Moral Development.* Much of this work advanced what he discovered in 1958 while researching for his doctoral dissertation at the University of Chicago.[26] His achievements have been dimmed by criticism that his data derived from populations of males, a gender bias that tainted his generalizations about human behavior.

Evolving stages of moral development are the nexus with the work of Gülen.[27] Education of emotional intelligence and moral development are deemed goals of education according to this influential teacher and author whose ideas have permeated so many start-up schools around the world and currently in charter schools in several cities of the US.

Piaget did not view himself as an educator, but his work clearly informed education of the vital importance of three overarching concepts. Firstly, Piaget's model of the limits and possibilities of his four stages of cognitive growth gave educators a blueprint for what children can be expected to do and not yet be ready to do. This expectation derived from educators particularly in the US, where the pragmatic inclination has led to attempting to hasten natural development, an intervention that Piaget would consider absurd. As a cat is programmed for agility, the turtle isn't. A genetically encoded cat adapts to its environment; it is hardwired to assimilate and accommodate to constraints of its world. To intervene pedagogically to hasten genetic development would be like trying to train the turtle to emulate the cat's agility.

Piaget taught that intelligence is not the same as cognitive development, that children are not stupid when they cannot understand in the same way as another child. Many listened when Piaget said that adults make assumptions about how children learn and what they can understand based on their own mature cognitive abilities. Piaget offered an organizational structure that helped education organize curriculum in line with the reality of the young child, thus preventing frustrating children who might otherwise be expected to grapple with concepts that their minds are not yet sufficiently developed to master.

Secondly, Piaget empathized how important it is for children to engage with the physical world in order to acquire the organizational schemata that allows them to continue a path of growth in learning. The schemata at each stage are not automatically brought into play by the child's increasing age but by the interaction of the learner and the physical and social environment. Concerning the fourth cognitive stage, researchers differ in their estimates of how many college students actually develop proficiency in either breadth or depth: percentages ranging from thirty and fifty percent and limiting in many cases to a single discipline, few exhibiting the Renaissance personality. This indicates that the schemata for each stage develop only through the individual's personal interaction with the real world rather than as a matter of course or curriculum. The natural companion to that idea is that more interactions will form more schemata, and thus more ability to learn effectively.

A child's play thus became a serious endeavor and a central focus in the educational systems of Maria Montessori and Rudolph Steiner. It was also the guiding force behind the kindergarten movement (see Chapter 2). Early childhood education was quick to understand that Piaget's work tells us that young children do not learn from pieces of paper with symbols that represent numbers, weight, volume, area, and time, and that children need to have real experiences before they can learn vocabulary that symbolizes those experiences. Especially in the pre-operational stage, children must repeatedly move and manipulate objects to begin to accommodate a new reality by creating a new schema. This takes place through play, which is the essential learning tool. A child will roll a ball over and over to experience its possibilities and limits, or use a crayon, or drop food over the edge of the table. Later, the child may pull a blanket on which a toy rests until he realizes that the two are connected and that pulling the blanket will net him the toy. Piaget called "circular reaction" this pattern, in which the child performs an act, perhaps randomly, then becomes interested in the result, and, subsequently repeats the action, and thus develops a new scheme.[28]

Thirdly, Piaget continually emphasized the need for children to be challenged by solving problems, with which their developing minds are ready to grapple. He brought to education a concept lauded by Shakespeare that "readiness is all."

A question still being hotly debated since Piaget's groundbreaking research entails if and how educators can offer experiences for a child at the stage of a cognitive development that fosters advancement toward the next stage. David Elkind would suggest that there is no hurry; the child herself will be internally motivated to move to the next stage if rich choices are provided.[29] Both John Dewey (see Chapter 1) and Maria Montessori (see Chapter 2) would reaffirm Elkind's advice. On the other hand, Vygotsky (see Chapter 3) argued that teacher intervention fosters growth, given the teacher's understanding of the student's zone of proximal development. The instructor may orchestrate dialectically what Vygotsky called the student's spontaneous concepts with the teacher's scientific concepts, resulting in marginal fluency and maturity of ratiocination.

In his analysis, Vygotsky departed from what he perceived as the inability of Piaget's theory to reconcile the spontaneous character of a child's reasoning with the scientific—and the adult—nature of concepts learned at school. Where Piaget saw confrontation, Vygotsky sought dialogue.[30] However, Vygotsky's difference from Piaget is only partial. Contingent upon student growth was the teacher's mastery of Vygotsky's three concepts in interactive dialogue: spontaneous concepts, scientific concepts, and the zone of proximal development. Some influenced by Vygotsky, those discussed in the chapter on Situated Learning (Chapter 9), infer mistakenly that advances are possible by radically nurturing to hasten developing thought.

In the US since the 2001, Congressional legislation known as "No Child Left Behind Act" has exerted immense pressure for children to learn early and quickly. This has resulted in teachers teaching to the test and relying on worksheets and right/wrong quiz formats as ubiquitous pedagogy. Many educators are calling for a return to curriculum based on Piaget's concepts.

Piaget, Vygotsky & Gülen

Piaget did not consider himself an educator or an educational psychologist in the tradition of practices in the United States. As noted above, he was a genetic epistemologist, a philosopher and scientist committed to research that validated hypotheses derived from his theory. Fethullah Gülen on the other hand is both teacher and educator, and even though he has not participated in clinical research, though, his ideas have stimulated empirical studies.[31]

Piaget published early in a long career. Like Gülen, his words captured the attention of many first in his native country and soon around the world. Though Gülen holds biology in considerable regard, Piaget is a strict empiricist who sought to find evidence in biology. The two share a common influence in German metaphysics. Piaget's rumination about schema, the clustering and patterning of concepts derives from Kant, whom Gülen also studied in his reading of Western thought.[32] Aslandoğan acknowledges that Gülen has not studied many of the works of major Western educators, though " . . . it is interesting to note that many principles and practices in Gülen's educational model are indeed supported by modern theories of learning and their associated pedagogical models."[33]

Keeping in mind that Piaget's model mapped thought and speech evolving by genetic code from the same root, it is safe to say that Gülen would align with Vygotsky's alternative model. Gülen's copious advice to parents, his explicit methodology, reveals greater reliance on how the social environment guides young minds. Closer to the ideas of Vygotsky and Montessori, Gülen argues, "In order to provide our children with a perfect education, we must also make sure that there is a perfect environment for education in place. Indeed, every child is shaped by the environment in which he lives and even he can be said to be the child of that environment."[34] Vygotsky criticized Piaget: child thought is not first autistic; from which emerges egocentric thought and only later manifests public speech. Vygotsky explicitly rejected how Piaget conceptualized the origins of language acquisition as "egocentricity."[35] Inclined viewing nature the source of thought rather than nurture, Piaget argued that thought begins egocentrically and becomes social in the language of the community. Piaget was overly deterministic in his adherence that the hardwiring of mind governs thinking stages, although acknowledging that to some extent external stimulation played an important role in speech and thought.[36]

Vygotsky, in challenging Piaget's genetic model, stressed that thought and speech have different roots; Vygotsky emphasized that social speech becomes inner speech, and then thought, surfacing as a result of reciprocity of speech and thought by way of inner speech. Incidentally, later in maturation, writing joins as triumvirate to shuttle among thought and speech to achieve the deepest thinking.[37] Beholden to Piaget for daring to buck the Watsonian hegemony that adhered to Locke's notion that mind is a tabula rasa, Vygotsky further investigated mind with empirical studies of children. He substituted Piaget's hierarchical stages for a model of dialectic of culture and mind. And, his model extended beyond theory to pedagogy that fosters learning. Moreover, Vygotsky's model is not limited to the unraveling of thought and language during early states but posits the machinations of mind and verbal expression from womb to the aging of syntax. He, like Dewey (see Chapter 1), wed pedagogy with theory. Here is where Gülen's instructions to teachers and parents overlap with Vygotsky in modifying Piaget's developmental model.

Piaget is best thought of as being an empirical philosopher who has been appropriated by education psychology, especially in the US; Gülen, in relief, can be portrayed as one whose personal experiences as a teacher and as philosopher, with a Sufi heritage, discourses and proscribes about ethical and spiritual issues.

Conclusion

Jean Piaget was always wary of any attempt to imprison the child's autonomous thinking with ready-made answers that would call on memory and docility rather than on intelligence and critical reflection. Piaget illustrated how knowledge is possible only because learners actively strive for mastery and understanding. He offered evidence for a constructivist and developmentalist understanding of intelligence, that is, a view

of cognitive development as not merely the fruit of biological maturation, or of simple cumulative self-experience, or of the direct internalization of cultural transmissions, but as interplay among all of these different factors. Gülen agrees, "Each person is influenced by and influences
others. Distance and proximity determines the degree of this influence in
cultivating a child, along with the influence of culture and traditions."[38]

Early in life, Piaget wrote down a principle that would continue to
guide him throughout his career: "In all fields of life (organic, mental,
social) there exist 'totalities' qualitatively distinct from their parts and
imposing on them an organization.[39] Piaget's lifelong interests ranged over
many fields of study, including philosophy, logic, metaphysics, the natural
sciences, and even theology. In all of these fields, he sought to find the
underlying organizational structure that emanated from biology. In later
years he concentrated his efforts on discovering and describing the common structural ground in many of the fields that interested him from the
beginning: physics, biology, psychology and epistemology[40]

Piaget's research findings have become the basis for much study in
teaching, cognitive psychology, remedial education, moral development,
and socialization. Debate continues about the effects of nurture on the
speed and quality of cognitive development within Piaget's stages, and in
fact on all of his findings. His ideas have penetrated so deeply into almost
all higher education programs in education and psychology that many
have accepted them simply as common sense; a belief in common with
how Gülen envisions the way teachers should construct their pedagogy.

6
Domains of Knowledge
Gülen and Benjamin Bloom

B ENJAMIN BLOOM'S SEMINAL hypotheses, research, and suggested pedagogy have considerably influenced graduate teacher preparation
programs in colleges and universities in the United States, especially
influencing the testing and textbook publishing industries. The following
discussion compares Bloom's work and Fethullah Gülen's many discussions of education. It juxtaposes how the ideas of the foremost psycho-
metrician of measuring cognition resonate with the educational insights
of a Muslim scholar influenced by Sufism. These comparisons highlight
greater common ground than differences, since neither scholar accepts
that genes determine success or failure, and both believe that when students are provided adequate time, pedagogical attention, and modeled
ethical behavior they can succeed in any subject.

Theories + Comparison with Fethullah Gülen
Benjamin Bloom was born February 21, 1913, in Lansford,
Pennsylvania, and died September 13, 1999 at his residence in Chicago.
He earned his bachelor's and master's degrees from Pennsylvania State
University, both in 1935, and a PhD in Education from the University of
Chicago in 1942.[1] Bloom began his teaching career in the Department of
Education at the University of Chicago in 1944, prior to which he had
been a staff member on the Board of Examinations (1940-1943), and a
University Examiner (1943-1959). Bloom developed the Measurement,
Evaluation, and Statistical Analysis (MESA) program at the University
of Chicago, helped to create the International Association for the
Evaluation of Educational Achievement (IEA), and helped organ-
ize the International Seminar for Advanced Training in Curriculum
Development.[2] He also served as an educational adviser in several other
countries, including India and Israel.[3] In 1970, Bloom was appointed
Charles H. Swift Distinguished Service Professor.

Bloom was an educational theorist particularly interested in thought
processes and development. He focused his studies on cognitive behavior
and learning, by innovating a think-aloud technique to study the thought
processes of college students while they were in class, from which he developed his theories of time-on-task.[4] After attending the 1948 Convention of
the American Psychological Association in Boston, Bloom was inspired
to work with a group of thirty-four educators and psychologists, which
included his mentor, Ralph W. Tyler in developing a classification system

or taxonomy.[5] The finished product, the handbook now widely referred to as "Bloom's Taxonomy," was published as *Taxonomy of Educational Objectives, The Classification of Educational Goals, Handbook I: Cognitive Domain* in 1956.[6] Bloom's Cognitive Taxonomy is a classification system that organizes educational objectives hierarchically, according to complexity. This system was described by one of Bloom's former students as the "operationalization of educational objectives."[7] Bloom also published a handbook that dealt with the affective domain.

After 1959, Bloom turned his attention to problems in learning rather than testing and evaluation. He wanted to develop a way for educators to provide high quality and more appropriate instruction for students of different ages and abilities. He developed this model dependent on feedback, correctives, and enrichments. In 1964 Bloom published *Stability and Change in Human Characteristics*, for which he had conducted longitudinal studies on the ability of the environment to influence knowledge, achievement, and personality. He found that environment was of maximum importance during a child's earliest years and gradually decreased through time. He discussed his findings with then President Lyndon Johnson and gave testimony before the US Congress. This led directly to the establishment of the Head Start Program, part of Johnson's Great Society, to help low-income children and families to improve their chances for learning and development, particularly from birth through five years of age. From his research in early childhood education, Bloom came to believe that all children could learn at high levels when the appropriate practices and environment are provided at home and in school.

The Domains of Knowledge

Bloom was interested in providing a guideline or tool for teachers and those designing curriculum, so they could appropriately categorize instructional objectives. He particularly wanted to avoid overemphasis on lesser skills, which are easily measured, at the expense of more complex learned competencies that are more difficult to test. His taxonomy identifies three major, interconnected domains: the cognitive that deals with thinking and intellectual capacity, the affective that has to do with emotions and behaviors, and the psychomotor that encompassing physical abilities and skills.[8] Psychometrics, the quantification of mental or intelligence data, was for Bloom a primary focus early in his career. Bloom divided processes in the cognitive domain into six tiers, according to increasing complexity. Each level of cognitive performance builds cumulatively on the lower tiers, so that a student first masters each lower level in order to reach the higher tiers.[9] The levels, in order of increasing complexity, are as follows:

1. Knowledge, which includes memorization, recognition, recall, and definition of basic facts, terms, methods, and principles;
2. Comprehension, which is being able to understand, paraphrase, extrapolate from, and interpret knowledge;
3. Application, which is a process of taking learned material and putting it to use in new situations, or of applying abstractions and theories to concrete situations;
4. Analysis, which is being able to separate a subject into its component parts and identifying relationships and patterns among them to understand the structure and organization of the material. For example, it is the ability to separate facts from opinions and to discern logical flaws;
5. Synthesis, which is a creative process of putting together parts into a novel sum, which can involve taking the analyzed component parts and relating them to each other in a new construction; and
6. Evaluation, which deals with making judgments and comparisons using determined criteria and standards (either internal or external).[10]

Following Bloom's lead, each level requires the teacher to apply different methods of teaching (reading, lecture, experiments, comparisons, writing, hands-on, etc.) and then to evaluate the student's proficiency.[11] A student first masters the lower cognitive level before advancing on to the next. Some educators have termed the first three of these levels as lower-level thinking and the final three as higher-level thinking.[12] Others consider any level above "knowledge" to involve higher order thinking. Bloom himself did not specifically use the terms "lower" and "higher order thinking," although the terms developed out of studies in his Taxonomy.[13] Moreover, his categorizations have reinforced traditional teaching and education methods that focus on facts and frequent measurement.

Bloom also developed a theory of Mastery Learning, based on a conviction that virtually all students are capable of achieving the same goals and performing at the same academic level if appropriate encouragement and conditions are provided for them. Students, therefore, should not be graded or evaluated in comparison to one another but instead should be encouraged individually to achieve the goals set forth by the curriculum and according to their particular aptitudes. Bloom believed that standard grading systems did not properly allow for varying abilities and the complex cognitive processes involved in learning. He advocated teaching "each child with the basic assumption that he or she can learn well when given the support and encouragement needed."[14] This focusing on the student as an individual finds an analogue in Gülen's theory that it is the teacher's responsibility to help identify and encourage each student's individual aptitudes. The educational goal should be to promote learning for all students rather than to accept that some students will fail.

One way that Bloom proposed to resolve this pedagogical failing was to focus on "alterable variables," which he defined as those factors that can be changed before the teaching and learning process begin or that can be modified during or through those processes to better suit an individual student's needs.[15] To rank time as an alterable variable, Bloom distinguished between "time available" and "time-on-task." Seldom is there flexibility in classroom-allotted time. But the amount of time a student spends actively learning (i.e. on task) is one variable, which can be altered, depending upon teaching method and the student's cognitive abilities. Any circumstance that can be changed to improve students' time-on-task, and, therefore, overall learning experience, is an alterable variable. Bloom attributed discrepancies in student learning to variables such as available resources, quality of teaching, and school and home environments, with the implication that under the best conditions almost all students can achieve academic excellence.[16] To have greater success, Bloom advocated classrooms in which students work independently, with the teacher, and collaboratively with one another. Bloom was outspoken in defense of his Mastery Learning proposals, stating, "It is a crime...to deprive children of successful learning when it is possible for virtually all to learn to a high level."[17]

Bloom's theories have often been called optimistic, a term he himself eschewed, because they are based upon an understanding of "giftedness" as a quality to be developed in all students. Bloom believed that, given the right environment, support, and type of instruction, success for all students is attainable. Perhaps Bloom's ideas have been deemed optimistic by some because of his focus upon what is "possible" rather than what is "probable." His ideas fall squarely on the nurture side of the learning debate, rejecting genetic determinism, which assumes that some students are naturally gifted while others are not.[18] Even Bloom, however, did not expect that it was likely that such positive changes, which would enable all students to succeed, would occur in the American education system.[19] Although Bloom had a diversity of ideas and theories, it is with his strict behavioral theories that he has most been associated, and these have been used to support traditional teaching and testing practices.

Comparison to Gülen

From his early work with school children and education near Izmir, Gülen conceived his dream of education for the future not only for youth of Turkey but also for youth across the planet as a hope for ushering in peace and tolerance. As decades passed and with new developments in learning, including those of Benjamin Bloom, he realized how technology was changing the shrinking world:

> In this time of rapidly increasing information, as distinct from knowledge, we need to instill in ourselves and our children the desire to acquire useful knowledge and then use it to benefit ourselves and humanity at large. Knowledge acquired for a right purpose is an inexhaustible source of blessings for the learner . . . Therefore, science and knowledge should seek to uncover humanity's nature and creation's mysteries. Any knowledge, even 'scientific,' is true only if it sheds light on the mysteries of human nature and the dark areas of existence."[20]

Insights like the above adumbrated how knowledge from his heritage and developments in the West could fuse into a holistic and global program that has been realized since the 1980s.

Knowledge: Application, Analysis, and Synthesis

The educational model espoused by Fethullah Gülen bears many similarities to Bloom's educational theories. At the core of each is the application of knowledge. Gülen believes that applying learned concepts and values to situations within and outside of school is a crucial component of the educational process. It is the responsibility of educators to teach in such a way that knowledge and its implications will become a part of a student's existence and character. Gülen wrote, "although knowledge is a value in itself, the purpose of learning is to make knowledge a guide in life."[21] Like a student who has achieved the ability to evaluate in Bloom's hierarchy, a successful student in Gülen's estimation is one who can analyze and synthesize learned information and integrate it into her life, using it as a guide for making value judgments and decisions. If knowledge is not integrated in the individual, says Gülen, it is like a weight on her shoulders, which will cause difficulties in the future. Knowledge should illuminate one's mind and soul; if it remains at the level of memorization, it can be even damaging.[22]

Students in Gülen-inspired schools are instructed in traditional curriculum as well as science and ethics. For Gülen, ethical values are not mere abstractions but are meant to be put into practice, or to use Bloom's terminology, made operational. This implies that Gülen assesses education as helping the learner negotiate through a maze of impinging and possibly conflicting demands. So, while education begins with knowledge, it must expand to include experience and analysis and extend beyond the classroom into ethical behaviors in lived situations. Robinson has described the type of values education, which Gülen promotes.

Concepts of values education involve teaching students to be able to recognize right social action and cognitive thinking including the ability to comprehend, internalize, assimilate, and evaluate information in social environments. The value represented in values education is best understood as reasoning used to distinguish a common ethic within the routines of daily life"[23]

The application of hierarchical knowledge is not a concept unique to Gülen and Bloom, nor did it evolve solely from educational theorists. In Sufism, the term *yaqin*, meaning certainty, represents a school of thought akin to Behaviorism, especially Bloom's hierarchical structure of cognitive processes and Gülen's emphasis on putting synthesized knowledge into practice.[24] There are three levels of *yaqin*, each building upon the previous level:

1. Certainty derived from knowledge – study leads one to this first level of *yaqin*. Attainment of knowledge-based certainty requires an understanding of the fundamental teachings of Islam.
2. Certainty derived from direct observation—once one has achieved the first level of *yaqin*
3. Certainty derived from direct experience – this empirical level of *yaqin* moves beyond knowledge and observation and is attainable only through the direct application of what is gained in the previous two stages. It requires one to experience directly God's presence, thereby affirming one's faith to the highest degree of certainty.[25]

This concept of certainty built upon knowledge and augmented through observation and experience is evident throughout Gülen's teachings, and is akin to the organizational structure of thought processes and learning presented in Bloom's Taxonomy.

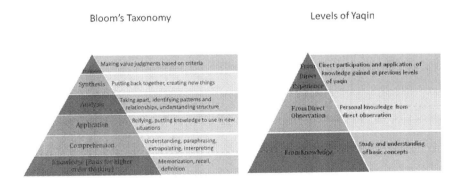

Figure 1.Yıldırım's comparison of Bloom's Taxonomy and Levels of *Yaqin* in Gülen's teachings.[26]

How Robinson describes Gülen's theory is analogous with Bloom's Taxonomy, in which application is equally imperative. It illustrates the simplest forms of learning as depending on knowledge of basic facts, and then, moving beyond to cognitively more complex analysis, it addresses the ability to synthesize and to evaluate. Putting knowledge into practice is only the third step of six in Bloom's hierarchy of cognitive processes; all the other stages require students not only to know and understand but also to apply that knowledge—to utilize it in some specific, relational manner. Both Gülen and Bloom believe that education must move beyond knowledge to understanding, applying, analyzing, synthesizing, and evaluating.

For Gülen, this process is articulated clearly in the Holy Qur'an, which encourages scientific inquiry for the purpose of awakening our moral conscience. The Qur'an encourages the study of the galaxy because such knowledge "impresses upon us the Magnificence of the Creator, exhorts us to wander among people, and directs our attention to the miraculous nature of our . . . creation." In the Qur'an, knowledge is the first stage of a religious journey that leads us toward an awareness of God.[27]

Aside from its emphasis on the application of knowledge, Gülen's educational theory contains several other analogues to Bloom's taxonomy. Gülen believes that what students learn has many component pieces. Each piece is like a guide that students may reconfigure into a new concept or knowledge.[28] The analytical process involves taking apart something already learned, breaking it down into its elemental pieces, after which a student may fuse some of these components with other, new ones, to create new permutations of knowledge. One of Bloom's former students credited him with "[teaching] me . . . the importance of supporting students in difficult times."[29]

Gülen acknowledges that in today's society, young people face a constant barrage of information from myriad sources – including the media, personal electronic devices, TV, politics, and sports – and that this profusion of information supersaturates the minds of students and adults alike. Even more threatening is recent argument that computer use essentially rewires the brain.[30] In such an over-stimulated state, the mind is often unable to process appropriately this influx of facts. Information overload may pose serious hindrances for the mind to appropriate cognitive development, muting student competencies like the ability to evaluate information, to distinguish facts from opinion, and to judge what is important and what isn't. Digitized distractions occupy students' thoughts and feelings, imposing stress and unnecessarily burdening youth emotionally, which many students are not able to handle.[31] Students may find it difficult to maintain the level of focus necessary in order to comprehend what is taught at school, apply it to life, analyze it, and synthesize it into new combinations of knowledge. Gülen stresses that to facilitate a student's ability to analyze and synthesize what she learns, the teacher must exhibit a steadfast commitment to the process of mentoring and educating. Emphasizing testable facts and theories, so convenient in satisfying a superficial demand for accountability and so enhanced by recent commuter-assisted methods, rarely gets beyond the lowest levels of Bloom's taxonomy.

Environment in School and at Home

An essential means for applying knowledge in the learning process is collaboration. Bloom encouraged his students to work together to learn from each other, an often-overlooked aspect of his theories.[32] Moreover, Bloom believed that "the basic differences among human beings are really very small," a conviction also held by Gülen, whose educational model promotes dialogue among students, encouraging them to cooperate in order to meet their common educational goals.[33] At Gülen-inspired schools, students of different backgrounds work together in small groups. Though not explicitly asserted in the official curriculum, it is evidenced sporadically in classes and in community/school events relating to learning projects and after school programs. Such collaborative learning instills ways to avoid conflict and to transcend differences in order to finish a project or create something together. Gülen underscores the value of respecting differences, be they socio-economic, religious, or cultural, and of focusing on areas in which students are able to agree and work with one another. For both Gülen and Bloom, learning should be collaborative and not solely an individual activity.

For students to learn cooperatively and constructively, they need to be provided with an academically salubrious environment. The educational reform ideas of both Gülen and Bloom focus on the importance of environment in cognitive development. In Gülen-inspired schools, a primary commitment is to enhance student engagement and increase learning by minimizing distractions that erode class time. Because Gülen-inspired schools attract and cater to a culturally and religiously diverse student body, teachers and students alike are called upon to model tolerance and practice conflict resolution. Educating and learning in such a diverse environment are two attractions of Gülen schools and help to prepare students for the outside world. Thus, common values held by teachers at Gülen-inspired schools involve celebrating diversity, working together, and giving one's best effort.

Bloom placed great importance on a student's educational environment, believing that "under favorable learning conditions most individuals can attain a level of excellence."[34] His educational theory is founded on the primacy of nurture, rather than nature. Bloom did concede that there are some inherent differences in human beings from birth, but that these differences can be overcome by appropriately altering the environments in which students grow and learn.[35] Bloom and Gülen pay particular attention to students' home environments. Bloom carried out a longitudinal study of children from birth through age six. Findings included that environmental influences have maximum impact in the earliest years and that gradually they decrease as the child ages. In the 1960s, he urged the US President and Congress to help low-income families maintain adequate nutritional, health, and home environments to permit proper growth, development, and learning to occur. The result was the Head Start program, which today annually provides these services to more than 900,000 low-income children in the US.

Bloom believed that conditions at home encompass a variety of alterable variables that impact a student's performance.[36] When parents encourage or model reading, ask questions, listen intently to each other, and show curiosity about new experiences or information, children are more likely to value those same activities in school than children whose parents simply send them to school each day and place the entire responsibility of education upon the teacher. Examples of unalterable, or static, constants are the socio-economic status of the student's family and the level of education of his or her parents. Since school districts cannot change these conditions, state and federal programs have been created in the US to provide meals, transportation and other services for economically disadvantaged students to improve their readiness to learn.[37]

Gülen likewise believes that the most important environment is the student's home, followed by the school and his social and academic interactions with peers. During the formative childhood years, Gülen explains that educators must consider all aspects of a child's environment, the impact of which might have on the child's education, and how teachers can shape any setting to promote growth and learning.[38]

Regardless of their own educational histories, though, all parents can have a positive effect on their children's education simply by promoting curiosity, creativity, and cooperation at home. Education is a collaborative effort requiring equal input from the teacher, the student, and the parents, the last of which is discussed extensively in the writings of both Bloom and Gülen. In his study of exceptionally talented sculptors, concert pianists and tennis players, Bloom found that many had chosen sculpture, the piano or tennis to emulate their parents' interest in that instrument or sport. Bloom observed "the parents of the pianists would send their children to the tennis lessons but they would take their child to the piano lessons."[39] This observation suggests that when parents take an active interest in or share an activity with their children, the child is more likely to be more successful in those activities than children whose parents do not share the interest with their child.

Gülen, too, stresses the importance of parental involvement in their children's education, as well as participation in the affairs of the entire community. Individuals who care about their children's future "cannot be indifferent to how they are educated," states Gülen; therefore "a family must provide a warm and supportive environment in which to rear children."[40] He notes that when children observe inappropriate behavior or conflict in their home, it can be permanently etched in their minds. Even when parents think their child does not understand a situation, such adverse memories may later resurface, impeding progression in education and emotional development. Gülen encourages parents to be circumspect in their interactions with and in the presence of their children and to be as transparent as possible, taking their children seriously and treating them as complete human beings.[41]

Education and Educators' Roles

This emphasis on environmental influence is integral to both Bloom's and Gülen's approaches to education. Bloom focused on problems in learning; his goal was to develop a method for teachers to provide higher quality and more appropriate instruction. He believed learning was influenced by opportunity and effort and that it was impeded by inadequate curriculum design and teaching methods. For five years Bloom and a group of colleagues investigated exceptionally talented individuals in a variety of vocations, including research mathematicians, Olympic swimmers, and concert pianists in order to find what these high achievers had in common.[42] One of their important findings was coined in the term "automaticity"— the ability to perform a skill without conscious thought. Mastery of a skill such as performing successfully math problems frees up parts of the brain to advance to higher levels of the both the skill itself and of learning in general. Bloom believed that this process applied to all learners and was fundamental to the learning process.

From these observations, Bloom and his team developed their ideas on mastery learning, an approach that focuses on advancement through demonstrated proficiency. He therefore advocated that teachers should encourage each student to pursue and excel in whatever area he or she has ability or about which they express an interest. Doing so will increase proficiency in one subject, bolster the student's confidence, and increase their overall interest in learning. Bloom stressed, however, that the role of an educator is not to identify talent or giftedness in a few select students. In order to maximize the possibility for all children to realized their full potential, educators should encourage each and every student to pursue their own particular interest and hone their specific talents.

The other commonality among the gifted individuals that Bloom and his team discovered was the importance of nurture. Talent, they found, requires facilitation by the entire family and the family's cohesiveness. All the highly gifted intellectuals and performers, studied by Bloom, reported that they had someone whom at a young age gave them an appreciation of learning or the love for the game. Bloom calls upon teachers to serve as role models and to give caring encouragement. He explained that teaching by example is necessary because, in many cases, ideas are "too complex to represent verbally" and can better be shown.[43] Bloom's concept of giftedness as a trait to be developed in each student places on teacher's responsibility. Teachers must recognize and cater to students' individual needs and abilities to help each student realize and maximize his or her full potential. Sometimes teachers are unable to perform at the level of their exceptionally talented students, and therefore turn to older stellar students to serve as models for the younger ones. In his research on pianists and successful tennis players, Bloom attested,

> As students learned from these observations of others, they also learned to observe and analyze their own performances. This critical and analytical skill applied to their own performances became highly developed and served the talented individuals long after the master teacher was no longer available for consultation and advice.[44]

Gülen's scope of teacher responsibility and nurturing of student exceeds that of Bloom. His model is explicitly holistic, for it includes the student's emotional, familial, and social life. For Gülen, this means nurturing both the academic and spiritual needs of each student in order to rear intellectually and morally competent individuals. He believes that schools must give equal attention to the sciences and to ethics and moral values, explaining that "we are creatures composed of not only a body or mind or feelings or spirit; rather, we are harmonious compositions of all these elements."[45]

The reader will find at Gülen-inspired schools a concerted endeavor to develop well-rounded young people whose scholastic achievements are also accompanied by a strong, scrupulous set of ethical values. An effective teacher is one who is able to discern and respond to the unique abilities each student.[46] Gülen asserts, "Patience is of great importance in education" and that "the best way to educate people is to show a special concern for every individual, not forgetting that each individual is a different 'world.[47] Gülen believes that the answer to today's overload of information is mastering some specific area of expertise. Every individual should master at least one facet of life and devote their effort to exploring and discovering within that area how to perform competently, so as to benefit from such performances. Thus, it is the teacher's responsibility to help identify and encourage each student's individual talents.[48]

Bloom and Gülen agree that, most importantly, teachers must serve as positive role models for their students. What Gülen sees as a critical weakness in the scientific curricula at many schools is the lack of moral guidance. To address this problem, he suggests that teachers serve as moral models for their students. This does not mean eschewing academic learning. On the contrary, if teachers instruct their students in academics while outwardly modeling moral behavior, students will pick up on these behaviors without teachers having to preach them. Teachers influenced by the writings of Gülen believe it is their responsibility to practice tolerance and understanding, thereby inculcating these values in their students.

Throughout his discourses on education, Gülen iterates that life itself provides experiences and is, thus, the real teacher, guiding endlessly lessons from which we may learn and better ourselves. Young people need teachers to serve as intermediaries who will help interpret the lessons of life.[49] Teachers must function as conduits of knowledge, of reading and analyzing the details of life, and then of channeling this information to the students in a relatable manner. Gülen expects much of educators, maintaining that they must continually search for new methods and occasions to teach. He likens them to alchemists in whose hands ore is turned to pure silver and gold.[50]

Bloom and Gülen are forward looking, proposing methods and values that will serve students in their future professional and personal lives. When children learn to value diligence, understand subsequent rewards, comprehend that they can succeed, they will go on to promote and uphold such ideals outside of the schools as well. Gülen notes, "A school . . . speaks even when it is silent. Because of this, although it seems to occupy only one phase of life, school actually dominates all times and events."[51] Gülen believes that parents must focus on building trust with their children, which can then be manifested in the future.[52] When parents and educators set a positive example for children, they provide an invaluable service to society, helping to shape young people into capable and informed adults.

Therefore, summing up, both Bloom and Gülen believe that all children are capable of academic success when provided with the proper encouragement and environment at home and at school. It is the teacher's responsibility to create a productive learning environment at school, recognizing individual student aptitudes and interests, while parents should model appropriate behavior and share talents and interests with their children. Bloom and Gülen emphasize the importance of collaboration.

Students should work together with other students and with the teacher, as well as working independently, to achieve their maximum potential. Teachers, on the other hand, are expected to serve as positive role models, to recognize each student's giftedness, and to approach education holistically. The goal of education, according to these two theorists, should be the cultivation of knowledgeable and competent individuals who are motivated and able to make positive contributions for the greater good of society.

7
Social Modeling and Self-Efficacy

Bandura and Gülen

SOCIAL LEARNING OCCUPIES a significant place in a discourse on Fethullah Gülen and Albert Bandura. The latter is considered one of the founders of the school of social learning theory, along with Lev Vygotsky, Julian Rotter, and Jean Lave. Bandura. However, later in his career, Bandura broadened the scope of his work to develop a social cognitive theory that encompasses the thought processes involved in the transmission and acquisition of knowledge and resulting behavior. His writings focus on the importance of observational learning, vicarious learning from symbols and symbolic environments, and modeling in learning. Bandura sees human functioning as explained through the reciprocal interaction of behavior, cognitive, and environmental events, and he considers both behaviorism and developmental determinism too narrow. He has researched, written, and testified extensively on self-efficacy and people's perception of their capability to exercise influence over events that affect their lives and how this empowerment affects their psychological functioning and behavior. Much of Gülen's career has been focused on advancing positive social change through education; social learning through modeling and environmental events play an integral role in Gülen's world of education. Gülen and Bandura have focused their ideas on many of the same intractable issues.

"The Diehard Optimist"

Albert Bandura was born on December 4, 1925, near Edmonton in Alberta, Canada. He is the youngest of six children born to immigrant parents of Eastern European heritage. His father was a railroad worker, and his mother worked in the local general store.[1] His parents greatly valued education, although neither had the benefit of formal education. In an interview for *Stanford Magazine,*[2] Bandura related that he had never forgotten his mother saying, "You have a choice. You can work in the fields and get drunk in the beer parlor, or you might get an education."[3] After graduating from the local high school, Bandura enrolled at the University of British Columbia in Vancouver. He had not intended to be a psychologist, but during his freshman year he enrolled in an early morning psychology class just to occupy his time since he carpooled with other students who had early classes. During the semester he became captivated by the subject matter and decided to major in psychology.[4] Bandura has since emphasized the role that luck or fortuitous events can play in one's life, using this and other examples. After graduating in 1949, Bandura attended the University of Iowa, known for its graduate program in theoretical psychology. There he earned an M.A. in 1951 and a PhD the following year. He completed a post-doctoral clinical internship at the Wichita Guidance Center, Kansas, after which he joined the psychology faculty at Stanford University in 1953, retiring in 2010. In 1964 he was promoted to full professor. Ten years later, in recognition of his academic achievements, he was awarded an endowed chair and became David Starr Professor of Social Science in Psychology. During the 1976-77 academic year, Bandura served as chair of the Department of Psychology. During his career at Stanford, Bandura was honored with many awards and titles. He was elected a Fellow of the American Psychological Association (APA) in 1964, and by 2002, the *Review of General Psychology* ranked him as the fourth most influential psychologist of the twentieth century, ranking only behind B.F. Skinner, Jean Piaget, and Sigmund Freud. In 2008, Bandura won the Grawemeyer Award in psychology for his work in cognitive theory and behavior modification, one of five annual awards given to individuals in different fields who are cited as making the world a better place.[5] According to Foster, he is frequently referred to as "the greatest living psychologist,"[6] because of his pioneering work on behavior modification and social cognitive theory, which has influenced the direction of the field of psychology since the mid-1980s.

Bandura's Early Work on Aggression

Over his long and distinguished career, Bandura has made significant contributions in psychology and human development. One of his initial research interests, which he undertook with his first doctoral student, Richard Walters, was to explain aggression in children, particularly why children in middle class families showed tendencies toward violence. Their research revealed that the parents of these children modeled aggressive behavior in front of their children. In 1959 Bandura published *Adolescent Aggression*, which documented how child-training practices and family interrelationships influence violent behavior in children. His research showed that children do not inherit violent tendencies; they learn aggression from observing others, both personally and through media. His research also showed that when aggression appears to reward and violence is glamorized on television, this behavior exerts a stronger influence on some children than the threat of punishment.

Bandura is well known for the Bobo doll experiments that he conducted with Ross and Ross in 1961 and 1963. In these studies an adult physically and verbally battered a life-sized plastic doll in the presence of a group of preschoolers. Afterward, many of the children began to engage in the same abusive behavior they had witnessed in the adult. The research also demonstrated that children could learn new patterns of behavior and not immediately act or perform. Bandura thereafter differentiated between the acquisition of cognitive effects of learning and imitative action or performance. In 1963, he published these theories and the research that supported them in *Social Learning and Personality Development*. Learning, he showed, does not occur primarily through trial and error or because of reward and punishment, but through social modeling, a process that can account for a variety of types of learning and enables educators to develop richer approaches to facilitated learning. Bandura's work on social learning constituted a rejection of the prevailing theories in human development, which on the one side involved interpretations of strict behaviorists such as Skinner, and on the other hand those of determinists such as Freud and Piaget. In later work Bandura demonstrated how variety in social modeling influences invention and occurs in the creative process; an individual will synthesize known elements or knowledge and then cognitively add new ones to generate a unique new construction.[7]

Bandura amplified the findings from Bobo studies with research that focused on symbolic media and non-human models such as cartoon characters, animals depicted as talking, puppets, and robots, or electronic sources like audio players, television, movies, computer displays, and printed materials. His findings furthered understanding about how these enactments influenced violence observed in children.   His work came to the attention of U.S. legislators. In the late 1960s Bandura testified before a number of Congressional committees and the Federal Trade Commission reporting on the documented evidence that televised violence affects aggressive behavior in children. As a result federal restrictions were placed on use of violence in television commercials and other programming. Bandura's ongoing work has included both the positive and negative influences of behavior shown on television and other media.

Social Learning Theory

In 1973 Bandura published *Aggression: A Social Learning Analysis,* in which he more comprehensively explained how aggressive patterns develop, why people engage in aggressive behavior, and why some stimuli elicit aggression and others do not. Based on his multifaceted research activities in a wide spectrum of phenomena, he elaborated an agentic perspective in which people are producers as well as products of the environment. Bandura demonstrated that children learn something about which they are cognitively aware but may not act accordingly until there is a compelling reason to act. He also found that people learn little from consequences if they are unaware of or do not to associate results with their actions.

In 1977, Bandura elaborated the theoretical aspects of his work on social learning in the text *Social Learning Theory*. This theory is based around observational learning through modeling, Bandura's innovative concept, in which "people derive conceptions from observing the structure of the behavior being modeled."[8] Such modeling behavior includes observing a live model, auditing instructions, or perceiving a symbolic model through various media. Learning and therefore behavioral change is dependent on what Bandura identified as four variables: attention, that is attending to the model; retention, being able to remember what has been observed; reproduction, being able to imitate the observed behavior; and motivation, having a reason to adopt the behavior. An array of conditions—the developmental status of the learner, the prestige and competence of the model, the learner's like or dislike of the model, the learner's expectations, the consequences of the modeled actions, the learner's goal-setting and learner's outcome expectations, and finally the perceived self-efficacy of the learner—affect observational learning and performance. Social modeling and perceived self-efficacy of Bandura's social learning theory are more congruent with Gülen's educational philosophy than most of the ideas of other theorists analyzed in this book.

Social learning theory may be considered as transitional between behaviorism, in which one's environment causes one to behave in certain ways, and cognitive learning theories, in which psychological factors are foremost in influencing behavior. But, Bandura soon came to reject "social learning theory" as too confining a label. Although the theory encompasses psychosocial phenomena, it does not recognize or include the thought processes involved. Bandura believed the cognitive component to be crucial, as Gülen also emphasizes.

Beyond the fact that both Bandura and Gülen discuss the social dimension of learning, there is another similarity in missions of their careers: both are champions of the educational use of mass media for improving the human condition, believing in the power of audio-visual and digital media to influence social change. Both have put their ideas, directly or indirectly, into practice to solve concrete social problems. These include the curbing aggression, confronting self-destructive behavior, and promoting educational opportunities for women in communities with a history of denying girls an education. Bandura's ideas have been implemented in cultures indigenous to Bolivia, Mexico, Kenya, Tanzania, China, Ethiopia, Pakistan, and the Philippines. The scholarly journal Population Communications International (PCI) that works to improve the status of women and increase the use of birth control is influence by Bandura's concepts on modeling. Its efforts utilize film mini-series and strategies of symbolic role modeling to influence individuals into going to local health clinics in Ethiopia, Tanzania and other countries. Gülen-influenced entrepreneurs have established television channels such as STV in Turkey, which model nonsmoking and non-abusive behaviors and their rewards in a country where smoking and abuse of women is widely accepted and practiced.[9]

Social Cognitive Theory

Perhaps Bandura's most significant contribution to psychology has been to demonstrate through an extensive body of ongoing research that children, and adults, can learn new behaviors and skills simply by observing others, without performing the actions themselves and without reinforcement. Learning in the absence of performance is termed latent learning. By observing others, learners may acquire declarative knowledge, procedural knowledge, or conditional knowledge, but they may not internalize in order to demonstrate what they have been exposed to at the time.

Observational or vicarious learning is the social aspect of Bandura's theory; it takes place through the subject observing others in various social settings. Moreover, there is a cognitive aspect of innate human psychology that accounts for bi-directional influences between the person's behavior and external factors. For Bandura, observational learning is primarily a process in which "information about the structure of behavior and about environmental events is transformed into symbolic representations that serve as guides for action."[10] He does not consider the person's innate psychological state as fixed. Instead, he believes that human beings, unique among animals, are capable of self-reflection and self-regulation, which, in turn, influence both behavior and development. He incorporates functions such as self-evaluation, self-regulation, inner rewards and punishments as aspects of self-reflection and thought.

> In the social cognitive view people are neither driven by inner forces nor automatically shaped and controlled by external stimuli. Rather, human functioning is explained in terms of a model of triadic reciprocity in which behavior, cognitive and other personal factors, and environmental events all operate as interacting determinants of each other.[11]

Bandura's research and theories are at odds with traditional behavioral theories, in which learning is consequences of stimuli and responses. Until Bandura's work, psychologists had focused on learning through trial and error. Bandura, with his colleagues, sought to free explanations of social learning from the behaviorists' assumption of the need for direct reward as well as from the other extreme, Freudian assumptions about identification and catharsis. Bandura's theories on social cognitivism do not deny the fact that people learn a great deal by doing, or enactive learning, but he maintains that human learning would be limited considerably if it were *only* possible through doing. His work has shown that people primarily learn by observing others.

Bandura's interest in how a child's self-regulatory and self-reflective capabilities develop led to a series of studies in which children observed peers and adults rewarding themselves for performances. These activities, which included bowling among other engagements, featured those observed receiving a variety of rewards, from small immediate to larger, long-term rewards. The research revealed that children weigh results when they decided how, when, and how much to reward themselves in similar circumstances. In making their decisions, Bandura found children to be reflective in choosing to either change their behavior or not, in fact they were more than just reactive, the tepid theory in vogue at the time of the studies. Bandura's inference put more emphasis on the learner as a more prominent agent in the learning process. Bandura's empirical and reproducible experiments essentially shifted psychology away from behaviorism to cognitive theory.[12] His emphasis on the relationship of observation and modeling for the young coincide with recurrent exhortations from Gülen: "Moreover, children need ideal models to follow. Parents are those chosen naturally as models by their child. If the child is unable to find a model in his parents, the child misses an inborn focus on the parents that causes certain conflicts of spirit. The child who finds a model in the family is most likely headed toward a happy and peaceful life."[13]

Self-Efficacy

In the 1990s, Bandura's work in cognitive development became more focused on what he termed self-efficacy, which bears on learning and acting. In 1995 and 1997 respectively, he published two books: *Self-Efficacy in Changing Societies*, the conference proceedings of a 1994 international conference he had organized; and *Self Efficacy: The Exercise of Control*. Bandura defines self-efficacy as one's beliefs about one's capabilities to exercise influence over events that affect one's life as well as the strength of those beliefs that can lead to action. Such beliefs determine how one thinks, feels, behaves, and motivates one's self, processes that form identity. These beliefs produce effects through cognitive, motivational, affective and selection processes.[14] Self-efficacy beliefs are item specific; Bandura therefore distinguishes self-efficacy from self-esteem, or self-worth, and confidence, a catchword as opposed to a specific construct embedded in a theoretical system. One can possess high self-efficacy in one situation but not in another, a differentiation lacking in notions of self-esteem or confidence. He and colleagues have addressed self-efficacy in relation to stressful life transitions, educational development, career choice, establishing proficiency, taking risks, and changing addictive behaviors by adopting healthy ones.[15]

Bandura demonstrated that self-knowledge about one's self-efficacy, whether accurate or not, comes from several sources. The most powerful influence is enactive attainment, in which a strong sense of self-efficacy is developed by way of repeated successes, and during which occasional failures are experienced, thus modifying or honing perception of one's capabilities. A second, less powerful source is vicarious experience from observing or visualizing notable people who perform actions for which they are famous. This raises self-percepts in the observer that he or she, too, has the capability to master comparable activities. Verbal persuasion, encouragement, and similar social influences may be used to persuade an individual into believing that he or she has the competence to achieve what they desire. This latter source of information is limited in producing enduring increases in self-efficacy but may contribute significantly to boosting effort and therefore produce successful performances. Finally, individuals use information from their own physiological states to judge capabilities. This information, regardless of source, is then processed cognitively.[16]

Bandura proposed that "mastery experiences," in which children successfully complete goals or projects, promotes self-belief and competency. Teachers contribute to positive self-efficacy in students by encouragement. By giving students problems to solve or achievable tasks, educators orchestrate for learners opportunities for positive reinforcement that enhance self-efficacy that leads to further cognitive and psychological progress. Bandura therefore cautioned about placing children prematurely in situations where they will experience failure. (Compare this with Vygotsky's and Britton's ideas on ZPG and scaffolding in Chapter 3).

Self-efficacy and goal setting are parts of the self-regulatory process in which humans self-organize proactively and self-reflectively as self-regulative beings rather than as beings that merely react to inner cognitive-affective forces, as elaborated in Freudian theories or explained by social environmental forces according to Skinnerian theories. Self-efficacy affects both attention and motivation of the observer with respect to learning and reproducing actions observed. Bandura and colleagues have applied findings of self-efficacy studies to treat intractable and debilitating phobias, compulsions, sexual dysfunction, and inhibitions. Participant modeling has been a successful way to obtain feedback quickly, which thus provides corrective experiences necessary for change.[17] These self-directed mastery experiences are now widely used in therapy.

The effectiveness of Bandura's theories and their practical applications in a variety of arenas is demonstrated by the fact that as of 2006, projects based on self-efficacy theories were underway in at least sixty countries.[18] Due to his belief that affecting one's cognitive state can and will increase physical and mental competencies, Bandura has been described as "a diehard optimist," a reputation that has undoubtedly been a contributing factor in his own personal and professional success and prominence.[19] His theories certainly attribute to human beings a greater degree of flexibility and plasticity than any major psychological theory to date.[20] Yet despite abundant existing and increasing empirical support, it is surprising how little social cognitive theory has permeated popular culture and psychology. However, this is the very *topos* that Gülen has entailed in his theories: how home, and local community evoke cognitively among youth the most promising and damaging potential in future adult behavior.

Home is the primary constituent, then friends and peer community, and finally by school and surroundings. The tailor shop, joiner's workshop . . . laundry, and other branches of work can also be regarded as societal environment. It is inevitable for pupil to "catch an infection" if the parents have been unable to develop or prepare child's environment adequately and are unable to understand the child's instincts. It is true that the child will certainly be corrupted if the environment is also corrupted. For this reason parents should make the environment at home, along with educators at each phase of the way and at any moment of life, suitable and appropriate for the child's benefit because it is extremely difficult to make amends once corruption has occurred. The environment must also be perfect for a perfect upbringing.[21]

Moral and Ecological Social Agency

Bandura's work in social modeling demonstrates how to facilitate effective learning and behavioral change. Today the importance of Bandura early contributions and his later insights in social cognitive theory are wide applicability to human learning competencies and behavioral modification. Modeling has been used to diminish aggression, to promote social functioning, to adopt standards of morality, to adjudicate moral dilemmas, and to influence ecological sustainability. Furthermore, "pro-social behavior such as empathy, sharing and altruism were learned through modeling."[22]

In recent years Bandura has given increased attention to moral agency as part of social cognitive theory. Individuals, he has shown, do not operate as autonomous moral agents, impervious to the social realities in which they live. Moral actions, therefore, are the product of reciprocal interaction of cognitive, affective, and social influences, already discussed above with regard to learning, aggression and other behaviors. Bandura, however, emphasizes that the self-regulation mechanism does not come into play unless it is activated.[23]

The exercise of moral agency has both inhibitive and proactive aspects. The inhibitive is the power to refrain from behaving inhumanely. Concerning the proactive aspect: "In it people invest their sense of self-worth so strongly in humane convictions and social obligations that they act against what they regard as unjust or immoral even if they incur heavy personal costs."[24] Gülen also has had much to say about moral agency:

> If the self is not well disciplined and is misused, there may be damage. In addition to the self, a person possesses cursory emotions, such as lust, anger, obstinacy and greed. It is possible that when they are disciplined they become very dangerous for the individual and for humanity. But, it is also possible that the self and that person's emotions may turn into human profundity when disciplined and may evolve and exalt eternal truths and spirituality.[25]

Bandura's recent writings, testimonies, and papers delivered at conferences have addressed and formalized nomenclature depicting contemporary acts of violence and inhumane behavior relating to events ranging from the Columbine High School shootings to torture at Ghraib prison, the U.S. wars in Iraq and Afghanistan, and national and international acts of terrorism. His and others' research findings have demonstrated the pervasive role of self-regulatory mechanisms and catalogued types of detrimental conduct.[26] These mechanisms punctuate across a spectrum from excuses for perpetuating inhumanities to rationalizations that impedes ecological sustainability and posit such categories as humans' moral justification or "cognitive reconstruction of behavior," their euphemistic labeling or "verbal sanitizing," their advantageous comparisons or "self-exoneration," their displacement or diffusion of responsibility or "disavowal of agency," their distortion or disregard of consequences or "minimizing harm," and their dehumanization or attribution of blame or "depersonalization."[27-29] The "proneness to moral disengagement predicts both felony and misdemeanor assaults and thefts across all class, sex, age and cultural boundaries," he writes.[30] He cites the tobacco and gun businesses and the National Rifle Association (NRA) as examples of industries and associations that involve many moral people despite abundant evidence of the harm resulting from their employment and affiliation. On the other hand, peer modeling and espousal of peaceable solutions to human conflicts can enhance moral engagement.[31] Bandura, therefore, places both personal and group moral agency firmly within a modeling and social cognitive context.

Gülen on Social Learning

Gülen emphasizes that, whether they desire it or not, parents are primary role models for their children; their actions, words, and their relationships with other people model examples for their children. Parents should always try to retain a noble status in their children's eyes so that their instructions and suggestions will carry weight. There should be no discrepancy between a person's intentions or thoughts and their observable behavior.

> If the beneficent words that parents utter are not going to be manifested in their behaviors and if these righteous attitudes do not become more valuable than just words, the influence of parents may end up with little and their hypocrisy may even have a counter influence. Parents who want their wise words to be influential for their children should first experience with a perfect sincerity what they say and what they mean, and then they might expect what they hope for in the child's behavior.[32]

If parents want their child's worldview to be based on trust, love, compassion and generosity, they should exemplify these traits in their own lives. Gülen suggests that instead of talking about virtues and why they are desirable, such virtues should be modeled vicariously by means of stories of past virtuous people.

For instance, a child who observes parents in tears over their sorrow for the sufferings of humanity will be more sensitive compared to a child who listens to the words of parents who lack emotive evidence for how deeply they feel. In this context Gülen tells of a traditional tale of parents who were concerned that their child's excessive consumption of honey was harmful. The parents approached a scholar of their culture for advice. Surprisingly, the scholar requested that the parents go home and in forty days return with the child. While puzzled, the parents obliged and in forty days did as requested. The scholar during the session explained clearly the risks of excessive honey consumption and chided the child. Later, after resolution, the parents asked the sage why he required a forty-day delay before addressing their issue; the scholar replied, "The day you brought in your child, I had eaten honey myself. With the honey in my body, my words would have no effect on him. I wanted to wait until no trace of honey remained so that my words would be sincere."

Parents should take the child seriously and to the degree possible treat them as adults while recognizing their limitations in fulfilling responsibilities. Gülen points out that while children may not immediately react when parents engage in lying or falsehoods, they are likely to retain this episode and act upon it later at an emotionally charged time. There are clear implications for teachers and curriculum:

> It should be regarded as important that when planning the education of youth to keep in balance, together in discipline, mind, heart, and spirit. Mistakes should be not cast in the student's face, to be humiliated in front of others. Such mistakes should be addressed through private counseling. If this approach turns out to fail, then the student should be provided extra concern in private, one-to-one interaction. Most important of what the student learns is how those providing appropriate models embody sound learning. Those who endure with troubles and difficulties should

be provided in their training examples with similar models of appropriate behavior. The heart of the learner should be instilled by discipline that protects noble ideals . . . . It is most important that the teacher models a behavior that reveals virtue and wisdom, beyond the teacher's words of wisdom and what strategies were learned for dealing with difficult challenges.[33]

Bandura and Gülen

For Gülen, parents are the most important and primary models for the child's education. It is of singular importance that parents maintain cred- ibility with their children through truthfulness and trustworthiness. It is positive modeling by parents, teachers and older peers, which in turn builds self-efficacy in the student. For instruction, Gülen recommends employing nonfiction stories about and by virtuous people. This peda- gogy provides narratives that model how virtue or good behavior results in rewards that benefit and satisfy personally and that society appreci- ates. Bandura has shown that when parents and teachers or other adults model certain behaviors and attitudes, they exert a powerful influence on the attitudes and behaviors of the children who have witnessed them. Unless it is corroborated with attitudes and behaviors, knowledge that parents and teachers impart has less impact on children.

Modeling can be differentiated as presentation and representation; the latter being more effective for inculcating desired results. Smoking in the Republic of Turkey, a widespread and long-practiced habit provides a sound example of this distinction. Nearly all adults agree that the habit is harmful and that young people should not start smoking. But over the years a majority of those adults in Turkey continued to smoke, often in the presence of their children. For decades government programs and mandated national curriculums in schools presented smoking's harmful effects, but these efforts have met with very limited success. Only recently has legislation banned smoking in enclosed public areas, including busses, restaurants, and government buildings. Gülen recommends that authority figures represent, or model, the virtue of not smoking: school administra- tors, inspired by Gülen's words, generally hire teachers who do not smoke. A recent study has examined the influence of Gülen-inspired schools in reduction of smoking in Turkey.[34]

The more credible the observed individuals, the more likely their actions will have an impact on the observer. Gülen-inspired educators at non-sec- tarian schools in ethnically diverse areas intentionally recruit students of different ethnic, religious or cultural backgrounds.[35] Hiring practices and personnel policies reflect awareness of the importance of character and self-efficacy modeling in learning and behavioral outcomes. At Gülen- inspired schools, in-service workshops on staff development emphasize for teachers how important is effective social modeling for character education.[36] Anecdotal examples of the modeling of moral behavior and high ethical standards are available.[37]

Both Bandura and Gülen are profoundly aware of the ability of mass media to affect social learning and effect positive change through symbolic modeling, and both have consulted with organizations on the use of this powerful tool for human good. For example in Turkey as well as anywhere, spousal abuse, drug abuse, and alcohol consumption are major social problems. Gülen was instrumental in establishing a socially responsible media company that now runs Samanyolu TV.[38] Gülen provided non-prescriptive input to the producers and scriptwriters of some programs on this channel.[39] For example, a family series entitled *The Great Reunion* (*Buyuk Bulusma* in Turkish) depicts characters who abuse their wives and children being held accountable by facing punishment in the hereafter. Another, *One Turkey* (*Tek Turkiye* in Turkish), addresses the issue of terrorism. Episodes involve characters who engage in terrorist activity and then face severe consequences, while characters who choose peace by reconciliation experience positive outcomes. The disaster relief agency, Kimse Yok Mu? (Isn't There Anyone Out There? in Turkish), arranges programs in which financially able families adopted "sister" families who need financial assistance. The outcomes, subsequently, have been long-term relationships among families of vastly different backgrounds.

Conclusion

Bandura and Gülen have long focused on the important role that parents and teachers play in modeling behavior and representing, with fidelity, those concepts that children are to learn. Both cite adults' own self-efficacy, and sincere belief, as factors determining effectiveness. Bandura has found empirically that those with high self-efficacy work harder, persist longer, persevere in the face of adversity, and ultimately achieve more. The key to high self-efficacy, which has now influenced a variety of fields from education to business to international affairs, is not so much knowledge or competence, but belief in positive outcomes and the presence of positive encouragement.

Gülen's writings emphasize the importance of how a person acquires the means to actualize a moral code in his or her life, a code that entails karma and harmonious balancing of justice and virtue. For him a school is much more than a building in which a set of subjects are taught; it is an environment in which the conduct of teachers and administrators, as well as the physical design and cleanliness of the building, impact students in multifaceted ways.

It is thought that schooling concerns only a particular time of life. In fact, that stage of learning, with a mission of showing how scattered issues can be related and understood as universals, is another, second, home that prepares students to be apprentices with an opportunity for continuous reading that provides lifelong discussions even when in silences. It is for this reason that even if it seems to be occupying just a part of early life, schooling is a figurative home of governance that governs for all times and sensitizes learners to the power of words. A student who goes to school with as an apprentice repeats lessons that can be used for the rest of life. School experiences can mingled with one's identity as fantasy, truth, or capability. Attaining an ability of turning actual issues into guides or keys for opening the mysterious doors on a way that advances towards virtue.[40]

Further and in a more poetic vein:

School is not only the place that the child gains his particular identity; he acquires also genuine set of skills and explores secrets of being at school. Thanks to schooling life attains an existence for most of an appearance of a river irrigating passages of land or the appearance of sparkling dew in the trees unified by the lights coming from the sun.[41]

In Bandura's social cognitive theory, children may learn behaviors when they are young but not act upon them until some trigger activates the behavior. Inherent in this theory is the human ability to self-reflect and self-regulate, which is the abilities to evaluate one's actions, to set one's own goals, and to respond wisely. Both Bandura and Gülen believe that human behavior is determined by an interaction of external environmental factors, innate psychological factors, and behavior. All individuals are both agentic as well as receptor, and reactive, beings.

In the writings and speeches of both Bandura and Gülen, there is a consistent thread concerning the betterment of both society and the environment. An academician, the work of Bandura is based on reproducible experiments, which have been replicated and applied by many other researchers in an array of disciplines. Volunteer participants in a social and faith-based movement, on the other hand, have implemented Gülen's ideas. There is a significant body of anecdotal evidence on the effectiveness of Gülen's ideas as evidenced in the success of institutions inspired by his philosophy.

Both Bandura and Gülen are optimists and each has spent his lifetime addressing a range of perplexing, even indomitable human issues, which include self-regulation, education, morality, and presence of violence. Bandura ultimately emphasizes the great plasticity of the human brain, the learnability of positive human behavior and conduct. Gülen is motivated by a charitable concern for doing good, helping one's neighbor, both near and far, to strive to reach the highest and best human potential.

8
Holism
Gülen and Moffett's Universe of Discourse

THE FOLLOWING CHAPTER DISCUSSES James Moffett's universe of discourse that aligns with many of Fethullah Gülen's ideas about education that appear in his more than sixty books.[1] Although Moffett found a home in the language arts, his theory applies to any discipline, from art, to math, social science, and science. Moffett reoriented the English language arts curriculum from a limited focus on only three domains: writing, grammar, and literature. His universe encompasses any subject of discourse. Research in England had confirmed that writing is a mode of learning, as well as reading, listening, and observing.[2] Moffett reoriented how teacher's methodologies subsequently expand to any oral or written expression used for learning—in addition to reporting on prior learning. Composing field notes for a biology teacher, essaying about one's genealogy linking to the Civil War for a history teacher, or responding over the Internet to voices of the Other both here and abroad, liberate both heuristics and responsibilities for teachers of every subject matter. Moffett changed teaching English from notional to relational, as the curriculum is anchored in both authorial / audience relationships and how an author abstracts subjects in various genres. Moffett believed that despite the open nature of his definition of language arts, the curriculum needed spirituality and stillness of meditative practices to reinvigorate students' mental activities. Such centering relates to ideas of Gülen, thoughts present in many of his copious essays dealing with holistic education.

A Sufi in the Sierra

James Moffett was born in Mississippi in 1929 to an itinerant family that followed the scheduled engagements of his jazz-musician father. Moffett received a pre-collegiate education in the public schools of Mississippi, Georgia, Tennessee, and Ohio. Upon graduation, he won a scholarship to Harvard, an award he had to pass up because, with his father ill and a brother overseas in WWII, his family needed him home. When conditions improved, he again applied and was accepted to Harvard. Before completing his graduate degree, he spent a year studying in France, and then finished that as well as a master's degree in French at Harvard before two years in the US military.

For a decade Moffett taught English and French at Philips Exeter Academy, the prestigious preparatory school in New Hampshire. There he participated in the school's innovation, the Harkness Table, in which nearly all classes were conducted around an oval table—an arrangement requiring teacher and students to be seated so that all maintain eye-engagement during discussions of the subject being taught.[3] This tradition had started in the 1930s when an alumnus gifted an oval table to the school, which led to the school's first class conducted in seminar style. The benefits of this intimate spacing were so immediately evident that eventually the school put oval tables in all classrooms.

Moffett's experience at Phillips Exeter and his childhood in the shadows of the entertainment industry greatly influenced his interest in innovative education and a lifelong interest in enhancing learning. Moffett spent a sabbatical year from Philips Exeter at San Francisco State where he worked with S. I. Hayakawa, whose book *Language in Thought and Action* had established the author among the foremost and best known semanticists.[4] While at San Francisco, Moffett wrote a review of Alan Watts' groundbreaking *Psychotherapy: East and West* for Hayakawa's journal.[5] When he returned to New England, Moffett reentered Harvard on a Carnegie Grant, where he began research on pedagogy and wrote his early major works, *Teaching the Universe of Discourse* and *A student Centered Language Arts Program: K-13*, both of which were published in 1968.[6]

Language Arts in a Decade of Change

Moffett's contributions to education coincided with two major social events: the Cold War years and desegregation in the United States, events that profoundly influenced educational policy and the country's schools. The 1956 Supreme Court decision in Brown vs. Board of Education guaranteed equal educational opportunity for all Americans, a decision that resulted in diversity of student populations.

Simultaneous with Brown vs. Board of Education was the success of the Soviet space program, Sputnik, which seemed to demonstrate its superiority to the US in science and math education. In 1958, the Federal government subsequently passed in 1958 the National Defense Education Act (NDEA) in an attempt to bolster these curriculums.

Two years later, Project English joined math and science under the NDEA. Twenty-eight curriculum centers at colleges and universities were established to upgrade curriculum and instruction through increased rigor in retraining K-12 teachers and reforming teacher training programs. After eight years, it became evident that university-level professors and experienced teachers from a variety of rural, suburban, and inner city schools were not working together effectively. The centers were producing materials inaccessible to large percentages of those teachers' student populations. Whereas poorly performing students had previously been allowed to drop out of school, the new mandates required students of a greater range of abilities and competencies to persist through to graduation. Now all students were to stay in school and graduate.

One who first recognized Moffett's promise was James R. Squire, then Executive Secretary of the National Council of Teachers of English (NCTE), and a central force behind Project English. He was among the first to realize that the Project's materials and methods did not fit the increasingly diverse American student population. In 1966 Squire organized an Anglo-American conference at Dartmouth to address this misfit of pedagogy and pupils.[7] It was at Dartmouth that Moffett's paper, "Drama is What is Happening," galvanized those in attendance from both countries into a reform movement identified as 'The New English'.[8] [9] [10] Moffett's ideas achieved such widespread acceptance that they eventually influenced governance and accreditation policies. In California, for example, the Dartmouth Conference led directly to reform in teacher preparation requirements. California's State Department of Education issued new curricular frameworks and established measures to research and evaluate the effectiveness of education. The Direct Writing component of the California Assessment Program, using Moffett's universe of discourse as domains of student writing, measured populations at two grade levels throughout the State for several years.[11]

A new level of professionalism emerged from both unions and teacher curricular associations, like the NCTE. The latter nominated exemplary teachers to work together with state specialists involved in writing, advising, and modeling instructional methods for classroom teachers.

In 1974, James Gray, Supervisor of English education, University of California at Berkeley (UCB), initiated what became the federally funded National Writing Project.[12] Gray earlier had co-directed an NDEA center and, like Squire, recognized problems. The credo of his writing project movement was Teachers Teaching Teachers, an effective peer-to-peer, teacher-led workshops for professional development and alternative to the model of universities' top-down teacher retraining of NDEA. Gray also served on the planning commission of California's Asilomar English Conferences, where participants engage in collaborative interaction of dialogue and on forums that resemble dialog centers associated with Fethullah Gülen.

It was at Asilomar that Gray met Moffett, who had been active with teachers at these conferences since relocating to California. Gray utilized considerably Moffett's pedagogical ideas to reform the ineffective NDEA model, based on instructors distributing information to students. Moffett recommended teachers encouraging students to keep journals, students to engage in collaborative writing and dialogues, curriculums subordinating literature to writing, and education promoting cross-cultural fluency within the US and abroad.[13] Today, thanks to continued Federal funding,

Gray's writing projects, organized around Moffett's methods, though often without awareness of his theory, are found in every state.

Moffett, so very much like Gülen, never accepted a traditional academic or organizational position but endured living as a freelance writer and consultant, following his catholic interests. He established an ashram in the foothills of the Sierra Nevada where he and his wife studied and conducted seminars. For a number of years the Moffetts followed the disciplines of Swami Sivalingam.[14] Insights from Buddhism, Hinduism, Christianity, and Islam gave him an understanding of how rationalism without the quieting influence of meditation got in the way of composing informed writing. His 1981 essay "Writing, Inner Speech, and Meditation" disturbed the publisher of *Interaction* but today does not seem so unconventional.[15]

Interaction, developed by Moffett in 1974, was an experimental program of print and analogue, published by a major textbook house, a K-12 program that networked instructional materials including fiction and nonfiction, composition prompts, and in-service staff development. *Interaction* augured the means to enhance student learning in the language arts for enhancing knowledge acquisition of all subjects, but its ambition far exceeded its mode of delivery at that time. Moffett, like many intellectuals of that period, combined his personal search and journey with innovative philosophical and practical pedagogical ideas. His co-author for the second edition of *Student Centered Student Language* echoed Rumi in describing the experience of working with Moffett as like "dancing with a man who had one foot on the earth and the other in the stars."[16] Four years before his death, Moffett's was honored with the NCTE–David H. Russell Award for Distinguished Research in the Teaching of English. He died at his home in the Sierra Nevada in December 1996.[17]

Moffett's Systemic Foundation Conforms with Gülen's Holism

Moffett's progressive ideas incorporated a holistic education for elementary, secondary and tertiary institutions.[18] In many ways he was a true Deweyan, though he never read Dewey.[19] His work and publications spanned theory, research, and pedagogy—a writing program across the curriculum,[20] four anthologies of student writing of different ages,[21] evaluation design,[22] and an anthology of nonfiction selections.[23] In 1968 he had co-edited a popular anthology of short fiction, the most popular anthology of literature,[24] which is still in print and used in college English classes around the Nation.

Scanning the table of contents of any of these works reveals Moffett's system. The system entails two progressions or axes of writings, abstractions and audiences, writing about and writing for. The axis of abstraction progresses from 1. What is Happening, to 2. What Happened, the 3. What Happens, and finally 4. What should / n't Happen. Writings for audiences range from self to incrementally more distanced and eventually remote public audiences. Moffett's ideas influenced curriculum in every state of the US and in many English-speaking nations. Somewhat reminiscent of Gülen's Hizmet Movement, Moffett's influence spread through the auspices of the classroom-teacher initiated, educational reform movement, the National Writing Project. This 35-year old, Federalization of the bottom-up movement exemplifies peer-to-peer engendering described recently by Steve Johnson's *Future Perfect.*[25]

One of Moffett's unique insights was that writing is another means for learning, in addition to reporting about prior learning. In this he carried on Vygotsky's earlier work. Moffett saw that writing, like dialoguing, witnessing, attuning, and collaborating, often results in new insights, as will be explained below. But the palimpsest upon which this research was based and foundational to all of his work is Moffett's theory of epistemology, as expressed in the essay "I / You / It."[26]

In addition to Moffett's attention to effective teaching of writing and reading, he also identified a need for public schooling to better complement cognitive development with ethical character and responsibility. His final publications Harmonic Learning: Keynoting School Reform[27] and The Universal Schoolhouse: Spiritual Awakening Through Education[28] addressed what he perceived as a lack in today's secular education. Here Moffett chimed with Gülen on how spirituality, not religion, complements reason, an ethereal mindedness gravely needed for returning wisdom to education. To operationalize his ideas in addressing this lack he used discourse, as Moffett elaborated:

> I gradually disengage myself from my sole point of view and learn to speak about myself, first, as if I were another person (objectification), then about others as if they were myself (identification), and finally about others without reference to myself (transpersonalization). Put another way, I evolve from passion to compassion to dispassion."[29]

Moffett advocated in-service teacher education, coincidentally a factor in the remarkable achievements of nondenominational schools inspired by Gülen.[30] In fact parenthetically, it was Moffett's series of VHS tapes of teachers modeling methods of instruction in the Interaction series that surfaced during the tenure of State Superintendent of Wilson Riles, California Department of Education, before the coining of the now-familiar phrase "staff development." Prospective teachers and current practitioners, in any language, would benefit from implementing Moffett's system, his writing pedagogy in teaching writing and reading not just in the language arts but also in the sciences and other subjects as well, for efficacy in foster learning.

Moffett's pedagogy centers on two key components. The first is "Orders of Knowledge." Moffett identified these orders as governing all discourse, a universe in both verbal and written expression, with each exhibiting specific grammatical and genre features. They are formalized quite simply, though deceptively, and as follows:

1. What is Happening
2. What Happened
3. What Happens
4. What (should / should not) Happen

Modals and verb tense in English mark the shifts across Moffett's four Orders of Thinking. The present progressive tense in English is usually indicated by "ing," such as "I'm talking on the telephone" or the sentence, "Barcelona is leading Chelsea with seven minutes left to play." It is the tense of a traffic reporter broadcasting live from a helicopter or an actor delivering lines that simulate live action, although the audience often already knows outcomes.

The past tense in English is characterizes by "ed," as in "Yesterday, Chelsea defeated Barcelona by one goal" or "I lived in Paris in 1994." "What Happened" tells about past actions. It is common in literary genres of memoir, biography, chronicle, history and all types of fiction. Fables, concluding with a moral, connect "what happens" with "what happened." They comprise a midpoint along the continuum from uniqueness of the singular What is Happening or Happened to plural generality of What Happens. Semantically these shift in orders of meaning occur in nearly all languages.

Moffett's Order "What Happens" is the mode to express generalization, signified by the ending "s" of English verbs, as in the phrase "Blood circulates" or "The Ottoman Empire rivals Rome's in grandeur." This tense is the language of hypothesis or of truisms that include adages or proverbs such as "an apple a day keeps the doctor away" or "Okumadan alim gezmeden seyyah olunmaz (One becomes a scholar by reading and traveling)." As with Turkish, French, or English, these shifts occur in all languages, which makes Moffett's system universal. Classroom assignments eliciting students writing What Happens include essays with subordinating narrative or logical buttressing of the generalization. In other words, this is the mode of science or research findings.

The fourth Order is "What Should or Shouldn't Happen;" note that in English, a modal precedes the verb to indicate exhortation or theorizing, as in "You must vote!" or "You shouldn't miss this sale." It is also associated with moral imperatives or wisdom as expressed in "Honor thy father and mother," or "Thou shalt not kill," or "In the United States, young people should exercise."

To further demonstrate the universality of how Moffett's theory applies to any language, consider the four Orders in Turkish: the verb "olmak" conjugates the four forms: "Oluyor," "Oldu," "Olmak," "Olmalı / olmalı değil"—four utterances that approximate "What is Happening," "What Happened," "What Happens," and "What should / n't Happen."

One might infer from the above that these orders are nothing more than Cicero's four modes of rhetoric—description, narration, exposition, and argumentation. Moffett unified naturally the orders around how the same subject advances to generalization or exhortation. Holding stable the subject of composition, say a horse, contrast a young author writing about a ride in a diary (intrapersonal communication with self) with the same writer the next day writing to a friend about the horseback ride. Next, envision that writer writing about that subject to readers of the school newspaper; and, finally, the writer writing on about riding in an essay in a competitive international writing contest. The rhetorical distances from self to unknown progress from the concrete and implicit to the abstract and explicit. Moffett defined in rhetorical and dialogic terms what Piaget did for the stages in a child's ability to attain perspective and to develop cognitively.

Moffett and Gülen

Moffett and Gülen share a conviction that dialogue is a context for tolerance at the heart of knowledge.[30] Each viewed the teacher as a model who elicits emulation.[31] Dialogue fosters responsible relationships, implicit in nexuses of performer and audience, or rhetor and reader, or informer and informed. These nexuses in the case of teacher relating to students include three potential stances: teacher performing "for," teacher performing "to," and teacher performing "with" learners. Teaching a class can be a soliloquy, "for" attending students. Other times, a teacher performs "to" students by asking questions of one for the edification of all, the Socratic method. A most powerful and least utilizes stance is when the teacher teaches "with" the students in hands-on projects as part of a learning community (see Chapter 9). Gülen and Moffett caution teachers to avoid only performing their knowledge "for" the class.

For Moffett and Gülen, the teacher assumes agency that dynamically models admirable behavior. But students are not passive audiences of "for," "to," or "with," as they engage aesthetically.[32] Rosenblatt has written about these transactions.[33] These philosophers consider the educator's responsibility to be not only to develop cognitive or artistic knowledge but also to model moral behavior that evokes and elicits what Rosenblatt called aesthetic responses.[34] The essence of which, Said articulated:

> Educating people is life's most sacred, but also it most difficult task. In addition to setting a good personal example, teachers should be patient enough to obtain the desired result. They should know their students well,

and address their intellects and their hearts, spirits, and feelings. The best way to educate people is to show a special concern for every individual, not forgetting that each individual is a different "world."[35]

Moffett and Gülen share beliefs about training, or better yet, attuning the mind. Moffett from his earliest publications emphasized the need for ethics to complement the dual aims of affective and cognitive learning. He recommended a quality of thought that developed out of moral practices or of discipline that attuned the self for efficacious negotiation with one's environment. By following this, a student evolves from egocentric engagement, to distanced objectivity, and, finally, to transpersonal harmony. This regimen that complements cognition includes three metaphysical stages: 1. Attentive observation or engagement and utilizing imaging and imagination to heighten receptivity of intuition; 2. Concentration or contemplation of self and dispassionate reflection; and, 3. Distancing to the point of achieving a settled mind or attunement. Moffett's disciplines resonate with Gülen's admonition for youth to avoid seductive fads and media cacophony. Gülen advocates a discipline that parallels Moffett's regimen: According to Gülen, "the ideal *Aksiyon Insani* should possess . . . the ability to critically analyze ideas, the capacity for self-criticism, a dedicated focus on intellectually-stimulating work, and close relationships with those who also share an aspiration to service."[36]

As early as 1976, Moffett delivered his first inchoate methodology for disciplining mind, as fundamental in his canon of rhetorical theory. "Almost anyone can train their bodies, but few can educate their minds and feelings. The former produces strong bodies, while the latter produces spiritual people."[37] The aims of morally and heightened critical thinking are more likely to foster wisdom in students than dry intellectuality of the incomplete objectives of lessons that shy away from spirituality. Moffett's methodology belies any assertion that his lessons and theory teach religion, though no thinking person would object to the teaching about religions.

Morality most frequently appears as essential in Gülen's writings. He defines it as "...a set of noble principles that originate in high spirituality and govern human conduct. For this reason, people who neglect spirituality and are, therefore lacking in spiritual values cannot sustain conduct in accordance with these principles."[38] In Moffett's usage the word "ethics" has more traction. "Ethics" derives from the Greek future tense of the verb that denotes "having" or "possessing," an acquired or learned habit. An individual's ethics implies predictability, reliability, and validity based on internalized behavior. It grounds a student's character in consistent moral certitude. Referring to such an holistic education, Gülen states that a true educator, "must give due importance to all aspects of a person's mind, spirit, and self, and then raise each to its proper perfection."[39]

Although Moffett often was a guest lecturer and occasionally taught for a semester at various colleges, he believed, as does Gülen, that the goal of life is a search for meaning. In his pursuit of knowledge, Moffett embraced science while rejecting scientism and celebrated secularism without presupposing a denial of religion. In *Storm in the Mountains*, Moffett documented how religious members of a West Virginia community reverted to violence because a progressive school board denied their chance to have a say about adoption of their children's textbooks.[40] Moffett disparaged the violence but defended the rights of locals to be heard, in spite of the event contributing to the demise of his *Interaction* series.[41]

Both Moffett and Gülen opted to follow their own inner calling, opting for lives of austerity and autonomous engagement to effect better education. Moffett's contributions to student-centered education, individualization, writing before reading, collaborative writing, and cross-cultural fluency, while viewed by some as anti-establishment at the time, have not only become a standard, they are also squarely in the Deweyan and Vygotskian traditions of cognitive and aesthetic development and his own upbringing. Mohammed inspires Gülen's pursuit of knowledge, as he has testified,

> The Prophet...emphasized education and literacy. He understood what his contemporaries did not: The main duty and purpose of human life is to seek understanding. The effort of doing so, known as education, is a perfecting process through which we earn, in the spiritual, intellectual, and physical dimensions of our beings, the rank appointed for us as the perfect pattern of creation. Education through learning and a commendable way of life is a sublime duty... By fulfilling it, we attain the rank of true humanity and become a beneficial element of society."[42]

Moffett's Works as they Relate to Gülen's Holism

Interaction, integration, and individualization for Moffett replace the three Rs, of reading, writing and arithmetic. He forged a system that, on one level, deals with the subject of English but entails teaching any subject taught in English, and, on a global level, provides educators of any language with the means and methods for teaching their variety of subjects.[43] [44] [45] Moffett wrote *Active Voice* a systemic, structured curriculum that includes pedagogy for elementary through college teaching, which organizes lessons for teachers of nearly any discipline. Each exercise includes two axes, one relating to audience, the other to the subjects on which students are to write. By following these assignments, students intuitively broaden along one axis their rhetorical abilities to write—first for self, then teachers as audience, ultimately writing for peers and remote unknown audiences. The vertical axis designates increasing degrees of abstraction; they increase levels of generalization as they write about What is Happening through to What Should / Shouldn't Happen. He compiled four anthologies of representative student writings in another series *Active Voices*, one each for teachers at elementary, at middle, at secondary, and at college levels. In these four anthologies, student writers represent Moffett's different genres: 1. Writing about what is happening (drama); 2. Following investigation and reflecting on what happened (narrative); 3. Thinking through what happens and should or shouldn't happen (essays as rules or as argument); and 4. Imagining What Might Happen (creating fiction in plays, poems, and stories). Moffett postulated a universe of discourse and the orders of knowledge as bridges of the individual's life path:

> Once out of the womb, we have to differentiate ourselves from the world to defend ourselves in it, and we have to break down our thought to match the social and material breakdowns of the outer world that we have to make our way in...we resort to egocentricity in order to survive. But this egocentricity must also mature by expanding across the culture, to accommodate our humanity, and eventually across the cosmos, to accommodate our divinity. Otherwise, we survive materially only but not psychologically or spiritually. We have to develop both a first-hand, first person view in order to stand up for ourselves in the world and to fulfill our particular potential, meaning, or karma.[46]

Some who teach English criticize Moffett's schemata for neglecting the centrality of literature. Moffett, following Vygotsky, did advocate using literature but only after the student has written. First, have students write and, then, read collateral poems and stories rather than engage in the more common practice of students writing about literature they have read. Moffett's sequence heightens students' understanding of choice. An example might be students in two groups in biology observe heliotrope growth of a plant with each noting in journals of before and later developments. Subsequently, the students tally these notes into two paragraphs and then read Theodore Roethke's "Cuttings" and "Cutting Later." This sequencing of writing and then reading integrates modes of ratiocination and allows teachers to group or to individualize instruction. Perhaps all teachers—of social studies, of art, of language, of science, of physical education as well as English—might enhance learning by integrating writing and reading literature collaterally. Such "writing across the curriculum," early advocated after the Dartmouth Conference by James Britton has since been adopted widely in U.S. school systems.[47]

Moffett, like Gülen and most of the visionary philosophers examined in this book, viewed the learner as becoming, as an organism whose thinking included inspiration as well as ratiocination. Moffett embraced Wordsworth's model of individual growth and maturation in the Lake Poet's description of childhood as " . . . trailing clouds of glory do we come," to one's awakening in adolescence as "shades of prison-house begin to close" until the adulthood and the loss of the ability to perceive those clouds of glory as they "fade into the light of common day."[48] Moffett made concrete the Lake Poet's poetic reification in a holistic regimen that encompassed psychomotor, affective, cognitive growth and ethical behavior. He asserted that traditional education only partially addressed this growth model due to the fracturing of cognition into disciplines of study and almost completely ignoring feelings and spirituality.[49] Moffett viewed all development as patterns; following Wordsworth's account of how every seven years a maturing of inner and outer human's epistemology evolves from ripening, to shaping, to developing.

In *Detecting Growth through Language*, Moffett provided an assessment model that corrected a major misuse of Bloom's model. When applied in schools, the Bloom Model (see Chapter 6) emphasizes the cognitive over affective and psychomotor domains of knowledge, because testing cognition is first and foremost easy and cheap. Its effect on school district curriculum is proscription: "Teach the facts, Mam, nothing but the facts." Only if time permits, then it will be acceptable to teach the affective or emotional domain. Moffett assessment corrected this miseducation. Engagement emotionally leads to cognition, as Dewey summed it up:

> The conclusion is not that the emotional, passionate phase of action can be or should be eliminated in behalf of a bloodless reason. More "passions," not fewer, is the answer. To check the influence of hate there must be sympathy, while to rationalize sympathy there are needed emotions of curiosity, caution, respect for the freedom of others— dispositions which evoke objects which balance those called up by sympathy, and prevent its degeneration into maudlin sentiment and meddling interference. Rationality, once more, is not a force to evoke against impulse and habit. It is the attainment of a working harmony among diverse desires.[51]

Cognition follows affect; cognition does not precede affect, a fact that needs pondering when thinking about Bloom's domains of experience. This fact informs each of Moffett's twenty-three growth sequences, which warrant research for improving measurement validity and reliable accountability.[52]

Moffett's lessons incorporate Vygotsky's central finding that scientific concepts and spontaneous concepts function, evolve, and structure dialectically; interaction, fostered by a teacher orchestrating within a zone of proximal development achieves the most lasting knowledge (see Chapter 3). Aligning with caveats of Gülen, teachers concentrating on what Vygotsky called scientific concepts do well for testing but results in deadened scholarship for the brightest and a loss of the intuitive among any student population.

Moffett valued a student-centered curriculum. His growth sequences in *Detecting Growth* measure student thinking as it progress from personal to conceptual. As each learner is unique, the twenty-three sequences assess incremental developments across a continuum, of differentials occurring in rhetoric. Nearly all the results of classroom student writing exhibit newly informed students mimicking in writing the already-informed instructor, who is college educated and likely experienced in teaching for some years. This demand to inform the already informed inverts normal writing outside classrooms. Beyond schooling, ninety-nine percent of anyone's writing will be to inform others of what you know and they don't.[53] With teacher as examiner, many students desperately try to echo the informed teacher and are often compelled to plagiarize. This notorious teacher stance warps a student's understanding about school-situated rhetoric in contrast to job-situated rhetoric of real life. The more the teacher performs as examiner, the more she vitiates her potential for deepest learning by the student. Britton's longitudinal study (see Chapter 3) established that *trust* is a most essential feature in teacher-student relationships that allow students to acquire ratiocination at Bloom's highest levels: the classificatory, speculative, and evaluative. As the student matriculates through secondary, he typically loses a crucial relationship with the teacher as a trusted adult as school demands emphasizes acquisition of testable information. Moffett, Bloom and Gülen explicitly proclaim the validity and reliability of trust relationships.

Moffett passed away just as the digital revolution was making its impact. Yet, as with so many facets of education, Moffett was ahead of the curve in connecting by Internet students in one part with students in other parts of the world in what he called developing Cross-cultural Fluency ("CCF").[54] By 2012, students have teamed up across the globe to participate in joint research projects, like on problems facing youth, sharing artifactuals, food fashions, global issues, video casting or corresponding as pen-pals about their own lives and environments in vastly different cultures and regions (Some students in Gülen-inspired schools).[55]

Moffett writings on learning and ethics are congruent with those of Gülen, whose essays inspired others to realize important innovations in not only education but also in journalism, in medicine, in banking, and in disaster relief.[56] Moffett and Gülen both wrote to restore wisdom to education. They articulated, with Dewey, Bloom, and others in this book on how to prepare youth for citizenship and productivity in their communities. Their articulated philosophies are comparable in being student-centered, trust-based, integrative, interactive, individualized, and rooted in the local, while aiming to fulfill what parents expect in a well-rounded education, which includes moral acumen. As Moffett in his last publication asserted:

Spiritual education centers on personal growth, which will solve more social ills and material problems than any other sort of educational orientation. Unless the raising of consciousness and culture is the primary goal of education, people eventually betray their practical goals such as material improvement and social amelioration. Americans are losing both prosperity and democracy because they are too undeveloped to make freedom work. But aside from any worldly payoff, personal development may also be the main purpose of life.[57]

9
Culture & Social Contextualism

THIS CHAPTER DIVERTS in form from other chapters of the book and the number of theorists in different fields. All the others have dealt with a leading figure and followers whose subsequent influence on education and preparing teachers parallel in congruence various and sundry thoughts found in the many works of Fethullah Gülen. This chapter includes an: of disciplines, anthropology, sociology, literary theory, psychology, but especially culture, postcolonial, and postmodern studies. Learning theorists have expanded their scope to include a variety of social and cultural aspects of environment, as initially explored by Vygotsky, demonstrated in Bandura's work on social contexts, and elucidated in Bruner's late writings in cultural psychology.[1] Current theorists explore the complex and multidimensional nature of learning and the importance of settings. The dissonance between institutionalized Western education and current learning theory raises important and troubling new questions about praxis, pragmatism, and outcome measurement as well as a responsibility for education to place greater importance on filial-direction, self-direction, self-reflection, and collaboration of learners. From an altogether different tradition, Fethullah Gülen exhorts educators to model behaviors appropriate to situations, an encouragement that is congruent with much presently being advanced by contextualism.

Research: Behaviorism, Cognitivism & Social Constructivism

Current learning research heralds a theoretical shift, one that moves the focus beyond the perennial nature/nurture debate. This paradigmatic turn has emerged not only in psychology but also in anthropology, language arts, computer studies, and neuroscience and from Gülen's station can be expressed as an interactive triangle consisting of biology, the foundation innate capabilities; environment, physical resources; and society, sociocultural elements. As Bruner has expressed it, "the program of cultural psychology is not to deny biology or economics but to show how human minds and lives are reflections of culture and history as well as of biology and physical resources."[2] The focus of learning theory and our definitions of literacy have been expanded from what we know, that is skills and knowledge, to include emotional, social, and experiential dimensions, the contexts in which we learn and the type of person we are encouraged to become at home, in school, and in the world. This broadening of learning from the initial context of the family is more in accord with the education theories of Gülen, as elaborated in every chapter (see particularly Chapters 1, 3, 7, and 8).

In the last twenty years or so, constructivist theories have largely super-seded both predominant educational philosophies: developmentalism, in which genes, inherently influential in Piaget, adumbrate individual identity and potential competence for learning, as well as behaviorism, in which the environment is all important in shaping the individual.[3] The earliest challenges to Piaget's structuralism approach to a child's development came from Cole and Scribner[4] and Scribner and Cole.[5] These researchers administered cognitive tests, developed for individual students in Western school systems to individuals at non-Anglo American sites. They were troubled with paradoxes, of subjects' greatly disparate performances on these standard cognitive tests and these non-Western subjects impressive results in everyday cognitive activities that involved memory, calculation and reasoning.[6] They found heuristics in Vygotsky's theory and research that connected an individual's thinking to the local cultural traditions in which he or she was reared.[7] Lave, Myers, and Rogoff have subsequently shown that traditional, as opposed to formal, school-based learning, when observed in many cultures including our own, is not so much reception of knowledge as a process of social participation in cultural embeddings, of which school may be only one component.[8] [9] [10]

Rogoff, a cross-cultural psychologist, studied learning activities among the Maya in Guatemala. There, for example, she found that children at one to two years of age watched their mothers making tortillas and tried to do so themselves.[11] A survey showed similar "apprenticing" in many cultures, from learning weaving, tailoring, engaging in agricultural activities, work-ing in a store, and using tools and instruments to recounting group history or individual feats.[12] Children experienced explanation more often as part of participating at their parents' side than through instructors' discursive lectures. Lave, a social anthropologist, has conducted research on learning in diverse settings from war-torn communities in Africa to shoppers in US malls.[13] [14] Her contributions trace how protean identity is formatted and transformed in the everyday lives of those facing contentious and abrupt confrontations, such as people having to deal with the construction of light rail transit through their neighborhoods and emigrant survivors of blood-shed who endure to prevail in Canada.[15]

Rogoff's and Lave's results have been similar to those of Cole and Scribner as well as corroborate how observation and participation instanti-ated new learning rather than a subject learning from an agent in a passive environment. In her most well known work, Lave studied twenty-five women shopping in a California supermarket and documented how they decided on purchases. The women in this study were quite diverse, vary-ing in age from twenty-one to eighty, in education from eighth grade to completed earned graduate degrees, and in family income from $8,000 to $100,000 annually.[16] Lave's findings resulted in redefining the learner as the practitioner in a situated or contextualized engagement, in addition to and in contradistinction with an autonomous learner in a classroom.[17]

Lave was most interested in how the women occasionally relied upon arithmetical calculations to decide which items from an array of brands stacked on shelves landed in shopping carts.[18] Of the many utterances prior to selecting for purchase, seventy-seven voiced incidents occurred when the women made a mathematical calculation. Later, outside the market, each shopper then performed on a pencil and paper test, which included arithmetic, division, multiplication, fractions, and decimals. The test simulated most of the computations the women had performed *in situ*. The results indicated that in the store they accurately computed 98% of the time, while on the test fashioned for classrooms they performed accurately only 59% of the time. These shoppers embodied situated learning of a quality unattainable in the decontextualized classroom. There is a difference between getting the right answer and knowing the right answer.[19]

These findings, and others like them, have led scholars to reconsider both the components involved in learning and the structure and goals of Western education as reflected in the formal learning models of Piaget, Bloom, and Vygotsky. Rogoff analyzed these models: "Piaget's emphasis was on children's qualitative shifts in perspective on logico-mathematical problems, whereas Vygotsky was interested in children's development of skills and information useful for the application of culturally developed tools for thinking."[20] For Piaget, development moves from the individual to the social, and for Vygotsky, from the social to the individual. For Vygotsky as well as Gülen, from the beginning the child is a social being; each assumed that social guidance aids children in learning to communicate and to plan and remember deliberately from the first years of life, which permits children to internalize activities practiced socially thereby advancing their own capabilities to independently manage problem solving.[21] [22]

In terms of cultural variances, Rogoff concluded that focus on the individual "as an independent actor is quite culturally determined, a product of middle-class Western striving for individualism and independence, with an emphasis on the individual as the most important unit of human functioning.[23] Western parents orient their young children toward objects rather than toward other people, so early in life children begin to compete with siblings and playmates; this culture bias results in valorizing the concept of freedom. In the Middle Eastern culture of Gülen, parents tend to orient children toward people, especially family, so early in life children begin to bond with siblings and playmates; this culture bias results in valorizing the concept of justice. Vygotsky, and other mid-century educational and learning theorists, focused on the sorts of language and analysis that characterize academic learning, acquisitions consistent with the agendas of their countries during their own upbringings and subsequently when they wrote.[24] Such a unidirectional focus, which privileges academic, literate approaches, needs to be questioned in order to understand the sociocultural context of individual development. Myers affords a brilliant survey of how in the West social change and technology continually redefined the notion of literacy.[25]

Moll[26] and Bruner[27] demonstrate how Vygotsky's ideas have been interpreted by the education establishment in a very narrow fashion, giving the teacher total responsibility for organizing classroom activities. By the late 1980s there was a convergence in thinking among educators who encouraged teachers to search for alternatives to didactic teaching with the need to refocus education around the idea that knowledge should be at least partially constructed by the learners themselves, within a range of sociocultural constraints.[28] In such environments learners become active explorers and not the "recipients of ready-made knowledge from outside to the individual mind" so that "learning becomes an active construction to be resolved through experientially based problems."[29] This is a practice consistent with Lave's supermarket study.

Departing from formal processes prevalent today in Western education, contemporary researchers, therefore, envision learning as a multidimensional process that encompasses multiple perspectives. Jarvis describes learning as experiential and existential: knowledge is first constructed in a social context and then appropriated by individuals as members of that society.[30] By juxtaposing classroom and real world education, part of this new emphasis redresses traditional cognitive theory, which often discounts hands-on experiential learning. This new constructionist/constructivist/contextualist approach employs a varied nomenclature to describe a spectrum of learning, from reflective practice, situated cognition, transformative learning, and practice learning. Two elements seem worth emphasizing: first, that much of this learning takes place outside of the traditional classroom with its standard methods of lecture, listening, and regurgitating; and second, that the proposed definition of learning and literacy is now vastly more inclusive and complex than it was twenty-five years ago, especially with the advent of computers.

Practitioners in a range of disciplines have shown that learning is culturally variable and interactive. Lave writes, ". . . learning is ubiquitous in ongoing activity, though often unrecognized as such. Practice learning, learning in context, always involves changes in knowledge and action."[31] Yet, Western education systems still concentrate on formal knowledge transmission that privileges values and ways of a particular culture as a whole. Bruner has posed key questions about the nature of such education, asking whether "education should reproduce the culture or enrich and cultivate human potential,"[32] and he contends elsewhere that as currently structured, Western schools are simply one more institution that make the rich richer and the poor poorer.[33] Noddings, a feminist voice in educational philosophy, has concluded that "Liberal education is an inappropriate ideal for general education because it draws on only a narrow set of human capabilities; hence, prescribing one size to fit all students, a policy that ensures inequality of outcomes."[34] She and Bruner, with Rogoff, have been at the forefront calling for a complete re-examination of Western modes of teaching and educating.

Since the 1980s, Uri Treisman, Director of the Charles A. Dana Center at the University of Texas at Austin, has been pivotal in deemphasizing singular mastery of skills of math by emphasizing cooperative engagement.[35] Settings, contingent to skill acquisition, determine significantly how students from different ethnic groups learn in and beyond classrooms. Treisman compared behaviors of Asian American, African-American, and Anglo-American undergrads in first year calculus at the University of California at Berkeley. He found these groups of students valued different learning strategies. Following class, some avoided and some chose to discuss academic subjects in social settings. Some thought post class debriefing akin to cheating, a betrayal of individuality and American self-reliance. Others once leaving lectures, capitalized academically at social events by reviewing or checking on what the instructor highlighted. Some American cultural groups deem learning to be private and personal and not proper subjects of discourse in public, as documented in speech during after-class sessions. Different cultures value learning differently.

Noddings, a former high school mathematics teacher who taught at Stanford and Wellesley after taking a doctorate in education, believes that "the great strength of ... constructivism is that it urges people to think, to try things out, and not to depend on rote memory or set curriculum and predetermined outcomes."[36] She has concluded that in the US teachers have "paid lip service only to critical thinking and actually given its attention to basic literacy." As a result, Noddings has championed a more caring, global approach to education, in which students' interests and input determine what is studied. She warns, "Too many educators are wedded to a modernist view of progress and its outmoded tools."[37] Subject matter, she suggests, "cannot carry itself. Relation, except in very rare cases, precedes any engagement with subject matter ... Kids listen to people who matter to them and to whom they matter."[38] Such conclusions chime with Gülen's exhortations documented throughout this book. Current education practices, rather than embracing methods that deal with complexity and pragmatism, instead "reproduce the culture and promote individual above group effectiveness."[39]

Current theory calls for students in small groups learning to collaborate, negotiate meanings, abstract from evidence, engage in third space activities, and be systematic in dividing intellectual labor.[30] A redefinition of literacy includes sub-skills of collaboration, like identifying and analyzing problems, of maintaining resilience in the face of ambiguity; of proposing explanatorily adequate hypotheses, and advancing solutions while being open to alternative hypotheses, of designing means for testing for the best solution, and of disseminating the results of findings.[41] This redefinition of literacy, further, emphasizes students consciously testing generalization while abstracting from data; experimenting empirically those trials that enable prediction; resisting any erasing of the past; forging fields of co-existence rather that fields of battle; warranting how wealth and power function in contentious issues; and differentiating how local concepts are fallaciously generalized globally.[42] [43] In short, they call for bringing inside academe many conversations, subjects, and methods that have heretofore been ignored.

Attendant with research on learning in settings are insights into investigations of the brain, a line of inquiry requiring its own chapter.[44]

The Culture of Education and Education as Part of Culture

Literacy has traditionally encompassed what the mind/brain gained from schooling: the ability to manipulate numbers, to decode texts, to analyze between and beyond the lines of script, and to compose meaningfully in speech and writing. The missions of education have included developing cognitive growth of students, acquiring skills for jobs and upward mobility, and perpetuating the nation's cultural heritage.[45] Standardized courses under this trinity, Noddings has pointed out, ignore almost all of the world's population and give little attention or validity to students' own experiences and interests.[46] In truth, Western education has long functioned as a hierarchical system that focuses study on "government, management, laws, wars, and winners" across all disciplines.

Research in contextualized learning and apprenticeship have coalesced around the culture of education itself, the theory and guidance of classroom practices, in which the Western classroom has become fossilized in a classical mode that not only reinforces societal disparities but has also become an end in itself. Education, Bruner argues, invents durable ways of distributing skills, attitudes and ways of thinking in the same old unjust demographic patterns ... as in procedures for examining students, which are totally unfair to the less privileged.[47] Schools "tend to . . . perpetuate subcultures of poverty or defiance that nipped or diverted children's' natural talents of mind," practices that contribute to a polarization for which education is no longer a way out.[48] Liberal education, Noddings adds, is preparation for a particular class of occupations, themselves privileged in our society. "We have neglected the personal side of education," Bruner claims. The narrative mode, story-making, is part of what is needed to remedy this, for in the narrative mode, through song, fiction, theater, drawing, one can construct an identity and find a place in one's culture.[49] Bruner's and Noddings' caveats and recommendations parallel Gülen's guidance to those inspired by him to take up teaching the youth of the world:

> Reading and literary composition are two of the most important goals that should be taught the child. The child should certainly learn reading and writing for particular purposes and to deal with assignments and practical needs, but, moreover, children should attain from teachers' guidance the lifelong habit and knowledge that reading is as important as mastering the act of reading and writing.[50]

These constructionist criticisms of narrowness and extensions of literacy both align with what Gülen has criticized early in his career about the Republic of Turkey's excessively centralized education and adumbrated later in his essays and sermons as palliatives. His holistic philosophy encompasses home, school and community learning and apprenticeship, areas of knowledge acquisition elaborated by Rogoff, Lave, Noddings, and most recently by sociologist Charles Murray in *Coming Apart: The State of White America*, 1960-2010.[51]

Many other scholars have surfaced recently to explain how contextualism redefines the acquisition of learning. But it demands elaboration beyond the scope of this chapter to explore in depth writers such as Carl Bereiter and Mikhail Bakhtin, whose names recurrently appear in scholarship and research. Bereiter's conceptualization of mind and acquisition of knowledge can be deemed synchronic, as ubiquitous and atemporal phenomena.[52] Mikhail Bakhtin's life's work dealt with dialogic imagination of cultural linguistics, which can be deemed diachronic, as how forms of utterances historically shape accessible minds for knowledge acquisition. Bereiter translated Carl Popper's three Worlds of Knowledge: Knowledge of World 1 that represents how nearly all sentient beings know the objective world; Knowledge of World 2 that represents tacit understanding of human's subjective world; and Knowledge of World 3 that represents the public understanding, the knowledge that is exclusively fashioned by humans both in and out of schools. Foremost among those researching World 3 and advancing guidance for educators is Charles Bazerman and his students.[53] [54]

Mikhail Bakhtin like Vygotsky—both of whom suffered gravely under the Soviet Union—accepted how society is the source that infuses mind with utterance.[55] A philosopher of language and literary critic, Bakhtin challenged traditional synchronic theories of linguistics and led theorists of pedagogy towards heuristic lessons for classrooms.[56] Rather than an autonomous creator of thought independent of society, Bakhtin envisioned the mind of a person as negotiator of dialogic speech acts, framed by how a culture valued genres that informed utterance, and, ultimately, thought. His theory highlights history, or diachrony, as it bears on accessibility and learning. A speaker of any language is weaned by the culture's utterances and its language tradition or what Bakhtin called *heteroglossia*. This is a language stew, of words and utterances formed in valorized genres of a culture, from a drama to a treatise on biology; it is a stew ingested with the very oxygen breathed. This *heteroglossic* stew contains conflicting ideologies in a multivocality of voices heard or read that embodies Bereiter's and Popper's "World 3."

Bakhtin's novel contribution was to identify genre containing utterances as the key to how mind processes one's linguistic environment: limericks confound many speakers of English as a second language as the translated poetry of Li Po baffles readers of English. But beyond confusion, genre substantially determines identity, as Identity and learning derive time-out-of-mind. In Arab cultures genres are gender relegated: to the female, the narrative, to the male, exposition.[57] Cultures differ by how genres determine moral ideology. For the ancient Greeks, drama, lyric, and epic featured content involving gods, goddesses, and heroes. These characters' actions, rehearsed orally in speech and writing repeatedly by the culture, prepare moral standards for the young of each Hellenic generation. These genres centripetally inculcate value and belief systems from the past about what constitute correctness, for the present and future behavior. Above all, Greeks valorized epic, then drama, then dithyramb, and finally prose.

For modern times in the West, Bakhtin celebrated the novel, the narrative, as the governing genre.[58] Narratives feature what he called double-voicedness. This duality of perspective can deconstruct critically the ethos of the past to foray scenarios for the present and future. Gülen's warning against being preachy when teaching stories to model morals approximates why double-voicedness of stories may elicit among the young the means for learning values and for testing belief systems.[59]

Bakhtin above all recognized the creative potential of cultural narratives in fostering identity, not that youth should emulate Achilles but to critically analyze Achilles. For Bakhtin the story, or the novel, is foremost among genres in the Modern Period.[60][61] The novel's unique potential of double-voicedness provides palliatives for defusing ideology and dogma in repressive cultures.

Such narratives involve both social embedding as well as cultural adaptation and coping. As underscored by Gülen:

> Each child is shaped according to the environment and can be regarded as the child of that environment. Home is the primary constituent, then friends and peer community, and finally by school and surroundings. The tailor shop, joiner's workshop, ironing shop, laundry and other branches of work can also be regarded as societal environment.[62]

Learning in school or learning as apprentice extends beyond acquiring skills for work in later life. Acquiring identities, caring for others, adopting positive attitudes, and resilience before ambiguity are crucial in achieving the good and satisfying life. Many educators tell their students and the public that the mission of education, the purpose for studying and fulfilling required courses, is to obtain a job as if the sole the aim of schooling. During Spring Break some years ago, a class of undergraduates carried out an assignment to investigate real world practices of employers experienced in firing employees. Never invoked in these interviews were reasons such as the employee "can't read," "has bad spelling," and "didn't know grammar." Rather, the most frequent reasons for job termination had to do with negative attitudes and lack of moral reasoning: "lying," "bad vibes," "persistently late," "rudeness to customers," "ignoring new ways of approaching routine tasks" and "condescending attitude toward aged," the most frequent causes of firing.[63] One interviewed employer reported that when notifying a troublesome employee of termination, he couched the bad news in an explanation that the economy was forcing businesses to downsize. Motivated to avoid potential litigation, the employer indulged immorally when honesty might likely educate and modify for the future the employee's attitude. Morality is absent in both employee and employer behavior. Ethics, moral reasoning, and caring are not usually a part of any high school curriculum, but are central in the recommendations for policy makers for Noddings, Bandura and Gülen.

Ways of learning, therefore, need to reflect society itself: diverse formal and informal education offerings that respond to diverse interests and aptitudes. These offerings should replicate social activities and prepare students for life: to be parents, to debate the issues of war and violence, to engage with one another on ethnic, religious, and gender diversity.[64] Noddings has pleaded for schools to bring within their curriculums the oft-avoided conversations about today's critical and sensitive issues. Moreover, she argues that subject matter cannot carry itself. "Relation, except in rare cases, precedes any engagement with subject matter. Kids listen to people who matter to them and to whom they matter."[65]

Gülen, as with constructivists, has emphasized the importance of learning in and acquired outside school.[66] [67]He writes,

> Even if a person has a superior nature and outstanding intellect, if he or she is content with their own opinions and are not receptive and respectful to the opinions of others, then they are more prone to make mistakes and errors than the average person. The most intelligent person is the one who most appreciates and respects mutual consultation and deliberation (*mashwarat*), and who benefits most from the ideas of others.[68]

Anticipating Lave and seemingly to concur with Gülen, one Bakhtinian scholar conceptualized setting as contingent to utterance:

> . . . linguistic matter constitutes only a part of the utterance, there exists another part that is nonverbal, which corresponds to the context of the enunciation. The existence of such a context has not been unknown before Bakhtin, but it had always been looked upon as external to the utterances, whereas Bakhtin asserts that it is an integral part of it.[69]

But, as this chapter has advanced, children assimilate in both informal and formal narratives from their parents, older peers, from television and the rest of their environment from birth. These narratives often conflict with what is emphasized in school. School cannot continue to ignore these personal narratives and the experiences of children but need to find ways to incorporate them and discuss them in curriculum if education is to be relevant to many of today's youth, not only in the U.S. but also in the rest of the world.

Conclusion

> Rationalist, wearing square hats,
> Think, in square rooms,
> Looking at the floor,
> Looking at the ceiling.
> They confine themselves
> To right angled triangles.
> If they tried rhomboids,
> Cones, waving lines, ellipses –
> As, for example, the ellipse of the halfmoon—
> Rationalists would wear sombreros.

(Wallace Stevens, 1923)[70]

The poet captures an essence of what scholars such as Noddings, Bruner, Myers, Moffett, Dewey, Rogoff and Lave have contributed to learning theory. Their wisdom has yet to reach many classrooms and perhaps more importantly, those community leaders who must more activity direct education. Perhaps, the findings of two decades reported in the pre-publication draft of the National Research Council of the National

Academes will cause policy makers to attend to contextuals discussed in this chapter. Clearly incentives and test-based accountability have been hugely disappointing.[71]

For Bruner, Bakhtin, Dewey, and others, the new standards of learning entail an interrelated network linking people, events, culture and time.[72] No longer is the notion of a concept defined traditionally as a verbal construct. Wisdom is a mindset resulting from a dialectic that includes a history of engagements, patterned by initiation, and exposed to near infinite variation impinging from a global village. After which, the learner in school or in the field evolves to levels of mastery in roles and eventually as a competent authority in mentoring new initiates. This role-shifting-and-shaping results as a generative identity who continually furthers to be modified by endured happenings that frequently include jarring negotiations during disruptive events. This relational grid transforms the learner from a person to social practitioner.[73] Resulting from this reformulation, the poet's hat for the youth is not that which she wore in school but a hat as learning-qua-participant in society. Thinking is no longer a conceptual word but a contextual process that formulates "a more-encompassing view of social practices."[74]

The same would theoretically hold for teacher instruction as well. In other words, the implementation of research into policy and practice should conform to these same standards of learning. Gülen acknowledges the need for teachers to first be educated themselves: "Educators who have not been apprenticed to a master and have not received a sound education are like blind people trying to light the way of others with lanterns."[75] Unfortunately, the education establishment has generally adopted the square and archaic hat of current fashion. In time it is hoped that teacher training institutions and state-funded in-service programs, run by county, district, and school, will influence the philosophy and methods of new teachers. Rather than a continuation of an academic food fight or Oedipal attack upon the previous generations of scholars, most educators benefit from developments by taking from each, for each tradition is partially correct, but not one of them is complete. Today, society metaphorically dons nearly all students with job-related hats. Yet few include what Noddings, Bandura, Bruner, Moffett, and Gülen advocate: fostering caring, healthy attitudes. Skills learned in school and acquired on the job still neglect Noddings and Gülen's super ordinate principles of attitude, compassion, of moral certitude, of relevance upon which such learning needs to be based.

10
Conclusion

THE PREVIOUS PAGES HAVE investigated the work of prominent scholars in learning theory and education to compare them with the ideas and ideals of F. Gülen. The goal of this volume is to provide an introductory overview to the basic tenets of Gülen's educational philosophy and to situate them among the important ideas and developments in Western education during the Twentieth Century.

Teacher Training for Compassion

Gülen's vision of education is a triangular interaction among students, parents, and teachers, each of the bonds conforming to relationships that I describe as I/Thou.[1] This I-Thou interface entails productive engagement resulting from trust, caring, and candor—features strived for in Gülen-inspired classrooms.[2] This trinity of teacher, student, and parent engenders trust and respect that can be eroded when increasingly distanced parties impinge upon the magic of learning. Without a sense of a trusting audience, researchers in the United Kingdom have found that student writing, among age groups between 13 through to 18 in five different subjects, often does not reach the highest levels of thinking, as commonly relied upon by educators using Bloom's Knowledge in the Cognitive Domain (see Chapter 6).[3] Levels of speculative and theoretical discourse were evidenced in classes of language arts and religious education, the latter a required class in schools in England and Wales. Successful teaching and parenting is necessarily I/Thou.

In the US during that last half century, state and national mandated testing of students in local schools may had a profound effect on I/Thou education. When test scores become paramount for government bureaucrats, these competitive numbers join those who sit outside the community triangle of teacher, student, and parent, and, necessarily, dictate a forced negotiation of I/It deracination of the promising potential of an I/Thou heuristic. Concern over scores that may include funding or teacher rating cause loss of catharsis, nurturing, and trust.

Gülen distinguishes educators from instructors, the former encompassing a more holistic role. His charge to educators is to "know how to find a way to the student's heart and ...to leave indelible imprints upon his or her mind."[4] Such imprints would include evaluation of a student's individual needs, engaging all aspects of their beings, and imparting wisdom, tolerance, and moral values along with scientific knowledge (*'ilm*). The promise of Gülen-inspired schools around the world evolves from their centeredness in the local community and their close ties with family.

Referring to the essential qualities of education, Gülen states that educators "should test the information to be passed on to students by refining their own minds and the prisms of their hearts."[5] He advocates that educators be thoroughly qualified and carefully selected for their positions. He further stresses how all adults—but parents and teachers in particular, as well as older peers—serve as positive role models whom children will be inclined to emulate. By modeling respect and compassion for their children, adults and society in turn receive reciprocal respect and compassion from youth.

For Gülen, dialogue in the classroom should be democratic and non-hierarchical, bottom-up, in I/thou interactions that transact with subject matter. When interaction degenerates into one-way delivery of information where teacher performs for the class, the stance shifts to an I/It. In Gülen-inspired classrooms and forums, or in international diplomacy and interfaith dialogue, the methods employed foster respect, candor, and openness, all conditions necessary for the emergence of trust. In Montessori classrooms (see Chapter 2), a student is entrusted with the responsibility to choose her own activities and work at her own pace, a practice Noddings believes should be introduced in all levels of schooling (see Chapter 9). Hahn believed that the responsibility acquired while collaborating in outdoor ventures should be continued in regular classroom activities and exercises (see Chapter 4). This German philosopher's ideal educational system is an egalitarian community grounded in mutual respect and openness of expression. Through such physical activities and association in an egalitarian community, Hahn believed students learn to become productive members of society. Moffett's educational system embraces many of these same ideals: his specific pedagogy encourages a variety of writing activities—from journaling to collaborative writing—to center the learning experience and enhance meaningful self-expression (see Chapter 8). All of these educators advocated for education to be morally and ethically uplifting, a quality they believed to be lacking in school systems and needing to be revived as wisdom education.[6]

Parents enclose the third of three angles among the partners of the I/Thou interface. Gülen and the other educators here encourage parents to promote learning at home and to take an active interest in their children's schoolwork and other activities. Montessori, for example, discussed the importance of a trusting relationship between parents and children, from which a child is more likely to learn appropriate behavior. The Italian scholar believed parents need to encourage play, which is grounded in the real world so their children stay in touch with reality to help them distinguish between creativity and distraction. Bloom researched the effects of how much time parents devote to encouraging their children's learning, both in school and extracurricular activities, finding it to be of great importance (see Chapter 6). Vygotsky, and present-day constructivists who have built on the Russian's work, emphasize how a child's cognitive abilities develop primarily through peer and familial interactions within a socio-cultural context (see Chapters 3 and 9). The three components of the I/Thou triangle, the teacher, learner, and parent, augur the greatest educational efficacy advanced by Bandura for learning and well being, to use the Canadian-American's nomenclature (see Chapter 7).

Outside this triangle one can visualize a set of concentric circles, which I will call I/it nexuses, which affect and impinge on what goes on in classrooms. At the remotest arc of the I/It encirclement are the goals of a nation state, likely to impose a one-size-fits-all rigidity for youth. In the most horrific cases, this policy aims to prepare students for military service and war. Kitsikis documents how the early nationalistic states of Greece and Turkey produced textbooks that vilified the "other," so as to guarantee military budgets from their respective populations.[7] Hahn, a German Jew, personally survived Hitler's modifying of curriculum when imposed at the Salem School.[8]

Piaget's schemata of cognitive development have greatly influenced the US educational system, with curricular frameworks and grade level expectations based on his linkage of developmental categories (see Chapter 5). Both he and Bloom believed that not all children reach the final stage of mature thinking and that these could be measured. It was Vygotsky who developed the importance of socio-cultural influence on learning that has been further elaborated by Bruner, Rogoff, and others (see Chapters 3 and 9). Whereas Gülen makes a moderate statement regarding societal and cultural impact, Vygotsky believed that cognitive structures and processes are direct products of one's socio-cultural interactions and environment. He developed the two-fold nature of a child's cultural, cognitive, and logical development: these functions originate *inter*psychologically (through interactions and relationships with others), and are then internalized and further developed *intra*psychologically (within the child).

Cumulative Knowledge, Interaction, Holism, and Locality

Gülen apparently intuited insights on how knowledge is cumulatively acquired, and he envisioned the implications that peer and student-educator interactions have for curriculum and learning. For him, knowledge is both experiential and cumulative. The concept of *yaqin* approximates the way in which Dewey explained impulse, thought, and interaction (see Chapter 1). During stages of growth, as hypothesized by Piaget and Bloom, children develop different functions and abilities, most of which build upon or refine earlier understandings. Piaget predicated that a child, for example, must first understand how to classify objects into one group, red blocks or square blocks, before she is able to comprehend that an object might be both red and square at the same time. Bloom's taxonomy formally categorized these levels of learning and thinking, a classification that reflected the cognitive influence that predominated in education from the 1960s until nearly the turn of the century.

Cooperation and collaboration are among Gülen's core educational principles. He believes that learning to work together is essential in the classroom and is an important means toward achieving community cohesion and ultimately toward solving world problems and achieving regional and global peace. In Gülen-inspired schools, students work together on projects and common goals, learning to respect and honor one another regardless of external cultural and economic differences including an understanding of the dangers of addiction that threaten their futures. Bloom and Moffett emphasized classroom collaboration as a way for students to provide mutual feedback, thus learning from one another as well as from the teacher. Vygotsky's pedagogical method advocated students working with more capable peers, to enable learners to internalize inner speech and thought; his entire theory of learning was based on social interaction.

Gülen faults present-day school systems for failing to provide students with the precepts of a sound moral education. He advocates teaching ethical knowledge by example but not by proscription. His educational ideal is a holistic one that treats each student as a being comprised of mind, body, and soul. Gülen-inspired schools do not teach religion; rather, they work to foster uplifting attitudes and engender students with moral sensitivity without inculcating any religious doctrine. A similar commitment to moral education is evident in Montessori's inclusive pedagogy and in Moffett's holistic 'meta-science,' which incorporates morality, ethics, and spirituality alongside cognitive, physical, and emotional knowledge. Hahn's educational model aims at holism, though he envisioned students experiencing spirituality through physical communion with nature; for him the weaknesses of modern youth are countered through incorporating physical education. Hahn linked physical health to mental health, believing that a physically fit body would lead to a healthier, more active mind and that physical education would counter restlessness and lack of discipline. Hahn saw education as more than just enriching the mind; it was his particular genius to add fitness training, physical activity, and community service to the curriculum. Service learning is experiencing a rapid expansion in US schools, a testament to Hahn's vision and a reaffirmation of the importance of community in the educational process.

Teachers at Gülen-inspired schools are expected to adhere to high ethical standards, so that students will emulate these observed behaviors. Older students also serve as role models for their peers and younger students. Bloom's longitudinal studies focused on gifted professionals in a variety of fields and how they had been influenced by role models and involved parents. Bandura's research demonstrated how both violent and benevolent behavior engaged in by adults was later manifested in those child witnesses. Like Gülen, Moffett viewed the teacher as what Gülen termed an *aksiyon insani*, the model of behavior set forth for students to emulate. There are three stances relating to teacher/student negotiations:

1. Performing *for*,
2. Performing *to*, and
3. Performing *with*.

The teacher, in each of these stances, serves as active role model. Teachers in the third stance of working with students and this parents approach I/Thou attunement.

Gülen holds tolerance, dialogue, and compassion, features most promising in such attunement are foremost human values to be practiced in schools. Students with a peaceful and tolerant environment are facilitated in their ability to work together toward common goals. Bloom worked toward eliminating the negative effects of poverty on learning and advocated minimizing any inherent disparities among students both at home and in school. Montessori, a proponent of positively altering the academic environment, created student-centered classrooms, hoping to provide students with a suitable environment in which to live and learn. While well-designed curriculum and a positive learning environment can greatly help student learning and development, Gülen, with Montessori and the other educators in this volume, believe that parents and the family environment are keys to their children's future.

Gülen is an education philosopher in the old tradition, before American administrators of schools deserted wisdom to emulate CEOs of industry. Gülen's mission derives from the heart in pursuit of knowledge and wisdom rather than efficiency. He cautions about addictions and health-threatening influences. He embraces local standards and those curricular requirements of communities hosting schools inspired by his words. Void of any religious content or *teblig*, he advocates only teaching *temsil*, the secular knowledge commonly taught in modern curriculums.

A palimpsest of curriculum unites the educational ideas of Gülen with the modern ideas among the caravanserai of educators in this book. An ancient model of at least a millennium and a half years undergirds both, a model institutionalized in accreditation and licensure today. Rooted in *temsil* of Islam and the trivium and quadrivium of late Roman times, Ibn

Rushd first, then St. Thomas Aquinas, upgraded the curriculum that eventually became that which children and adolescents study in school. This palimpsest is evidenced in the art of the Middle Ages.

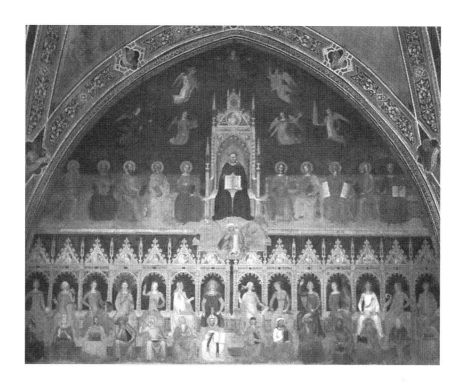

"Triumph of St. Thomas" by Andrea di Bonaiuto, Spanish Chapel,
Santa Maria Novella, Florence Italy
The seven niches on the Saint's left are *temsil* and the
trivium and quadrivium.

A 14th century painting in Florence distinguishes what to Muslims are *temsil* and *teblig*. Andrea di Bonaiuto's "The Triumph of St. Thomas" in Santa Maria Novella documents one common feature of both Christian and Muslim intellectual orientation. The painting also depicts Ibn Rushd, known as and beholden by Thomas Aquinas as Averroes. The painter arranges horizontally two sets of seven icons beneath both these 13th century thinkers. On the right are seven idealized figures above seven historical masters, the pairs symbolizing each of the rational subjects studied commonly in elementary schools today. Third to the right, a woman with a square hovers over Euclid or geometry. These secular knowledges of *temsil* are separated from religious curriculum, or *teblig*, arranged on the left, the sacred curriculums.

The subjects of *teblig*, or religious education of sacred or transmitted knowledge, are never included in Gülen-inspired, nondenominational schools anywhere in the world. Gülen has persistently advocated only teaching the *temsil*, the secular sciences, in the same tradition of the US, which conforms to the separation of church and state (Afsaruddin, 2005, p. 5). Considering this review of today's curriculum, one soon realizes that St. Thomas' arithmetic and computational numeration was in Latin, but today children compute with Arab numbers, which only allows for division and makes multiplication easier. Upon further reflection, the subject of algebra from the Islamic world has since been added to music, astronomy, arithmetic, geometry, grammar, rhetoric, and logic. In other words, today's curriculum is the fusion of the two heritages, not exclusively, by any means, of that of ancient Rome alone.

Knowledge among these subjects in elementary and secondary school curriculums entail different structures, which warrant degrees for successful completion. This fact influences how different subjects in school are taught differently.[9] Mathematics and language are processes; astronomy and the sciences are products, substantives with databases and with methodologies that include the possibility of replicating for testing and predictably. This feature of predictability is an attribute of science knowledge that is lacking in the arts. Yet, in any subject area, the pedagogy of a lesson involves students interplaying particulars and generalizations. At university, the scholar of science, physical or social, graduates with a B. S. degree, recognition of competence in discovering generalizations of predictive value after study of a host of particulars. Her friends earning a BA degree have exhibited their competence to create art that evokes feelings or competence in expressing rationally generalizations about a particular, a singular work of literature or design. A poem, painting, or concert evokes responses from the engaged student who can competently generalize critically in well-formed elaboration of how particulars or features of the artwork manifest his or her asserted generalization. Essential to these subjects are feelings, language and number, by which a student masters environment by internalizing mind patterns for negotiating the world.[10] Curriculums and instruction encountered in Gülen-spired schools around the world avoid religion and only deal with *temsil* in developing in students knowledge and competence.[11]

Epilogue

Some readers of this book may wish to know more about how Gülen influences the schools around the world that are affiliated with the *Hizmet* movement, whose adherents have gone out into world to do the good works that Gülen advocates. If these searchers look for some headquarters or bureaucratic department or commission, they search in vain.

The *Hizmet* tradition is neither centralized nor hierarchical but rather manifests itself bottom up in locally rooted peer-to-peer network in different communities. When establishing a new school, a local community of parents and educators come together to elicit each other's points of view and discern community needs. Some of Gülen's extensive writings and talks have been gathered and edited on the Internet that provides a fine database for such research.

Notes

Preface

1 Edward Said, *Orientalism*, (New York, NY: Vintage, 1987).
2 Jill B. Carroll, *A Dialogue of Civilizations: Gülen's Islamic Ideals and Humanistic Discourse*. With foreword by Akbar S. Ahmed. (Somerset, NY: Light, 2007).
3 Edward Said, *Culture and Imperialism*, (New York, NY: Knopf, 1993), 74-80.
4 Bruce Novak and Jeffrey D. Wilhelm, *Literacy and Wisdom: "Being the Book" and "Being the Change*, (New York, NY: Teachers College Press of Columbia University, 2011).
5 Steven Johnson, *Future Perfection: The Case for Progress in a Networked Age*, (New York, NY: Riverhead Book, 2012), 94-96, 158, 199-294.

Introduction

1 Helen R. Ebaugh, *The Gülen Movement: A Sociological Analysis of a Civic Movement Rooted in Moderate Islam*, (New York, NY: Springer, 2009).
2 Muhammed Çetin, *The Gülen movement: Civic Service without Borders*. (New York, NY: Blue Dome Pr, 2010), 20.
3 *Foreign Policy Magazine*, http://www.foreignpolicy.com/articles/2008/08/03/meet_fethullah_guelen_the_worlds_top_public_intellectual).
4 Time Magazine. (2013). http://time100.time.com/2013/04/18/time-100/slide/fethullah-gulen/
5 Jill B. Carroll, *A Dialogue of Civilizations: Gülen's Islamic Ideals and Humanistic Discourse*. With foreword by Akbar S. Ahmed. (Somerset, NY: Light, 2007).
6 Anne Solberg, The Gülen Schools: A Perfect Compromise or Compromising Perfectly? http://www.kotor-network.info/papers/2005/Gülen.Solberg.pdf
7 Muhammed Çetin, *The Gülen Movement: Civic Service without Borders*. (New York, NY: Blue Dome Pr, 2010), 91.
8 Yüksel Aslandoğan and Muhammed Çetin, The Educational Philosophy of Gülen in Thought and Practice." Ed. Robert A. Hunt and Yüksel Aslandoğan. *Muslim Citizens of the Globalized World: Contributions of the Gülen Movement*. (Somerset, NJ: The Light, 2006), 35.
9 Joseph O'Neill, *The Blood-Dark Track*. (London, UK: Granta, 2001).
10 Orhan Pamuk, "The Souring of Turkey's European Dream." http://www.guardian.co.uk/commentisfree/2010/dec/23/turkey-european-dream-migrants-minorites
11 Yüksel Aslandoğan and Muhammed Çetin, The Educational Philosophy of Gülen in Thought and Practice." Ed. Robert A. Hunt and Yüksel Aslandoğan. *Muslim Citizens of the Globalized World: Contributions of the Gülen Movement*. (Somerset, NJ: The Light, 2006).
12 (Ibid).

13 Jeton Mehmeti, "Religious Ethics, Spirituality and Public Life: The Contribution of Fethullah Gülen. *East and West Encounters: The Gülen Movement.*
   Pacifica Institute. USC, Los Angeles, 4-6 Dec. 2009.
14 Gülen Feb. 22 2006 http://www.infinitelight.org/content/view/722/4/
15 Father Thomas Michel, http://www.thomasmichel.us/gulen-educator.html
16 Fethullah Gülen, *The Statue of Our Souls: Revival in Islamic_Thought and
   Activism.* (Rutherford, NJ: The Light, 2005), para. 7 following Transforming
   character.
17 Fethullah Gülen, (http://www.fethullahGülenconference.org/houston/read.
   php?p=fethullah-Gülen-vision-transcendent-education).
18 Fethullah Gülen, http://www.fethullahGülenconference.org/houston/read.
   php?p=fethullah-Gülen-vision-transcendent-education).
19 Fethullah Gülen, http://www.fethullahGülenconference.org/houston/read.
   php?p=fethullah-Gülen-vision-transcendent-education).
20 Fethullah Gülen, Wed. 14 June 2006http://en.fGülen.com/love-and-
   tolerance/274-education/1855-education-from-c1adle-to-grave.html).
21 Fethullah Gülen, *Toward a Global Civilization of Love & Tolerance.*
   (Somerset, N.J.: Light, Inc., 2004), 194.
22 John Dewey, *Human Nature and Conduct.* (New York, NY: Modern Library,
   1950), 171-2, IV, para. 4.
23 Fethullah Gülen, *Toward a Global Civilization of Love & Tolerance.*
   (Somerset, N.J.: Light, Inc., 2004), 194.
24 Ibid.,193-201.
25 Fethullah Gülen, http://www.fethullahGülen.org/love-and-tolerance/274-
   education/1855-education-from-cradle-to-grave.html
26 Fethullah Gülen, *Fethullah Gülen: Essays, Perspectives, Opinions.*
   (Rutherford, NY: Light, Inc., 2002), 78.

Chapter One: Dewey

1 Samuel Taylor Coleridge, *Aids to Reflection.* http://archive.org/details/aid-
   storeflectio01marsgoog, 58.
2 Jay Martin, *The Education of John Dewey: A Biography*, (New York, NY:
   Columbia U Pr, 2002), 49.
3 John Dewey, The Metaphysical Assumptions of Materialism (1882), 208-213.
4 Stephen Rockefeller, (1991) *John Dewey: Religious Faith and Democratic
   Humanism. (*New York, NY: Columbia U Pr, 1991), 83-83.
5 Fethullah Gülen, (2002), http://www.fethullahGülen.org/Gülens-works/
   319-questions-and-answers/1118-submission-sense-and-reason.html
6 Fethullah Gülen, (Saturday, 07 March 2009 10:17), http://www.fethullahgulen.
   org/recent-articles/3248-implications-of-the-birth-of-the-prophet.html
7 Fethullah Gülen, "Education from Cradle to Grave." (2004), Fethullah Gülen's
   Website. <http://www.fethullahgulen.org/love-and-tolerance/
   274-education/1855-education-from-cradle-to-grave>
8 Thomas Michel, (2002), "Gülen as Educator and Religious Teacher." http://
   www.youtube.com/watch?v=FSC3NNuzky4

9 Miles Myers, *Changing Our Minds* (National Council of Teachers of English, 1996), 157-169.

10 Anya Topolski, and K. U. Leuven, (2/15/2008) <http://www.ethical-perspectives.be/page.php?LAN=E&FILE=ep_detail&ID=125&TID=1110>.

11 Fethullah Gülen, (2005), "Contributions to the Turkish Education System," http://www.fethullahgulen.org/about-fethullah-gulen/an-analysis-of-the-gulen-movement/3040-the-contribution-to-the-turkish-education-system. html

12 Wilford Aikin, (October 18, 2000), *8-Year Study*. http://www.8yearstudy.org/ index.html

13 Progressive Education Association, Commission on the Relation of School and College. (1943). *Thirty Schools Tell Their Story* (New York, NY: Harper, 1943).

14 Faculty of University School. *The Philosophy and Purposes of the University School*, (Columbus, OH: The U of Ohio Pr, 1948).

15 Class of 1938, University High School, Ohio State University, *Were We Guinea Pigs?* (New York: Henry Holt, 1942).

16 Margaret Willis, *The Guinea Pigs After 20 Years*, (Columbus: Ohio State University Pr, 1961).

17 Lewis Terman, and Melita Oden, *The Gifted Child Grows Up: Twenty-five Years Follow-up of a Superior Group* (Stanford: Stanford U Pr, 1948), 12.18Frederick O. Flener, (2009). "The "guinea pigs" after 60 years: more than 70 years ago, the United States conducted a very successful large-scale experiment in progressive education. How did it affect students over the decades? And why has it seemed to be forgotten?" *Phi Delta Kappan.* 1, no. 1 (Sept. 2009): 4.

19 Fethullah Gülen, Bringing up the Young." Fethullah Gülen's Website. (2006) <http://en.fGülen.com/pearls-of-wisdom/1096-bringing-up-the-young.html>.

20 John Dewey, Experience *and Nature*. Chicago, Ill: Open Court, 1925).

21 John Dewey, *Art as experience*, (London, UK: Allen & Unwin, 1934).

22 John Dewey and Arthur F. Bentley. *Knowing and the Known*. Boston, MA: Bacon, (1949).

23 Fethullah Gülen, "Cekirdekten Cinara: Bir Baska Acidan Ailede Egitim," *Seed to a Cedar Tree: Another Perspective of Family Education*, in Turkish, (Nil A.S., Izmir, Turkey, 2002b).

24 Fethullah Gülen, (August 13-23, 1995) http://www.fethullahgulen.org/about-fethullah-gulen/gulens-thoughts/1249-sunni-islam-and-free-thought.html

25 Thomas Alexander, (2010) <http://muse.jhu.edu/journals/transactions_of_ the_charles_s_peirce_society/summary/v046/46.4.alexander.html>.

26 Jay Martin, *The Education of John Dewey: A Biography*, (New York, NY: Columbia U Pr, 2002), 319-320.

27 John Dewey, *The School and Society, John Dewey: the Middle works*. Vol 1 ed. JoAnn Boydston. (Carbondale, IL: Southern Illinois U Pr, 1976).

28 John Dewey, "My Pedagogic creed." John Dewey: The Early works. 5, ed. JoAnn Boydston. (Carbondale, IL: Southern Illinois U Pr, 1972), 77.

29 John Dewey, *The School and society, John Dewey: the Middle works*. Vol 1 ed. JoAnn Boydston. (Carbondale, IL: Southern Illinois U Pr, 1976), 19-20.

30 John Dewey, *My Pedagogic creed*. (New York, NY: E. L. Kellogg, 1897).

31 Fethullah Gülen, "Bringing up the Young." Fethullah Gülen's Website. (2006) <http://en.fGülen.com/pearls-of-wisdom/1096-bringing-up-the-young.html>.

32 Fethullah Gülen, http://www.fethullahgulen.org/conference-papers/323-gulen-conference-in-indonesia/3712-gulens-educational-philosophy-striving-for-the-golden-generation-of-muslims.html

33 Fethullah Gülen, "Education from Cradle to Grave." Fethullah Gülen's Website. (2004)<http://www.fethullahgulen.org/love-and-tolerance/274-education/1855-education-from-cradle-to-grave>.

34 Ibid.

35 Thomas Michel, "Gülen as Educator and Religious Teacher." Fethullah Gülen's web site. (2002) <http://www.fethullahGülen.org/press-room/review/1054-Gülen-as-educator-and-religious-teacher.html>.

36 Sherry L. Santos, "The Urgency of Educational Reform in the United States of America: Lessons Learned from Fethullah Gülen." Fethullah Gülen's Web Site (2006), <http://www.fethullahGülen.org/conference-papers/the-fethul-lah-Gülen-movement-iii>.

37 Ibid.

38 John Dewey, Democracy and education: an Introduction to the philosophy of education. (New York, NY: The Macmillan Company, 1916).

39 John Dewey, Interest in relation to training of the will. Ed. by Charles A. McMurry. (Chicago, IL: University of Chicago Press, 1899).

40 John Dewey, *German Philosophy and Politics*, (New York, NY: Henry Holt & Co., 1915). <http://www.archive.org/details/germanphilosophy002600mbp 7/19/10>.

41 John Dewey, Democracy and education: an Introduction to the philosophy of education. (New York, NY: The Macmillan Company, 1916).

42 John Dewey, German Philosophy and Politics, (New York, NY: Henry Holt & Co., 1915). <http://www.archive.org/details/germanphilosophy002600mbp 7/19/10>.

43 Zürcher Erik. *Turkey: A Modern History*. 3rd ed. (London: Tauris & Co Ltd., 1993), 194.

44 Fethullah Gülen, (2002), http://en.fGülen.com/pearls-of-wisdom/1097-art. html), 65.

45 John Dewey, "Late Works." John Dewey: the Early works. 5, Ed JoAnn Boydston. (Carbondale, IL: Southern Illinois U Pr, 1972), 10 and 110.

46 Fethullah Gülen, *Pearls of Wisdom*. (Somerset, NJ: The Light, 2005), 31.

47 Novak, Bruce and Jeffrey Wilhelm. *Literacy for Love and Wisdom: 'Being the Book' and 'Being the Change.'* New York: Teachers College Pr. (2012).

48 Louise Rosenblatt, The Reader, the text, the poem: transactional theory of literary work. (Carbondale, IL: So Ill U Pr, 1978).

49 Ibid., 86. Fethullah Gülen, "Criteria or Lights of the Way," Izmir, 7th ed., 4, (1997), http://www.fethullahgulen.org/about-fethullah-gulen/gulens-thoughts/1287-pearls-of-wisdom-or-philosophy.html

50 Louise Rosenblatt, Literature as exploration. New York, NY: D. Appleton-Century Co., Inc., 1938), 92.

51 John Dewey, Logic: The Theory of Inquiry (1938).

Chapter Two: Montessori

1 Mary Alice Hornberger, The Developmental Psychology of Maria Montessori (Italy). E. D.D. Dissertation, (New York, NY: Columbia University Teachers College, 1982), 43. http://proquest.umi.com/pqdweb?index=0&did=75021373 1&SrchMode=2&sid=1&Fmt=6&VInst=PROD&VType=PQD&RQT=309& VName=PQD&TS=1277758412&clientId=48776 June 24, 2010.

2 Valeria Babini, Sarah Morgan, and Daniel Pick, "Science, Feminism and Education: the Early Work of Maria Montessori, *History Workshop Journal*, No. 49 (Oxford, UK: Oxford University Press, Spring 2000): 44-67.

3 Ibid., 47.

4 Mary Alice Hornberger, The Developmental psychology of Maria Montessori (Italy). E. D.D. Dissertation, (New York, NY: Columbia University Teachers College, 1982), 19.

5 Valeria Babini, Sarah Morgan, and Daniel Pick, "Science, Feminism and Education: the Early Work of Maria Montessori, *History Workshop Journal*, No. 49 (Oxford, UK: Oxford University Press, Spring 2000): 45-47.

6 Jacqueline Cossetino, "Culture, Craft & Coherence: the Unexpected Vitality of Montessori Teacher Training," *Journal of Teacher Education*, *60*(5) (Nov/Dec 2009), 520-1. http://ezproxy.lib.utexas.edu/login?url=http://vnweb.hwwilson-web.com/hww/jumpstart.jhtml?recid=0bc05f7a67b1790e25dfedf00b111595 69a5cb2a9898618a893d7ec0a54d94d1dd9ef229434ea956&fmt=C. June 18, 2010.

7 Hermann Rohrs, "Maria Montessori." *UNESCO: International Bureau of Education* (2000), 2.

8 Julia Van Deusen Fox, "The Self-Actualizing Teacher," *Improving College and University Teaching*, *13*(3), (Heldref Publications, Summer 1965), 147-148. http://www.jstor.org/stable/27562459. June 16, 2010.

9 Jerome W Barryman, "Montessori and Religious Education," *Religious Education*, *75* (May/June 1980), 294-307. http://ezproxy.lib.utexas.edu/login?url=http://vnweb.hwwilsonweb.com/hww/jumpstart.jhtml?recid=0bc05f 7a67b1790e25dfedf00b111595cc9498aa47d03b68544d1b6b02ad97a5fc897ca cffbf463b&fmt=C. June 22, 2010.

10 Mary Alice Hornberger, The Developmental Psychology of Maria Montessori (Italy). E. D.D. Dissertation, (New York, NY: Columbia University Teachers College, 1982), 43.

11 Montessori, Maria, *What You Should Know About Your Child.* Interpreted and edited by A. (Adyar, India: Gnana Prakasam. Kalakshetra, 1966b), 131.

12 Mary Alice Hornberger, The Developmental Psychology of Maria Montessori (Italy). E. D.D. Dissertation, (New York, NY: Columbia University Teachers College, 1982), 30.

13 Montessori, Maria, *Education for a new world* (Thiruvanmujar, India: Kalakshetra Publication, 1946).

14 Mary Alice Hornberger, The Developmental Psychology of Maria Montessori (Italy). E. D.D. Dissertation, (New York, NY: Columbia University Teachers College, 1982), 45-7.

15 Ibid., 49.

16 Ibid., 86-8.

17 Ibid., 90-3.

18 Bob Chapman, Nepal Volunteer. Personal correspondence, 30 September 2009.

19 Maria Montessori, *The Secret of Childhood* (New York: Ballantine Books, 1966a), 42.

20 Ibid., 35.

21 Mary Alice Hornberger, The Developmental Psychology of Maria Montessori (Italy). E. D.D. Dissertation, (New York, NY: Columbia University Teachers College, 1982), 40.

22 Hermann Rohrs, "Maria Montessori," *UNESCO: International Bureau of Education* (2000), 2.

23 Fethullah Gülen, *Sızıntı*. Bizim Maarifimiz -1, (Trans. in press) C:9, 1(1) October 1979

24 Maria Montessori, *The Absorbent Mind* (New York: Dell Publishing, 1966), 216.

25 Fethullah Gülen, "The Necessity of reflection and self-criticism," *Fethullah Gülen's Web Site* (December 2002b). http://en.fGülen.com/recent-articles/1202-the-necessity-of-reflection-and-selfcriticism.html. July 12, 2010.

26 Valeria Babini, Sarah Morgan, and Daniel Pick, "Science, Feminism and Education: the Early Work of Maria Montessori, *History Workshop Journal*, No. 49 (Oxford, UK: Oxford University Press, Spring 2000): 54.

27 Jacqueline Cossetino, "Culture, Craft & Coherence: the Unexpected Vitality of Montessori Teacher Training," *Journal of Teacher Education, 60*(5) (Nov/Dec 2009), 522.

28 Fethullah Gülen, "Education from Cradle to Grave," *Fethullah Gülen's Web Site* (2004) http://en.fGülen.com/love-and-tolerance/274-education/1855-education-from-cradle-to-grave.html. 2 September 2010.

29 Julia Van Deusen Fox, "The Self-Actualizing Teacher," *Improving College and University Teaching, 13*(3), (Heldref Publications, Summer 1965), 147-148. http://www.jstor.org/stable/27562459. June 16, 2010.

30 Fethullah Gülen, "Universal Mercy and Education," *Fethullah Gülen's Web Site* (September 2002c). http://en.fGülen.com/recent-articles/1082-universal-mercy-and-education.html. July 12, 2010.

31 Irene Hope Gazza, "Reinventing the Wheel: Seeking Excellence in Education," *Delta Kappa Gamma Bull, 76*(1) fall 2009), 34-36. http://vnweb.hwwilsonweb.com/hww/results/external_link_maincontentframe.jhtml?_DARGS=/hww/results/results_common.jhtml.42. June 16, 2010. Also see Lockhorst, Daan, Theo Wubbles, and Bert van Oers, "Educational Dialogues and the Fostering of Pupils' Independence: the Practices of Two Teachers," *Journal of Curriculum Studies*, 42(1) (July 2009), 99-121. http://dx.doi.

org/10.1080/00220270903079237. June 18, 2010; and Jacqueline Cossetino, "Culture, Craft & Coherence: the Unexpected Vitality of Montessori Teacher Training," *Journal of Teacher Education*, *60*(5) (Nov/Dec 2009), 520-525.

32 Mary Alice Hornberger, The Developmental Psychology of Maria Montessori (Italy). E. D.D. Dissertation, (New York, NY: Columbia University Teachers College, 1982), 158.

33 Ibid., 190.

34 Irene Hope Gazza, "Reinventing the Wheel: Seeking Excellence in Education," *Delta Kappa Gamma Bull*, *76*(1) fall 2009), 34-36. http://vnweb. hwwilsonweb.com/hww/results/external_link_maincontentframe.jhtml?_DARGS=/hww/results/results_common.jhtml.42. June 16, 2010.

35 Ibid.

36 Ibid.

37 Mary Alice Hornberger, The Developmental Psychology of Maria Montessori (Italy). E. D.D. Dissertation, (New York, NY: Columbia University Teachers College, 1982), 61-2.

38 Montessori, Maria, *The Absorbent Mind*, (New York, NY: Dell Publishing, (1967).

39 Montessori, Maria, *The Absorbent Mind,* (New York, NY: Dell Publishing, (1967), 181.

40 Hermann Rohrs, "Maria Montessori," *UNESCO: International Bureau of Education* (2000), 3.

41 Montessori, Maria, *Secret of Childhood*, (New York, NY: Ballantine Books, 1966, 216; also see Faryadi, Qais, The Montessori Paradigm of Learning: So What? (2007), http://ezproxy.lib.utexas.edu/login?url=http://search.ebsco-host.com/login.aspx?direct=true&db=eric&AN=ED496081&site=ehost-live

42 Fethullah Gülen, "The Rights of Children," 17 September 2001. http://www. fethullahGülen.org/about-fethullah-Gülen/166-as-a-teacher/818-the-rights-of-children.html. 3 September 2010. and Fethullah Gülen, "Universal Mercy and Education." *Fethullah Gülen's Web Site* (September 2002c). http:// en.fGülen.com/recent-articles/1082-universal-mercy-and-education.html. July 12, 2010.

43 Fethullah Gülen, "Bringing up a Child with Multiple Abilities," *Fethullah Gülen's Web Site*. (26 November 2006) http://www.fethullahGülen.org/content/view/1883/11/. 2 September 2010.

44 Mary Alice Hornberger, The Developmental Psychology of Maria Montessori (Italy). E. D.D. Dissertation, (New York, NY: Columbia University Teachers College, 1982), 97; also 143-46.

45 Hermann Rohrs. "Maria Montessori," *UNESCO: International Bureau of Education* (2000), 9.

46 Montessori, Maria, *The Absorbent Mind*, (New York, NY: Dell Publishing, (1967), 189.

47 Gülen, Fethullah. "Bringing up a Child with Multiple Abilities," *Fethullah Gülen's Web Site*. (26 November 2006) http://www.fethullahGülen.org/content/view/1883/11/. 2 September 2010.

48 Montessori, Mario, "Maria Montessori's contribution to the cultivation of

the mathematical mind," *International Review of Education / Internationale Zeitschrift für Erziehungswissenschaft / Revue Internationale de l'Education*, Vol. 7, No. 2, The Teaching of Mathematics, Springer (1961): 134-141. http://www.jstor.org/stable/3441716. June 22, 2010.

49 Polat, Cemen, "Gülen-Inspired Schools in Australia and their Funding." (Papers presented at the East Meets West Conference, University of Southern California, December 12, 2010).

50 Steven Levy, *In the Plex: How Google thinks, works, and shapes our lives*, (New York, NY: Simon & Schuster, 2011).

51 Kendra Dwelley, Personal communication, 10 December 2010.

Chapter Three: Vygotsky

1 Lev Vygotsky, *Language in Thought and Mind*, E. Hanfmann & G. Vakar, (Cambridge, MA: MIT Pr, 1962).

2 Lev Vygotsky, *Mind in Society: The Development of Higher Psychological Processes. Thought and Language*, Ed. Alex Kosulin, (Cambridge, MA: MIT Pr, 1986).

3 Stephen Toulmin, "The Mozart of Psychology," *New York Times Review* (28 September 1978). 51-57.

4 Lev Vygotsky, *Language in Thought and Mind*, Ed. Alex Kosulin, 6th Edition, (Cambridge, MA: MIT Pr, 1992), p. 233.

5 Ibid., 249.

6 Ibid.

7 Wayne Au, "Vygotsky and Lenin on Learning: The Parallel Structures of Individual and Social Development." *Science and Society*, Vol. 71, No. 3, July 2007. http://lchc.ucsd.edu/MCA/Paper/AuVygotskyandLenin.pdf.

8 Lev Vygotsky, *Mind in Society: The Development of Higher Psychological Processes. Thought and Language*, Ed. Alex Kosulin, (Cambridge, MA: MIT Pr, 1986), 186-7.

9 Lev Vygotsky, (http://www.marxists.org/archive/vygotsky/works/1926/educa-tional-psychology/ch12.htm).

10 Lev Vygotsky, "Esthetic Education," *Educational Psychology*. Tr. Robert Silverman, (Florida: St. Lucie Press, 1992), http://www.marxists.org/archive/vygotsky/works/1926/educational-psychology/ch13.htm

11 Lev Vygotsky, *Mind in Society: The Development of Higher Psychological Processes. Thought and Language*, Ed. Alex Kosulin, (Cambridge, MA: MIT Pr, 1978), 57.

12 Noam Chomsky, "A Review of B. F. Skinner's *Verbal Behavior*." Linguistic Society of America. Reprint from *Language*, Vol. 35, January-March, 1959, 142.

13 Noam Chomsky, *Syntactic Structures,* (Cambridge: MIT Pr, 1957).

14 James T. Zebrowski, *Thinking Through Theory* (Portsmouth, NH: Boynton/ Cook Heinemann, 1994), 293-297.

15 Carol Chomsky, *Children's Acquisition of Syntax from 5 to 10.* (MIT Pr, 1969), 19.

16 Walter Loban, *Language Development: Kindergarten through Grade Twelve.*

No. 18 Series of Research Reports, (Urbana, Il: NCTE. 1967).

17 James Britton, Nancy Martin, Alex McCloud & Harold Rosen, *Development of Writing Abilities*, London Schools Council, (London, UK: Macmillan, 1975).

18 James Britton, Nancy Martin, Alex McCloud & Harold Rosen, *Development of Writing Abilities*, London Schools Council, (London, UK: Macmillan, 1975), 168, Table 18.

19 Lev Vygotsky, *Language in Thought and Mind*, Ed. Alex Kosulin, 6th Edition, (Cambridge, MA: MIT Pr, 1992), 96-210.

20 Arthur Applebee, *Child's Concept of Story: Ages Two through Seventeen.* (Chicago, Il: U of Chi Pr, 1978).

21 Brian Boyd, *On the Origin of Stories: Evolution, Cognition, and Fiction. Cambridge*: Belknap Pr, 2009).

22 Arthur Applebee, *Child's Concept of Story: Ages Two through Seventeen.* (Chicago, Il: U of Chi Pr, 1978), 58. Fig 2.

23 M. F. Gülen, *The Statue of Our Souls,* (Somerset, NJ: The Light, 2005), 42.

24 Judith Langer, and Arthur Applebee, *How Writing shapes thinking: a Study of Teaching and Learning*. Research Report No. 22. (Urbana, IL: NCTE, 1987), 139-144.

25 Lev Vygotsky, *Language in Thought and Mind*, Ed. Alex Kosulin, 6th Edition, (Cambridge, MA: MIT Pr, 1992), 96-145.

26 Lev Vygotsky, *Language in Thought and Mind*, Ed. Alex Kosulin, 6th Edition, (Cambridge, MA: MIT Pr, 1992), 245.

27 Ibid., 148.

28 Lev Vygotsky, *Language in Thought and Mind*, Ed. Alex Kosulin, 6th Edition, (Cambridge, MA: MIT Pr, 1992), 110-130.

29 Arthur Applebee, *Child's Concept of Story: Ages Two through Seventeen.* (Chicago, Il: U of Chi Pr, 1978), 56-72.

30 Andrey Maidansky, "The Russian Spinozists." *Studies in East European Thought*, Vol. 55, No. 3 (Sep., 2003): 199-216. http://www.jstor.org/stable/20099832.

31 Fethullah Gülen, (14 June 2006). http://en.fgulen.com/religious-education-of-the-child/1883-bringing-up-a-child-with-multiple-abilities March 19, 2011

32 Fethullah Gülen, *Cekirdekten cinara: Bir baska acidan ailede egitim* [From a Seed to a Cedar Tree: Another Perspective of Family Education]. (Izmir, Turkey: Nil AS, 2002), 72.

33 Andrew Pollard, *Social World of Children's Learning.* (New York, NY: Continuum, 2001), 113.

34 Fethullah Gülen, *Cekirdekten cinara: Bir baska acidan ailede egitim* [From a seed to a cedar tree: Another perspective of family education]. (Izmir, Turkey: Nil AS, 2002).

35 Ibid.

36 Fethullah Gülen, "Yaqin (Certainty)." *The Meaning of Life*, January 9, 2006. http://www.mlife.org/content/view/176/69/. May 11, 2010.

37 Wayne Au, "Vygotsky and Lenin on Learning: The Parallel Structures of In-

dividual and Social Development." *Science and Society*, Vol. 71, No. 3, 290. July 2007. http://lchc.ucsd.edu/MCA/Paper/AuVygotskyandLenin.pdf.

38 Lev Vygotsky, *Language in Thought and Mind*, Ed. Alex Kosulin, 6th Edition, (Cambridge, MA: MIT Pr, 1992).

39 Fethullah Gülen, "Yaqin (Certainty)." *The Meaning of Life*, January 9, 2006. http://www.mlife.org/content/view/176/69/. May 11, 2010.

40 Lev Vygotsky, *Mind in Society*. (Cambridge, MA: Harvard University Press, 1978).

41 Fethullah Gülen, (2008 http://www.fethullahGülen.org/recent-articles/2557-language-and-thought.html)."

42 Lev Vygotsky, 1992: http://www.marxists.org/archive/vygotsky/works/1926/educational-psychology/ch12.htm).

43 Y. A. Aslandoğan, "Pedagogical Model of Gülen and modern theories of learning." 2006 Conference Proceedings.

44 Lev Vygotsky, "Consciousness as a Problem for the Psychology of Behavior." *The Collected Works of L. S. Vygotsky*. Vol. 3, (New York, NY: Plenum, 1997), 339.

45 Lev Vygotsky, 1992: http://www.marxists.org/archive/vygotsky/works/1926/educational-psychology/ch12.htm).

46 Fethullah Gülen, *Cekirdekten Cinara: Bir Baska Acidan Ailede Egitim* [From a seed to a cedar tree: Another perspective of family education]. (Izmir, Turkey: Nil AS, 2002).

47 Lev Vygotsky, "Ethical Behavior." *Educational Psychology*. Trans. Robert Silverman. (Florida: St. Lucie Press, 1992), http://www.marxists.org/archive/vygotsky/works/1926/educational-psychology/ch12.htm

Chapter Four: Hahn

1 Fethullah Gülen, http://creativecommons.org/licenses/by/3.0/

2 James, Thomas. (2000) Kurt Hahn and the Aims of Education. 2000), 6. <www.kurthahn.org/writings/james.pdf>. (Retrieved 7/7/10).

3 Ibid.,191. This enthusiasm at that time was manifest in the *zeitgeist*, as evidenced in E. M. Butler's *The Tyranny of Greece Over Germany*, (Cambridge, UK: Cambridge U Pr, 1935).

4 Charles Stetson, "An Essay on Kurt Hahn, Founder of Outward Bound: Genius of Experimental Education in the Twentieth Century. (1941), 2. <www.kurthahn.org/writings/stet.pdf>. (Retrieved on 7/7/10).

5 Kurt Hahn, "Dr Kurt Hahn at the Forty-eighth Annual Dinner of Old Centralians. (1959), 1. <www.kurthahn.org/writings/oldcentral.pdf>. (Retrieved on 7/7/10).

6 Heidi M. Anderson, "An Articulation and Formalization of Kurt Hahn's Model of Adventure Education." Diss. (La Sierra University, May 2007), 430.

7 (Hahn, 1936, 2)

8 Heidi M. Anderson, "An Articulation and Formalization of Kurt Hahn's Model of Adventure Education." Diss. (La Sierra University, May 2007), 531.

9 James, Thomas. (2000) Kurt Hahn and the Aims of Education. 2000), 4.

<www.kurthahn.org/writings/james.pdf>. (Retrieved 7/7/10).

10 Charles Stetson, "An Essay on Kurt Hahn, Founder of Outward Bound: Genius of Experimental Education in the Twentieth Century. (1941), 4. <www.kurthahn.org/writings/stet.pdf>. (Retrieved on 7/7/10).

11 Heidi M. Anderson, "An Articulation and Formalization of Kurt Hahn's Model of Adventure Education." Diss. (La Sierra University, May 2007), 306.

12 James, Thomas. (2000) Kurt Hahn and the Aims of Education. 2000), 11. <www.kurthahn.org/writings/james.pdf>. (Retrieved 7/7/10).

13 Ibid.,11.

14 Heidi M. Anderson, "An Articulation and Formalization of Kurt Hahn's Model of Adventure Education." Diss. (La Sierra University, May 2007), 529.

15 Heidi M. Anderson, "An Articulation and Formalization of Kurt Hahn's Model of Adventure Education." Diss. (La Sierra University, May 2007), 326-8.

16 National Outdoor Leadership School, NOLS http://www.nols.edu/.

17 Heidi M. Anderson, "An Articulation and Formalization of Kurt Hahn's Model of Adventure Education." Diss. (La Sierra University, May 2007), 334, item 14.

18 Heidi M. Anderson, "An Articulation and Formalization of Kurt Hahn's Model of Adventure Education." Diss. (La Sierra University, May 2007), 200.

19 James C. Harrington, *Wrestling with Free Speech, Religious Freedom, and Democracy in Turkey: The Political Trials and Times of Fethullah Gülen,* (New York, NY: University Press of America, Inc., 2011.

20 Heidi M. Anderson, "An Articulation and Formalization of Kurt Hahn's Model of Adventure Education." Diss. (La Sierra University, May 2007), 186.

21 Jill B. Carroll, *A Dialogue of Civilizations: Gülen's Islamic Ideals and Humanistic Discourse.* With foreword by Akbar S. Ahmed. (Somerset, NY: Light, 2007), see chapters on Gülen and Plato.

22 Heidi M. Anderson, "An Articulation and Formalization of Kurt Hahn's Model of Adventure Education." Diss. (La Sierra University, May 2007), 282.

23 Heidi M. Anderson, "An Articulation and Formalization of Kurt Hahn's Model of Adventure Education." Diss. (La Sierra University, May 2007), 274-293.

24 (Ibid, 3).

25 James Neill, "Dr Kurt Hahn: On the Life and Philosophy of an Inspirational Educator." 2008 < wilderdom.com/sixdeclinesofmodernyouth). (Retrieved 7/7/10).

26 In Anderson footnoting Hahn "Pre-service Training: Compulsion? Attraction? Persuasion? A Criticism of the Conservative Sup-Committees Report on Education (Elgin, Scotland: Gordonstoun School, October 1942), 3.

27 Ibid., 191- 215.

28 Heidi M. Anderson, "An Articulation and Formalization of Kurt Hahn's Model of Adventure Education." Diss. (La Sierra University, May 2007), 412-14.

29 Lawrence Bains, Carr, 2010, 179-197). see above et al, Carr, 2010, pp. 179-197; Joseph Bogen, "Some educational implications of hemispheric

specialization." *The Human Brain.* Ed. M. C. Wittrock. (Englewood Cliffs, NJ: Prentice-Hall, 1977). Also see Stephan D. Krashen, 1977). "The Left hemisphere." *The Human Brain.* Ed. M. C. Wittrock. (Englewood Cliffs, NJ: Prentice-Hall, 1977), Antonio
Damasio, *The Feeling of What Happens: Body and Emotion in the Making of Consciousness.* NY: Harcourt, 1999); Nicholas Carr, *The Shallows: What the Internet is Doing to Our Brains.* New York, NY: Norton, 2010); and Clay Shirky, *Cognitive Surplus: Creativity and Generosity in the Connected Age.* (New York, NY: Penguin, 2010).

30 Kurt Hahn, Wikipedia 24/11/10 http://en.wikipedia.org/wiki/Kurt_Hahn 26/11/10) (http://wilderdom.com/sixdeclinesofmodernyouth.html; http://wilderdom.com/KurtHahn.html).

31 Richard Louv, *The Last child in the woods.* (New York, NY: Workman Publishing, 2008).

32 Heidi M. Anderson, "An Articulation and Formalization of Kurt Hahn's Model of Adventure Education." Diss. (La Sierra University, May 2007), 263.

33 Fethullah Gülen, http://www.fethullahgulen.org/pearls-of-wisdom/646-life-human-character-and-virtue.html

34 Kurt Hahn, "Dr Kurt Hahn at the Forty-eighth Annual Dinner of Old Centralians. (1959), 5. <www.kurthahn.org/writings/oldcentral.pdf>. (Retrieved on 7/7/10).

35 Heidi M. Anderson, "An Articulation and Formalization of Kurt Hahn's Model of Adventure Education." Diss. (La Sierra University, May 2007), 342.

36 Fethullah Gülen, Preparing the Environment for Education, 2 C. "The Role of Environment in Education, Ed. A. A. Adem Akinci. Tr. A. Aydin (2010). Unpublished.

37 Kurt Hahn, "Education and peace: the foundations of modern society." *The Inverness Courier* (Inverness, Scotland: March 1936), 3.

38 Kurt Hahn, "Dr Kurt Hahn at the Forty-eighth Annual Dinner of Old Centralians. (1959), 6. <www.kurthahn.org/writings/oldcentral.pdf>. (Retrieved on 7/7/10).

39 James, Thomas. (2000) Kurt Hahn and the Aims of Education. 2000), 3. <www.kurthahn.org/writings/james.pdf>. (Retrieved 7/7/10).

40 James Neill, "Dr Kurt Hahn: On the Life and Philosophy of an Inspirational Educator." 2008 (http://wilderdom.com/sixdeclinesofmodernyouth.html; http://wilderdom.com/KurtHahn.html). (Retrieved 7/7/10). Also see http://en.wikipedia.org/wiki/Kurt_Hahn 26/11/10)

41 James Neill, "Dr Kurt Hahn: On the Life and Philosophy of an Inspirational Educator." 2008 (http://wilderdom.com/sixdeclinesofmodernyouth.html; http://wilderdom.com/KurtHahn.html). (Retrieved 7/7/10).

42 Heidi M. Anderson, "An Articulation and Formalization of Kurt Hahn's Model of Adventure Education." Diss. (La Sierra University, May 2007), 193.

43 http://www.fethullahgulen.org/pearls-of-wisdom/649-personal-integrity.html

44 James Neill, "Dr Kurt Hahn: On the Life and Philosophy of an Inspirational

Educator." 2008 (http://wilderdom.com/sixdeclinesofmodernyouth.html; http://wilderdom.com/KurtHahn.html). (Retrieved 7/7/10).

45 Karen Carlton and Chalon Emmons. "Every Moment Meditation: Teaching English as Spiritual Work." *The Academy and the Possibility of Belief: Essays on the Intellectual and Spiritual Life*. Eds. Mary Louise Buley-Meissner, Mary McCaslin Thompson, and Elizabeth Bachrach Tan. Cresskill, NJ: Hampton Press, 2000. 17-38. Also see Karen Carlton "Silence in Discourse." Diss (New York University, 1988).

46 Ahmet Orhan Polat, Keys Factors to the Success of Gülen-inspired Schools, http://www.fethullahgulen.org/conference-papers/323-gulen-conference-in-indonesia/3732-ahmet-orhan-polat-the-key-factors-behind-the-success-of-gulen-inspired-schools.html

47 John Raines, "The Poverty called Starvation." (Proceeds of Dialog of Civilization Platform 1/23/2010), 3. http://www.Güleninstitute.org/index. php/Dialog-of-Civilizations-Platform/ 10/1/10

48 Heidi M. Anderson, "An Articulation and Formalization of Kurt Hahn's Model of Adventure Education." Diss. (La Sierra University, May 2007), 499-500.

49 Charles Stetson, "An Essay on Kurt Hahn, Founder of Outward Bound: Genius of Experimental Education in the Twentieth Century. (1941), 7. <www.kurthahn.org/writings/stet.pdf>. (Retrieved on 7/7/10).

50 Heidi M. Anderson, "An Articulation and Formalization of Kurt Hahn's Model of Adventure Education." Diss. (La Sierra University, May 2007), 101-103.

51 Ibid., 334, Item 16.

52 Fethullah Gülen, "Educational services spreading throughout the world." (2010A) <http://fethullahGülenchair.com/index.php?option=com_content &view=article&id=501%3Aeducational-services-spreading-throughout-the-world-&catid=64%3Aeducation&Itemid=201&lang=en >. (Retrieved on 7/7/10).

53 Heidi M. Anderson, "An Articulation and Formalization of Kurt Hahn's Model of Adventure Education." Diss. (La Sierra University, May 2007), 331-486.

54 Shirley Brice Heath, *Words at Work and Play: Three Decades in Family and Community Life*, (Cambridge, UK: Cambridge U Pr, 2012).

55 Fethullah Gülen, "Love for Humankind." *The Fountain*. (April 2004, Issue 46).

56 Gülen, Fethullah. (2010A) Educational services spreading throughout the world. <http://fethullahGülenchair.com/index.php?option=com_content& view=article&id=501%3Aeducational-services-spreading-throughout-the-world-&catid=64%3Aeducation&Itemid=201&lang=en >.

57 Kurt Hahn, "Dr Kurt Hahn at the Forty-eighth Annual Dinner of Old Centralians. (1959), 1. <www.kurthahn.org/writings/oldcentral.pdf>. (Retrieved on 7/7/10).

58 Charles Stetson, "An Essay on Kurt Hahn, Founder of Outward Bound:

Genius of Experimental Education in the Twentieth Century. (1941), 7. <www.kurthahn.org/writings/stet.pdf>. (Retrieved on 7/7/10).

59 YetkinYıldırım, "Ethics in Engineering and Science: Fethullah Gülen's Model." Gülen Symposium, (Conference Proceeds: 7 October 24, 2009), 7.

60 Tom Gage, "Cross-Cultural Fluency: The Rhetoric of Dialogue." (July, 2007), 398. *The Journal of the Humanities*. Vol. 6 www.humanties-journal.com.

61 Kim, Heon C. (2010) Making Peace with the World: the Role of the Gülen Movement in the Task of Eco-justice. 23/10/10 http://fGülenconference.org/ Welcome.html 14/11/10

62 (Gülen, 2010,< www.fethullahGülen.org/about-fethullah-Gülen/education>).

63 Fethullah Gülen, "Education from Cradle to Grave." Fethullah Gülen's Website. (2004), 208.<http://www.fethullahgulen.org/love-and-tolerance/274-education/1855-education-from-cradle-to-grave>.

64 (Ibid, 207)"

65 (Ibid, 208)"

66 Elif Batuman, "The Memory kitchen," (*New Yorker Magazine*. April 19, 2010), 56-69).

67 (Ibid 207)"

68 (Ibid, 204)"

69 (Ibid, 204)

Chapter Five: Piaget

1 Richard I. Evans, *Jean Piaget, the Man and His Ideas*. Tr. Eleanor Duckworth, (New York, NY: E. P. Dutton, 1973).

2 Jean Piaget, *Autobiography*, tr. Donald MacQueen, Eds. M. Piercy & D. Berliner, Vol. 4 (New York, NY: Russell & Russell, 1952), 225-37.

3 Ibid.

4 Ibid.

5 Ibid.

6 Jean Piaget, *Le Langage et la Pensée chez L'enfant*. (Paris, France: Delachaux et Niestlé, 1923).

7 Lev Vygotsky, *Thought and Language*. Ed. Alex Kozulin. (Cambridge, MA: MIT Pr, 1986),12-57.

8 Richard I. Evans, *Jean Piaget, the Man and His Ideas*. Tr. Eleanor Duckworth. (New York, NY: E. P. Dutton, 1973).

9 Jean Piaget, *Autobiography*, tr. Donald MacQueen, Eds. M. Piercy & D. Berliner, Vol. 4 (New York, NY: Russell & Russell, 1952).

10 Dorothy G. Singer and Tracey A. Revenson, *A Piaget Primer: How a Child Thinks*. (New York: Plume, 1996).

11 Richard I. Evans, *Jean Piaget, the Man and His Ideas*. Tr. Eleanor Duckworth, (New York, NY: E. P. Dutton, 1973).

12 Richard I. Evans, *Jean Piaget, the Man and His Ideas*. Tr. Eleanor Duckworth, (New York, NY: E. P. Dutton, 1973), 23.

13 Ibid.

14 Jean Piaget, Genetic Epistemology. Tr. Eleanor Duckworth. (New York,

NY: W.W. Norton & Company, Inc., 1971b). http://iaepedia.org/College_ Student%E2%80%99s_Guide_to_Computers_in_Education/Chapter_6:_ Learning_and_Learning_Theory

15 Jean Piaget, *Judgment and Reasoning in the Child*. Tr. Marjorie Warden (New York, NY: Harcourt, Brace and Company, 1928).

16 Richard I. Evans, *Jean Piaget, the Man and His Ideas*. Tr. Eleanor Duckworth. (New York, NY: E. P. Dutton, 1973).

17 B. F. Skinner, *The Behavior of Organisms: An Experimental Analysis*. (Cambridge, MA: Skinner Foundation, 1938).

18 Yüksel Aslandoğan, "Pedagogical Model of Gülen and Modern Theories of Learning." *Proceedings from the Conference on Islam in the Contemporary World: The Gülen in Thought and Practice*. (2006b), 131.Southern Methodist University, Dallas, March 4-5, 2006. http://www.fethullahGülenconference.org/dallas/proceedings/YAAslandogan.pdf

19 Fethullah Gülen, Ölçü Veya Yoldaki Işıklar, Chapter 3, (Ahlaki-İçtimai, Terbiye, 2004), http://tr.fGülen.com/content/view/885/3/

20 Fethullah Gülen, *Sızıntı Magazine*. Ed. A. A. Adem Akinci. Tr. A. Aydin (2010). Nesillerin Maariften Bekledikleri, 2007b). November 2007, No 346, P. 470-471 http://www.sizinti.com.tr/konular/ayrinti/maarifimizde-muallim. html. Also see Fethullah Gülen, *Sızıntı Magazine*. Ed. A. A. Adem Akinci. Tr. A. Aydin (2010). (Maarifin Vadettikleri, 2007a), October 2007, No 345, V 29, p. 418-419 http://www.sizinti.com.tr/konular/ayrinti/maarifimizde-muallim.html

21 Jean Piaget, *Autobiography*, tr. Donald MacQueen, Eds. M. Piercy & D. Berliner, Vol. 4 (New York, NY: Russell & Russell, 1952).

22 Fethullah Gülen, *Sızıntı Magazine*. Ed. A. A. Adem Akinci. Tr. A. Aydin (2010). 1 Aralık 1979, Maarifimizde Muallim, No 11, V 1-2. http://www.sizinti.com.tr/konular/ayrinti/bizim-maarifimiz.html

23 W.C. Crain, *Theories of Development*, (New York, NY: Prentice-Hall, 1985), 118-136.

24 Lawrence Kohlberg, *Essays on Moral Development*. (San Francisco, CA: Harper & Row, 1987).

25 Lawrence Kohlberg, (http://faculty.plts.edu/gpence/html/kohlberg.htm)

26 Lawrence Kohlberg, The Development of Modes of Thinking and Choices in Years 10 to 16. (*PhD Dissertation, University of Chicago, 1958).*

27 Fethullah Gülen, *Ölçü ve Yol*. Ed. A. A. Adembey. Tr. A. Aydin. Chapter 3. *Moral Assembly and Discipline*. (Unpublished, 2010).

28 Richard I. Evans, *Jean Piaget, the Man and His Ideas*. Tr. Eleanor Duckworth. (New York, NY: E. P. Dutton, 1973), 16.

29 David Elkind, *The Hurried Child: Growing Up Too Fast Too Soon*. (Reading, Mass: Addison-Wesley Pub. Co., 1981).

30 Lev Vygotsky, *Thought and Language*. Ed. Alex Kozulin. (Cambridge, MA: MIT Pr, 1986), xxxiv-vi.

31 Yüksel Aslandoğan, and Muhammed Çetin, "The Educational Philosophy of Gülen in Thought and Practice." Ed. Robert A. Hunt and Yüksel Aslandoğan. *Muslim Citizens of the Globalized World: Contributions of the Gülen Move-*

ment. (Somerset, NJ: The Light, 2006a).

32 Ibid.

33 Ibid.

34 Fethullah Gülen, *Çekirdekten Çınara* (Bir Başka Açıdan Ailede Eğitim), Terbiye Vasatı Hazırlama, Tr. Adem Akinci and A. Aydin (2010). (Nil Yayinlari, Izmir, 2006a), 83. Also see Chapter 3. Also see M. F. Gülen, *Çekirdekten Çınara* (Bir Başka Açıdan Ailede Eğitim), The Preparation of the Child for the Future. Chapter 3, Tr. Adem Akinci and A. Aydin (2010). (Izmir, Turkey: Nil Yayinlari, 2006b), 95-98 & 103. And Gülen, *Çekirdekten Çınara* (Bir Başka Açıdan Ailede Eğitim) Choosing Friends, Chapter 6. tr. Adem Akinci and A. Aydin (2010). (Izmir, Turkey: Nil Yayinlari, 2006d), 151-2.

35 Lev Vygotsky, *Thought and Language.* Ed. Alex Kozulin. (Cambridge, MA: MIT Pr, 1986),12-57.

36 Ibid., 231.

37 Ibid., 240.

38 Fethullah Gülen, *Ölçü ve Yol.* (2010) Ed. A. A. Adembey. Tr. A. Aydin. *Moral Assembly and Discipline.* Unpublished.

39 Jean Piaget, *Autobiography*, Tr. Donald MacQueen, Eds. M. Piercy & D. Berliner, Vol. 4 (New York, NY: Russell & Russell, 1952).

40 Jean Piaget, *Genetic Epistemology.* Tr. Eleanor Duckworth. (New York, NY: W.W. Norton & Company, Inc., 1971b). http://iaepedia.org/College_ Student%E2%80%99s_Guide_to_Computers_in_Education/Chapter_6:_ Learning_and_Learning_Theory

Chapter Six: Bloom

1 Mary Forehand, "Bloom's Taxonomy: Original and Revised," in M. Oney's *Emerging Perspectives on Learning, Teaching, and Technology*, 2005 XXX. 1942 was a fortuitous year, for at Chicago the Dewey-related 8-year Study was published, referred to in Chapter 1 above.

2 Ibid.

3 Elliot W. Eisner, "Benjamin Bloom: 1913-99." *Prospects: The Quarterly Review of Comparative Education,* Vol. 30, No. 3 (September 2000): 1-7. UNESCO: International Bureau of Education. http://www.ibe.unesco.org/ publications/ThinkersPdf/bloome.pdf. April 30, 2010.

4 Ibid., 3.

5 Mary Forehand, "Bloom's Taxonomy: Original and Revised," in M. Oney's *Emerging Perspectives on Learning, Teaching, and Technology*, 2005 XXX.

6 For a critical assessment, see Michael Booker, "A Roof without Walls: Benjamin Bloom's Taxonomy and the Misdirection of American Educa-tion," *Academic Questions,* Vol. 20, Issue 4 (2007): 348. Academic Search Complete. http://content.ebscohost.com/ContentServer.asp?T=P& P=AN& K=31160818& EbscoContent=dGJyMNXb4kSeprM4y9f3OLCmr0iep7NSrq 64SbSWxWX

7 Mary Forehand, "Bloom's Taxonomy: Original and Revised," in M. Oney's *Emerging Perspectives on Learning, Teaching, and Technology*, 2005, 2. XXX.

8 James Williams, "Hey, Big Thinker." *Times Educational Supplement*, Is-

sue 4853 (2009): 24-25. LexisNexis. http://sfx.lib.utexas.edu:9003/
sfx_local?sid=metalib:EBSCO_A2H&id=doi:&genre=&isbn=&issn=004
07887&date=2009&volume=&issue=4853&spage=24&epage=25&aulast
=Williams&aufirst=%20James&auinit=&title=Times%20Educational%20
Supplement&atitle=Hey%2C%20big%20thinker.&sici=&__service_
type=getFullTxt&pid=%3Cmetalib_doc_number%3E002484301%3C/met-
alib_doc_number%3E%3Cmetalib_base_url%3Ehttp://metalib.lib.utexas.
edu:80%3C/metalib_base_url%3E%3Copid%3E%3C/opid%3E. May 5, 2010.

9 Elliot W. Eisner, "Benjamin Bloom: 1913-99." *Prospects: The Quarterly
Review of Comparative Education,* Vol. 30, No. 3 (September 2000): 3.
UNESCO: International Bureau of Education. http://www.ibe.unesco.org/
publications/ThinkersPdf/bloome.pdf. April 30, 2010.

10 Christine Robinson, "Lessons on Learning." Journal for Quality & Participation, Vol. 32, Issue 1 (2009): 25. Business Source Complete. http://ezproxy.
lib.utexas.edu/login?url=http://search.ebscohost.com/login.aspx?direct=true
&db=bth&AN=39662761&site=ehost-live. May 5, 2010.

11 Edgar J. Manton, Donald E. English, and Courtney Russ Kernek. "Evaluating Knowledge and Critical Thinking in International Marketing Courses."
College Student Journal, Vol. 42, Issue 4 (2008): 1037-1044. SPORTDiscus.
http://ezproxy.lib.utexas.edu/login?url=http://search.ebscohost.com/login.asp
x?direct=true&db=s3h&AN=34876571&site=ehost-live. May 5, 2010.

12 Christine Robinson, "Lessons on Learning." Journal for Quality & Participation, Vol. 32, Issue 1 (2009): 25-26. Business Source Complete. http://
ezproxy.lib.utexas.edu/login?url=http://search.ebscohost.com/login.aspx?dire
ct=true&db=bth&AN=39662761&site=ehost-live. May 5, 2010.

13 Mary Forehand, "Bloom's Taxonomy: Original and Revised," in M. Oney's
Emerging Perspectives on Learning, Teaching, and Technology, 2005 XXX.
1942 was a fortuitous year, for at Chicago the Dewey-related 8-year Study
was published, referred to in Chapter 1 above.

14 Michael Booker, "A Roof without Walls: Benjamin Bloom's Taxonomy and
the Misdirection of American Education," *Academic Questions,* Vol. 20,
Issue 4 (2007): 352. Academic Search Complete. http://content.ebscohost.
com/ContentServer.asp?T=P& P=AN& K=31160818& EbscoContent=dGJy
MNXb4kSeprM4y9f3OLCmr0iep7NSrq64SbSWxWX

15 Benjamin S. Bloom, "A Response to Slavin's Mastery Learning Reconsid-
ered." Review of Educational Research, Vol. 57, No. 4 (1987): 508. JSTOR.
http://www.jstor.org/stable/1170434. May 7, 2010.

16 Ibid., 382

17 Ibid.

18 Ibid., 508

19 Elliot W. Eisner, "Benjamin Bloom: 1913-99." *Prospects: The Quarterly
Review of Comparative Education,* Vol. 30, No. 3, 4. (September 2000): 1-7.
UNESCO: International Bureau of Education. http://www.ibe.unesco.org/
publications/ThinkersPdf/bloome.pdf. April 30, 2010.

20 Lorin W. Anderson, "If You Don't Know Who Wrote It, You Won't Under-

stand It: Lessons Learned from Benjamin S. Bloom." *Peabody Journal of Education*, Vol. 71, No. 1, Mentors and Mentoring (1996): 79. JSTOR. http://www.jstor.org/stable/1492555. April 30, 2010.

21 Fethullah Gülen, Universal Mercy and Education (2002c) http://www.fethullahgulen.org/recent-articles/1082-universal-mercy-and-education.html

22 Ibid., 206.

23 Fethullah Gülen, Cag ve Nesil, (Izmir, Turkey: Nil A.S., 2000), 102.

24 Phyllis J. Robinson, "Defining Ethos in Global Values Education." *Fethullah Gülen's Web Site – Alternative Perspectives of the Gülen Movement.* (November 15, 2008), 5. http://www.fethullahgulen.org/conference-papers/gulen-conference-in-washington-dc/3114-defining-ethos-in-global-values-education.html. May 10, 2010.

25 Fethullah Gülen, "Yaqin (Certainty)." The Meaning of Life, January 9, 2006. http://www.mlife.org/content/view/176/69/. May 11, 2010.

26 Fig. 1. Bloom's Taxonomy By Heather Coffey and further modified by YetkinYıldırım http://www.learnnc.org/lp/pages/4719

27 Holy Qur'an, 35:28

28 Fethullah Gülen, Cag ve Nesil, (Izmir, Turkey: Nil A.S., 2000),105.

29 Ibid., 2.

30 Nicholas Carr, *The Shallows: What the Internet is Doing to Our Brains.* (New York, NY: Norton, 2010).

31 Fethullah Gülen, Cag ve Nesil, (Izmir, Turkey: Nil A.S., 2000), 107.

32 Elliot W. Eisner, "Benjamin Bloom: 1913-99." *Prospects: The Quarterly Review of Comparative Education,* Vol. 30, No. 3 (September 2000): 4. UNESCO: International Bureau of Education. http://www.ibe.unesco.org/publications/ThinkersPdf/bloome.pdf. April 30, 2010.

33 Ronald J. Brandt, "On Talent Development: A Conversation with Benjamin Bloom." *Educational Leadership,* Vol. 43, Issue 1 (1985): 33. Professional Development Collection. http://ezproxy.lib.utexas.edu/login?url=http://search.ebscohost.com/login.aspx?direct=true&db=tfh&AN=8524769&site=ehost-live. May 6, 2010.

34 Ibid., 34.

35 Lorin W. Anderson, "If You Don't Know Who Wrote It, You Won't Understand It: Lessons Learned from Benjamin S. Bloom." *Peabody Journal of Education*, Vol. 71, No. 1, Mentors and Mentoring (1996): 82. JSTOR. http://www.jstor.org/stable/1492555. April 30, 2010. ,

36 Elliot W. Eisner, "Benjamin Bloom: 1913-99." *Prospects: The Quarterly Review of Comparative Education,* Vol. 30, No. 3 (September 2000): 4-6. UNESCO: International Bureau of Education. http://www.ibe.unesco.org/publications/ThinkersPdf/bloome.pdf. April 30, 2010.

37 Lorin W. Anderson, "If You Don't Know Who Wrote It, You Won't Understand It: Lessons Learned from Benjamin S. Bloom." *Peabody Journal of Education*, Vol. 71, No. 1, Mentors and Mentoring (1996): 80. JSTOR. http://www.jstor.org/stable/1492555. April 30, 2010.

38 Gülen, Fethullah. Cekirdekten Cinara, Bir Baska Acidan Aile Egitimi (From

a Seed to a Cedar Tree: Another Perspective of Family Education, in Turkish), (Izmir, Turkey: Nil A.S., 2002b), 83.

39 Ronald J. Brandt, "On Talent Development: A Conversation with Benjamin Bloom." *Educational Leadership,* Vol. 43, Issue 1 (1985): 34. Professional Development Collection. http://ezproxy.lib.utexas.edu/login?url=http://search.ebscohost.com/login.aspx?direct=true&db=tfh&AN=8524769&site=ehost-live. May 6, 2010.

40 Fethullah Gülen, *Education from Cradle to Grave.* Fethullah Gülen's Web Site (2004b). http://www.fethullahgulen.org/love-and-tolerance/274-education/1855-education-from-cradle-to-grave.html. May 17, 2010.

41 Gülen, Fethullah. "Cekirdekten Cinara, Bir Baska Acidan Aile Egitimi" (From a Seed to a Cedar Tree: Another Perspective of Family Education, in Turkish), (Izmir, Turkey: Nil A.S., 2002b), 74-75.

42 Benjamin S. Bloom, "The Master Teachers." *The Phi Delta Kappan*, Vol. 63, No. 10 (June 1982): 664-668. JSTOR. http://www.jstor.org/stable/20386506. May 3, 2010.

43 Ibid., 668.

44 Ibid.

45 Fethullah Gülen, *Essays, Perspectives, Opinions*, (Rutherford, NJ, 2002), 78.

46 Fethullah Gülen, *Cag ve Nesil*, (Izmir, Turkey: Nil A.S., 2000), 106.

47 Fethullah Gülen, *Essays, Perspectives, Opinions*, (Rutherford, NJ, 2002), 75.

48 Fethullah Gülen, *Cag ve Nesil*, (Izmir, Turkey: Nil A.S., 2000), 108.

49 Ibid., 103.

50 Ibid., 104.

51 Ibid., 110.

52 Fethullah Gülen, *Education from Cradle to Grave.* Fethullah Gülen's Web Site (2004b). http://www.fethullahgulen.org/love-and-tolerance/274-education/1855-education-from-cradle-to-grave.html. May 17, 2010.

Chapter Seven: Bandura

1 F. Pajares, "Albert Bandura: biographical sketch." 2004 http://des.emory.edu/mfp/bandurabio.html 7/21/10

2 Christine Foster, "Confidence man," *Stanford Magazine*. Sept/Oct. 2006. http://www.stanfordalumni.org/news/magazine/2006/sepoct/features/bandura.html

3 Ibid.

4 Ibid.

5 F. Pajares, "Albert Bandura: biographical sketch." 2004 http://des.emory.edu/mfp/bandurabio.html 7/21/10

6 Christine Foster, "Confidence man," *Stanford Magazine*. Sept/Oct. 2006. http://www.stanfordalumni.org/news/magazine/2006/sepoct/features/bandura.html

7 Albert Bandura, 1986). *Social Foundations of Thought and Action.* (Englewood Cliffs, NJ: Prentice-Hall, 1986), 104-105.

8 Ibid., 111.

9 Helen R. Ebaugh, *The Gülen Movement: A Sociological Analysis of a Civic*

Movement Rooted in Moderate Islam, (New York, NY: Springer, 2009).

10 Albert Bandura, *Social Foundations of Thought and Action*. (Englewood Cliffs, NJ: Prentice-Hall, 1986), 51.

11 Ibid., 18.

12 Ibid., 344.

13 Fethullah Gülen, "Child-Parents Relation or Interactions," *Prizma-2* Tr. Adembey/Aydin 2010: 13, para 5.

14 Albert Bandura, "Self-efficacy," In V. S. Ramachaudran (Ed.), *Encyclopedia of Human Behavior* (Vol. 4, pp. 71-81). New York: Academic Press. (Reprinted in H. Friedman [Ed.], *Encyclopedia of mental health*. San Diego: Academic Press, 1998), 71-81.

15 Albert Bandura, *Self-efficacy in Changing Societies*. (New York, NY: Thomas, 1995).

16 Albert Bandura, *Social Foundations of Thought and Action*, (Englewood Cliffs, NJ: Prentice-Hall, 1986), 399-401

17 Albert Bandura, *Social Learning Theory*. (New York, NY: General Learning Press, 1977). Also see Albert Bandura, 1986). *Social Foundations of Thought and Action*. (Englewood Cliffs, NJ: Prentice-Hall, 1986), 258.

18 Christine Foster, "Confidence man," *Stanford Magazine*. Sept/Oct. 2006. http://www.stanfordalumni.org/news/magazine/2006/sepoct/features/ bandura.html

19 Ibid.

20 Ibid., 86.

21 Fethullah Gülen, "Çekirdekten Çınara ,"(*Bir Başka Açıdan Ailede Eğitim*), (*From a Seed to a Cedar Tree: Another Perspective of Family Education*, in Turkish), Trans. Adem Akinci and A. Aydin (2010). Izmir, Turkey: Nil Yayinlari, 2002), 20.

22 Albert Bandura & Ted Rosenthal, "Vicarious Classical Conditioning as a Function of Arousal Level." *Journal of Social Psychology*, 1966 3, 54.

23 Albert Bandura, "Moral disengagement in the perpetuation of inhumanities." *Personality and Social Psychology Review*. Vol. 3, 1999): 193-20

24 Albert Bandura, "Moral disengagement in the perpetuation of inhumanities." *Journal of Moral Education*, 2002) *31*(2), 101-120.

25 Fethullah Gülen "Fasıldan Fasıla 2," *Perspective*, tr. Adembey/Aydin 2010 (The Sign of Maturity on the Line of Justice, 2007), 13.

26 Scott Atran, *Talking to the Enemy: Faith, Brotherhood, and the (Un)Making of Terrorists*. (New York, NY: Harper Collins, 2010). Atran's systemic analysis of terrorists and those left behind bear findings rich in substantiation of Bandura's Social Learning Theory and Social Cognition Theory, as Atran's conclusions reveal less about Islam's influencing violent acts than camaraderie elicited by football and films.

27 Albert Bandura, "Moral Disengagement in the Perpetuation of Inhumanities," *Personality and Social Psychology Review*, (Vol. 3,1999). 193-209.

28 Albert Bandura, A. "Moral Disengagement in the Perpetuation of Inhumanities." *Journal of Moral Education*, (*31*(2) 2002),101-120.

29 Albert Bandura, "Impeding Ecological Sustainability through Selective Moral

Disengagement." *Journal of Innovation and Sustainable Development*. (*2*(1), 2007) 8-35.

30 Albert Bandura, USC Award acceptance speech, 2007. Available online from Annenberg school of Communication, University of South California. http://www.des.emory.edu/mfp/BanduraAPA2004.html

31 Albert Bandura, "Moral disengagement in the perpetuation of inhumanities" *Personality and Social Psychology Review*. (Vol. 3, 1999). 198.

32 Fethullah Gülen, "Çekir Çınara," Being a Good Model. Tr. Adembey/Aydin Chapter 2, 2010: 27.

33 Fethullah Gülen, "Maarifimizde Muallim, *Sızıntı*, (1 December1979) Tr. Adembey/Aydin C: 11, V:1) 2010: 24.

34 Fethullah Gülen, http://www.Güleninstitute.org/index.php/Research-Projects/Research-Projects.html

35 Fethullah Gülen (Kalyoncu 2008). 36Fethullah Gülen, Interview with an educator who studied with Gülen and worked at college-prep tutoring centers with teachers inspired by Gülen. The educator wished to remain anonymous.

37 Zeki Saritoprak, "Introduction: Special issue on the Gülen movement." *Muslim World*. Guest Editor. (July, 2005).

38 Helen Rose Ebaugh, 2009) *The Gülen Movement: a Sociological Analysis of a Civic Movement Rooted in Moderate Islam*. (New York, NY: Springer, 2009).

39 Fethullah Gülen, Interview with Dr Adem Akinci, former faculty at Harran University who studied under Gülen.

40 Fethullah Gülen, "Bizim Maarifimiz -1, *Sızıntı*, 1 October 1979, C. 9, V:1. Tr. Adembey/Aydin 2010: 23

41 Ibid.

Chapter Eight: Moffett

1 James Moffett, *Teaching the Universe of Discourse*, (New York, NY: Houghton Mifflin, 1968b).

2 James Britton, Tony Burgess, Nancy Martin, Alex McLeod, Harold Rosen. *Development of Writing Abilities (11-18)*. (London, UK: Macmillan, 1975).

3 Koshnick, Damian. "Koshnick's_Visual_Biblio_Representing_Moffett_Publications." (2010) http://jamesmoffettstudies.ning.com/page/library-of-moffett-pdfs. May 10, 2010.

4 S. I. Hayakawa *Language in Thought and Action*. (New York, NY: Harcourt, Brace & World, Inc., 1941).
Hayakawa, 1941)

5 James Moffett, "Turning Language Upon Itself." *ETC.: A Review of General Semantics*. Vol. XVIII, No. 4, (San Francisco, CA: February 1962): 486-90.

6 James Moffett, *Teaching the Universe of Discourse*. (New York, NY: Houghton Mifflin, 1968b), 60-120. And James Moffett and Betty Jane Wagner *Student-Centered Language Arts, K-12*, 4ed. (New York, NY: Houghton Mifflin, 1992d).
(These resource books for teachers have since become classics. Current research on his work and a biography of all of Moffett's oeuvre are online

from the Moffett Archives, at University of Santa Barbara at endnote "3" above.

7 John Dixon, *Growth through English*. (Oxford, UK: Oxford U Pr., 1967).

8 James Moffett, *Teaching the Universe of Discourse*. (New York, NY: Houghton Mifflin, 1968b), 60-120.

9 L. E. W. Smith, *Toward New English Curriculum*. (London, UK: J. M. Dent & Sons Ltd., 1972).

10 James Britton, Tony Burgess, Nancy Martin, Alex McLeod, Harold Rosen. *Development of Writing Abilities (11-18)*. (London, UK: Macmillan, 1975).

11 Irvin Peckham, *State Direct Writing Assessment*. (Sacramento, California: State Department of Education, 1987) http://www.jstor.org/pss/819410 11/22/10

12 National Writing Project. http://www.nwp.org

13 Janet Emig, 2006. In conversation with author 30 September 2006.

14 Swami Sivalingam, *Wings of Divine Wisdom*, (Berkeley, CA: Prana Yoga Ashram, 1977).

15 James Moffett, *Coming on Center*, (Upper Montclair, NJ: Boynton/Cook, 1981), 133-181.

16 Betty Jane Wagner, James Moffett Memorial, 1997 National Convention, National Council of Teachers of English, Detroit, Michigan

17 cunepress, www.jimmoffett.org, 2004

18 Koshnick, Damian. "Koshnicks_Visual_Biblio_Representing_Moffett_Publica- tions." (2010) http://jamesmoffettstudies.ning.com/page/library-of-moffett- pdfs. May 10, 2010.

19 James Moffett, Keynote address before English Teacher Specialists. (Asilomar, CA, 1968).

20 James Moffett, *Active Voice*. 2ed. (Portsmouth, NH: Boynton/Cook Heine- mann, 1992a). Moffett, 1992a

21 James Moffett, *Active Voices I: A Writer's Reader for Grades 4-6*, (Upper Montclair, NJ: Boynton/Cook, 1987a). James Moffett, *Active Voices II: A Writer's Reader for Grades 7-9*, (Upper Montclair, NJ: Boynton/Cook, 1987a). James Moffett, *Active Voices I: A Writer's Reader for Grades 10-12*, (Upper Montclair, NJ: Boynton/Cook, 1987a). James Moffett, *Active Voices I: A Writer's Reader for College*, (Upper Montclair, NJ: Boynton/Cook, 1987a).

22 James Moffett, *Detecting Growth in Language*, (Portsmouth, NH: Boynton/ Cook Heinemann, 1992b).

23 James Moffett, *Points of Departure: an Anthology of Nonfiction*, (New York, NY: Mentor, 1985).

24 James Moffett and Kenneth McElheny, *Points of View: an Anthology of Short Stories*. 2ed. (New York, NY: Mentor1995).

25 Steven Johnson, *Future Perfect: The Case for Progress in a Networked Age*, (New York, NY: Riverhead Books, 2012).

26 James Moffett, "I/You/It." *College Composition and Communication*, Vol.

16, No. 5, (NCTE, Urbana: December1965) 243-48.

27 James Moffett, *Harmonic Learning: Keynoting School Reform.* (Portsmouth, NH: Boynton/Cook Heinemann), 1992c.

28 James Moffett, *The Universal Schoolhouse: Spiritual Awakening Through Education.* (San Francisco, CA: Jossey-Bass Publ., 1994).

29 James Moffett and Kenneth McElheny, *Points of View: an Anthology of Short Stories.* 2ed. (New York, NY: Mentor1995), 593.

30 Yüksel Aslandoğan and M. Çetin "The Educational Philosophy of Gülen in Thought and Practice." R. Hunt & Yüksel Aslandoğan, Eds. *Muslim Citizens of the Globalized World: Contributions of the Gülen Movement* (Somerset, NJ: The Light, 2006), 49.

31 James Moffett and Betty Jane Wagner, *Student-Centered Language Arts, K-12,* 4ed. (New York, NY: Houghton Mifflin, 1968), 72-83.

32 YetkinYıldırım, "Ethics in Engineering and Science: Fethullah Gülen's Model." Gülen Symposium, (Conference Proceeds: 7 October 24, 2009), 7. 28. Also see A. Berleant, *Art and Engagement*, (Philadelphia, PA: Temple U Pr. 1991) and *Aesthetics of Environment*, 1993.

33 Arnold Berleant, *Art and Engagement.* (Philadelphia, PA: Temple U Pr. 1991).

34 Louise Rosenblatt, *Literature as Exploration.* Revised Edition, (New York, NY: Noble & Nobel, 1968).

35 Louise Rosenblatt, *The Reader, the Text, the Poem*, (Carbondale, IL: So. Illinois U Pr., 1978).

36 Magdy Said, "Reading the World In Fethullah Gülen's Educational Philosophy," Second International Conference on Islam in the Contemporary World: The Fethullah Gülen Movement in Thought and Practice. March 4-5, 2006, Southern Methodist University, Dallas, TX. http://fethullahgulenconference.org/dallas/read.php?p=reading-world-fethullah-gulen-educational-philosophy

37 YetkinYıldırım, "Ethics in Engineering and Science: Fethullah Gülen's Model." Gülen Symposium, (Conference Proceeds: 7 October 24, 2009), 7.

38 James Moffett, "Writing, Inner Speech, and Meditation." Delivered at the Annual Convention of the California Association of Teachers of English, San Diego, 1979.

39 Fethullah Gülen, "Sacred, Secular, Twin Tolerations and the Hizmet," http://www.fethullahgulen.com/Video-Yazilari-Musluman-Olarak-Olmek/thought/pearls-of-wisdom/24526-morals

40 Fethullah Gülen, 2002: http://www.fethullahGülen.org/recent-articles/1082-universal-mercy-and-education.html

41 James Moffett, *Storm in the Mountains: a Case Study of Censorship, Conflict, and Consciousness.* (Carbondale, Ill: U of So. Illinois Pr.,1988).

42 James Moffett, "Censorship and Spiritual Education," *English Education*, Vol. 21, No. 2, (NCTE, May, 1989), 70-87.

43 Gülen, 2002b: http://www.fethullahGülen.org/recent-articles/1082-universal-mercy-and-education.html

44 Moffett, James, *Harmonic Learning: Keynoting School Reform*. (Portsmouth, NH: Boynton/Cook Heinemann, (1992c).

45 James Moffett, *Detecting Growth in Language*, (Portsmouth, NH: Boynton/Cook Heinemann, 1992b).

46 James Moffett, *The Universal Schoolhouse: Spiritual Awakening Through Education*. San Francisco, CA: Jossey-Bass Publ., 1994).

47 Ibid.

48 James Britton, et al. *Development of Writing Abilities (11-18)*. (London, UK: Macmillan, 1975).

49 William Wordsworth, Ode: Intimations of Immortality from Recollections of Early Childhood. http://www.bartleby.com/101/536.html

50 James Moffett, *The Universal Schoolhouse: Spiritual Awakening Through Education*. San Francisco, CA: Jossey-Bass Publ., 1994), 278-81.

51 John Dewey, *The Nature of Deliberation Human Nature and Conduct* Part 3: The Place of Intelligence: III. The Nature of Deliberation pp. para 9. http://www.brocku.ca/MeadProject/Dewey/Dewey_1922/Dewey1922_17.html

52 James Moffett, *Detecting Growth in Language*, (Portsmouth, NH: Boynton/Cook Heinemann, 1992b). Moffet.t 1992b

53 Judith Langer, and Arthur Applebee, *How Writing shapes thinking: a Study of teaching and learning*. Research Report No. 22. (Urbana, IL: NCTE, 1987).

54 Tom Gage, "Cross-Cultural Fluency: The Rhetoric of Dialogue." (July 2007) *The Journal of the Humanities*. Vol. 6 www.humanties-journal.com.

55 Tom Gage, "A Steady Digital Dialogue: Youth Building Peace in a Dark Time." Peacebuilding Through Education Conference. October, 2012. Time Center, New York City, Peace Island Institute, Yale University, Fountain Magazine, New York Institute of Technology. CCF Teams include the following: Dogan Koc, President of Houston's Gülen Institute; Mark Hertz, Arcata, CA and Marie Cecille Bauchant, Tangiers; Robert Jeffers, English Dept. Chair, Dorsey HS, LA; Tara Nuth, Fortuna HS, Fortuna CA; Anne Lorenzini-Boyers, Lysee Regnault, Morocco and Mark Hertz, Six Rivers; and Dr Janet Crane, Salem HS, Salem, Mass. http://www.peaceislands.org/locations/new-york/144-for-global-affairs/467-peacebuilding-through-education-conference-september-24-2012

56 Helen Rose Ebaugh, *The Gülen Movement: a Sociological Analysis of a Civic Movement Rooted in Moderate Islam*, (New York, NY: Springer, 2009).

57 James Moffett, *The Universal Schoolhouse: Spiritual Awakening Through Education*. San Francisco, CA: Jossey-Bass Publ., 1994).

Chapter 9: Social Constructionists

1 Jerome Bruner, *The Culture of Education*, (Cambridge, MA: Harvard University Press, 1996).

2 Jerome Bruner, *Acts of Meaning*, (Cambridge, MA: Harvard University Press, 1990), 138.

3 Jerome Bruner, *The Culture of Education*, (Cambridge, MA: Harvard University Press, 1996), 285-288.

4 Michael Cole and Sylvia Scribner, *Culture & Thought: a Psychological Intro-*

duction. (New York, NY: John Wiley & Sons, Inc., 1974).

5 Sylvia Scribner and Michael Cole, *The Psychology of Literacy*. (Cambridge, MA: Harvard U Pr, 1981).

6 Ibid., 74.

7 Barbara Rogoff, *The Cultural Nature of Human Development*. (New York, NY: Oxford University Pr, 2003), 42.

8 Ibid., 50.

9 Miles Myers, *Changing Our Minds: Negotiating English and Literacy*, (Urbana, IL: NCTE, 1996).

10 Jean Lave, Michael Murtaugh, and Olivia de la Rocha. "The Dialectic of Arithmetic in Grocery Shopping." *Everyday Cognition: its Development in Social Context*. Ed. Barbara Rogoff and Jean Lave. (Cambridge, MA: Harvard U Pr, 1984).

11 Barbara Rogoff, *The Cultural Nature of Human Development*. (New York, NY: Oxford U Pr, 2003), 50.

12 Fethullah Gülen, "Preparing the Environment for Education," (Çek. Çın., Chapter 3). Tr. Adembey/Aydin 2010

13 Jean Lave (http://www.lifecircles-inc.com/Learningtheories/constructivism/Lave.html).

14 Barbara Rogoff and Jean Lave, *Everyday Cognition: Its Development in Social Context*. (Cambridge, MA: Harvard U Pr.1984), 67-93. Also see Seth Chaiklin and Jean Lave, *Understanding Practice: Perspectives on Activity and Context*. (Cambridge, MA: Cambridge U Pr, 1993).

15 Dorothy Holland and Jean Lave, *History in Person: Enduring Struggles, Contentious Practice, Intimate Identities* (Santa Fe, NM: School of American Research Pr. 2000).

16 Ibid, 69.

17 Jean Lave, Michael Murtaugh, and Olivia de la Rocha. "The Dialectic of Arithmetic in Grocery Shopping." *Everyday Cognition: its Development in Social Context*. Ed. Barbara Rogoff and Jean Lave. (Cambridge, MA: Harvard U Pr, 1984), 67-94.

18 Barbara Rogoff and Jean Lave, *Everyday Cognition: Its Development in Social Context*. (Cambridge, MA: Harvard U Pr.1984), 56-94.

19 Miles Myers, *Changing Our Minds: Negotiating English and Literacy*, (Urbana, IL: NCTE, 1996), 198.

20 Barbara Rogoff, *Apprenticeship in Thinking*. New York, NY: Oxford University Pr, 1990), 141.

21 Ibid., Rogoff, 146). Also see Gülen Fethullah Gülen, "Child-Parents Relation or Interactions," *Prizma-2* Tr. Adembey/Aydin 2010: 13, para 5.

22 Ibid., 208.

23 Ibid.

24 Barbara Rogoff, C. Mosier, J. Mistry & A. Goncü, "Toddlers' Guided Participation in Cultural Activity," In E. Forman, N. Minick & A. Stone (Eds.), *Contexts for Learning: Sociocultural Dynamics in Children's Development*. (New York, NY: Oxford University Pr, 1993).

25 Miles Myers, *Changing Our Minds: Negotiating English and Literacy*,

(Urbana, IL: NCTE, 1996), 39-157.

26 Luis Moll, et.al, "Vygotsky in Classroom Practice: Moving from Individual Transmission to Social Transmission," in *Contexts for Learning*, E.A. Forman, et. al. New York, NY: Oxford University Pr, 1993), 21.

27 Jerome Bruner, "Prologue to the English Edition" *L.S. Vygotsky: Collected works*. Vol. 1 (New York, NY: Plenum, 1987), 1-16.

28 Luis Moll, et.al, "Vygotsky in Classroom Practice: Moving from Individual Transmission to Social Transmission," in *Contexts for Learning*, E.A. Forman, et. al. New York, NY: Oxford University Pr, 1993), 156.

29 Ibid.,154.

30 Peter Jarvis, "Learning to be a Person in Society: Learning to be Me." In K. Illeris, Ed. *Contemporary Theories of Learning: Learning Theorists—in Their Own Words*. (New York, NY: Routledge, 2009).

31 Jean Lave and Etienne Wenger, 2003, http://pubpages.unh.edu/~jds/CofPractice.htm

32 Jerome Bruner, "Prologue to the English Edition" *L.S. Vygotsky: Collected works*. Vol. 1 (New York, NY: Plenum, 1987), 80.

33 Jerome Bruner, *The Culture of Education*, (Cambridge, MA: Harvard University Press, 1996), and Jerome Bruner, *Acts of Meaning*, (Cambridge, MA: Harvard University Press, 1990).

34 Nel Noddings, *The Challenge to Care in Schools.* 2nd ed. (New York, NY: Teachers College Pr, 2005), 28.

35 Uri Treisman (http://www.utexas.edu/opa/experts/profile.php?id=397).

36 Nel Noddings, *Critical Lessons: What Our Schools Should Teach.* (Cambridge, UK: Cambridge University Press, 2006), 284.

37 Nel Noddings, ed. *Educating Citizens for Global Awareness.* 2nd. Ed. (New York, NY: Teachers College Pr, 2005), 173.

38 Ibid., 38).

39 Gurkin Celik and Yusuf Alan, "Fethullah Gülen as a Servant Leader," Second International Conference on Islam in the Contemporary World: The Fethullah Gülen Movement in Thought and Practice, March 4-5, 2006 Southern Methodist University, Dallas Texas.

40 James Moffett, *Detecting Growth in Language*, (Portsmouth, NH: Boynton/ Cook Heinemann, 1992), 30-32.

41 Robert Reich, *The Work of Nations: Preparing Ourselves for 21st Century Capitalism*. New York, NY: Vintage, 1992), 228-233.

42 Edward Said, *Humanism and democratic criticism*. (New York, NY: Columbia U Pr. 2004), 141-143.

43 Walter Mignolo, *Local Histories/Global Designs: Coloniality, Subaltern Knowledges, and Border Thinking*. (Princeton, NJ: Princeton U Pr, 2000).

44 For further readings in brain, brain/mind, neuro-linguistics, and insights into learning see George Lakoff, *Moral Politics: How Liberals and Conservatives Think*. 2ed Chicago, IL: U of Chi U Pr, 2002); George Lakoff, *Women, Fire, and Dangerous Things: What Categories Reveal about the Mind.* Chicago, IL: U of Chi U Pr, 1987); George Lakoff and Mark Johnson, *Metaphor We*

Live by. (Chicago, IL: U of Chi U Pr, 1980).
George Lakoff and Mark Johnson, 1980; George Lakoff and Mark Turner, *More than Cool Reason: a Field Guide to Poetic Metaphor.* (Chicago, IL: U of Chi U Pr, 1989);
Mark Johnson, *Moral Imagination: Implications of Cognitive Science for Ethics.* Chicago, IL: U of Chi U Pr, 1993); Antonio Damasio, *The Feeling of What Happens: Body and Emotion in the Making of Consciousness.* (New York, NY: Harcourt Brace & Co., 1999); Jack Fuller, *What is Happening to News: The Information Explosion and the Crisis in Journalism.* Chicago, IL: U of Chi Pr, 2010), and Nicholas Carr, *The Shallows: What the Internet is Doing to Our Brains.* (New York, NY: Norton, 2010).

44 Miles Myers, *Changing Our Minds: Negotiating English and Literacy,* (Urbana, IL: NCTE, 1996), 4.

45 Nel Noddings, *Critical Lessons: What Our Schools Should Teach. Cambridge,* (Cambridge, UK: Cambridge University Press, 2006).

46 Jerome Bruner, *The Culture of education,* (Cambridge, MA: Harvard University Press, 1996).

47 Ibid, 28.

48 Jerome Bruner, *The Culture of education,* (Cambridge, MA: Harvard University Press, 1996), 67fn.

49 Fethullah Gülen, "Çekirdekten Çinara," Chapter 5, (The Meaning of Reading) eds. & tr. Aydin & Adembey Chapter 3. 2010), 43.

50 Charles Murray, *Coming Apart: The State of White America, 1960-2010* (New York, NY: Crown Forum, 2012).

51 Carl Bereiter, "Rethinking Learning." In David R. Olson & Nancy Torrance (Eds.), *The Handbook of Education and Human Development.* (Oxford, UK: Blackwells, 1998), 485-513.

53 Charles Bazerman, *Shaping Written Knowledge: the Genre and Activity of the Experimental Article in Science.* Madison, WI: U of Wisconsin Pr. 1988). http://wac.colostate.edu/books/bazerman_shaping/ shaping.pdf. Also see Terry Myers Zawacki and Paul M. Rogers, Writing Across the Curriculum: a Critical Sourcebook. (New York, NY: St. Martin's Press, 2012).

54 James Thomas Zebroski, *Thinking through Theory.* (Portsmouth: Boynton/ Cook Heinemann, 1994), 277-284. Also see David Lodge, *After Bakhtin: Essays on Fiction and Criticism.* (London, UK: Routledge, 1990).

55 John Hardcastle, "With Genre in Mind: The Expressive, Utterance, and Speech Genres in Classroom Discourse." *Learning and Teaching Genre.* Ed. Aviva Freedman and Peter Medway. Portsmouth, ME: Boynton/Cook Heinemann, 1994). Also see Charles Bazerman, "Where Is the Classroom?" In Aviva Freedman & Peter Medway (Eds.), *Learning and Teaching Genre.* (Portsmouth, ME: Boynton/Cook Heinemann1994).

56 Adonis, *An Introduction to Arab poetics.* Tr. Catherine Cobham. London, UK: Saqi, 1990).

57 David Lodge, *After Bakhtin: Essays on Fiction and Criticism.* (London, UK: Routledge, 1990).

58 Gary Saul Morson, *Bakhtin: Essays and Dialogues on his Work.* (Chicago,

IL: U of Chi Pr, 1984).

59 Fethullah Gülen, "Çekir Çınara," Being a Good Model. Tr. Adembey/Aydin Chapter 2, 2010: 27.

60 Charles Bazerman, *Shaping Written Knowledge: the Genre and Activity of the Experimental Article in Science.* Madison, WI: U of Wisconsin Pr. 1988). http://wac.colostate.edu/books/bazerman_shaping/shaping.pdf

61 Charles Bazerman, "Where Is the Classroom?" In Aviva Freedman & Peter Medway (Eds.), *Learning and Teaching Genre.* (Portsmouth, ME: Boynton/ Cook Heinemann1994), 25-30. Also see Brian Boyd, *On the Origin of Stories: Evolution, Cognition, and Fiction.* Cambridge, MA: Belknap Pr, 2009).

62 Fethullah Gülen, "Çekirdekten Çinara," (Preparing the Environment for Education) eds. & tr. Aydin & Adembey Chapter 3. 2010), 20.

63 Tom Gage, in progress

64 Nel Noddings, *Critical Lessons: What Our Schools Should Teach. Cambridge,* (Cambridge, UK: Cambridge University Press, 2006).

65 Ibid., 36.

66 Muhammed Çetin, *The Gülen movement: Civic Service without Borders.* (New York, NY: Blue Dome Pr, 2010), 20.

67 Mehmet Kalyoncu, *A Civilian Response to Ethno-religious Conflict: the Gülen Movement in Southeast Turkey.* (Somerset, NJ: Light, 2008). Kalyoncu, 2008).

68 Fethullah Gülen, "Çekirdekten Çinara," (Preparing the Environment for Education) eds. & tr. Aydin & Adembey Chapter 3. 2010), 44.

69 Tzvetan Todorov, *The Conquest of America: the Question of the Other.* (Norman, OK: U of Oklahoma Pr, 1999), 41.

70 Wallace Stevens, "Six Significant Landscapes" in *Collected Poems* of *Wallace Stevens* (New York, NY: Knopt Inc., 1923).

71 Michael Hout and Stuart W. Elliott, Eds. *Incentives and Test-based Accountability in Education.* National Research Council of the National Academes. (Washington, DC: National Academes Press, 2011). Hout & Elliott, 5/16/2011, Incentives and Test-Based Accountability in Education, National Research Council of the National Academes).

72 Jean Lave and Etienne Wenger, *Situated Learning.* (Cambridge, UK: Cambridge U Pr. 1991), 121.

73 Ibid, 121.

74 Ibid, 43.

75 Fethullah Gülen, http://www.fethullahgulen.org/pearls-of-wisdom/1096-bringing-up-the-young.html

Chapter Ten: Conclusion

1 I've modified a seminal idea of the existentialist philosopher Martin Buber who formulated the concepts "Ich-Du" and "Ich-Es." Rather than limiting it to the mutuality of two being, I use the English equivalent I/It and I/Thou as ends of a spectrum of a communication system in teaching and education.

2 (Scholz 1998).

3 James Britton, Nancy Martin, Alex McCloud & Harold Rosen, *Development of*

Writing Abilities, London Schools Council, (London, UK: Macmillan, 1975), Fig. 13, 134.

4 (School and the Teacher, para. 7)

5 Ibid.

6 Bruce Novak and Jeffrey Wilhelm, *Literacy for Love and Wisdom: 'Being the Book' and 'Being the Change.'* (New York, NY: Teachers College Pr, 2011).

7 Dmitri Kitsikis, "Forward," in *The Ottoman Mosaic: Exploring Models for Peace by Re-Exploring the Past*. Eds. Kemal Karpat and YetkinYıldırım. (Seattle, WA: Cune Press, 2010), 13-21.

8 Wendi H. A. Anderson, An Articulation and Formalization of Kurt Hahn's Model of Adventure Education. Diss. La Sierra University, 2007.

9 Philip Phoenix, *Realms of Meaning: a Philosophy of the Curriculum for General Education*, (New York, NY: McGraw Hill, 1964). Also see Earl Minor, "That Literature is a Kind of Knowledge," Critical Inquiry, Vol. 2, Issue 3, (Spring 1976), 487-519.

10 Carl Bereiter, "Rethinking Learning." In David R. Olson & Nancy Torrance (Eds.), *The Handbook of Education and Human Development*. (Oxford, UK: Blackwells, 1998), 485-513.

11 Tom Gage, "Gülen como educador," Iniciativas Transnacionales de Educacion, Dialogo y Ayuda Humanitiaria: Movimiento Gülen, eds. Ali R. Candir and Juan Manuel Portilla Gomez, (Univerrsidad Nacional Autónoma de México Facultad de Estudios, 2012). Also see Tom Gage, "Gülen as an Educator," in *Hizmet Movement*, ed. Martin Marty, (Chicago, IL: Niagra Press, pending).

Index

A

American Psychological Association (APA), 94

Ankara, Turkey, 8, 14, 21, 46, 49, 97, 119, 122-125, 128-129, 132, 161, 163-164

Applebee, Dr. Arthur, 7, 17-18, 21-22, 40-43, 45, 47, 49-51, 53, 58, 67-68, 76-77, 79-81, 89-90, 94-95, 97-98, 101, 106-111, 116-117, 119-120, 124-125, 128-129, 134, 137, 146, 154, 158, 161-162, 165

Asilomar Conference, Pacific Grove, California, 108, 159

Aslandoğan, Yüksel, 138, 152, 160, 161

B

von Baden, Prince Max (See "von")

Bakhtin, Mikhail (Bakhtinian), 44, 112, 125-126, 128-129, 164

Bandura, Albert, 7, 17, 44-46, 50, 52-53, 55, 61, 67, 69, 75-76, 79-83, 85-87, 93-101, 103-105, 110, 112-114, 116, 119-120, 122, 124, 127, 129-130, 132-134, 149, 156-158, 164

Bazerman, Dr. Charles, 7, 48, 93, 106-111, 113, 115, 117, 123, 130, 138, 148, 150, 158-159, 164

behaviorists (behaviorism), 46, 68, 72, 94-95, 145, 152

Bereiter, Carl, 125-126, 164, 166

Berkeley, California, 8-9, 11, 47, 49, 108-110, 123, 159, 172

Bloom, Benjamin, 7, 16-17, 46, 48, 52, 61, 80-91, 106, 108, 116-117, 121, 130-134, 153-156

Britton, James, 47-49, 61, 99, 115, 117, 146, 158-159, 161, 165-166

Brown vs. Board of Education, 30, 49, 107, 114

C

Carroll, Dr. B. Jill, 13, 138, 148

Çetin, Dr. Muhammed, 1 (flyleaf), 138, 152, 160, 165

Chicago, University of, 21, 23-26, 75, 80, 141, 152

Chomsky, Noam, 25, 46-47, 78, 145

cognitive theory, 7, 17, 93-101, 103-105, 119, 127, 129, 132, 134, 156-158

Coleridge, Samuel Taylor, 19, 139

Columbia University, New York City, 23, 25, 93, 138-140, 142-144, 163

Columbine High School, 101

concrete operations stage (conventional), 7, 11, 17, 39, 47, 50, 67-79, 94-95, 112, 120-121, 132, 151-153

Confucius, 13-14

cross-cultural fluency (CCF), 117, 161

D

Dartmouth Conference, New Hampshire, 108, 115

decline of modern youth, 7, 17, 50, 55-66, 131-133, 147-150, 166

developmentalism, 7, 11, 17, 39, 47, 50, 67-79, 94-95, 112, 120-121, 132, 151-153

Dewey, John (Deweyan), 7, 11, 15-17, 19-30, 37, 45, 56, 63, 75-76, 78, 109, 111, 114, 116-117, 128-129, 132, 139-142, 161, 172

dhimma (or millet in Turkish), 10

Dialogic, 125-126, 128-129, 164

domains of knowledge, 7, 16-17, 48, 52, 61, 80-91, 116-117, 121, 130-134, 153-156

E

Ebaugh, Dr. Helen Rose, 138, 156, 158, 161

egocentric speech, 17, 42-54, 68, 72, 76-78, 93, 99, 110, 115-116, 119-122, 125, 132-133, 145-147, 151-153, 163

expeditionary learning principles, 7, 17, 50, 55-66, 131-133, 147-150, 166

F

formal operations stage (autonomous), 7, 11, 17, 39, 47, 50, 67-79, 94-95, 112, 120-121, 132, 151-153

G

gestalt psychology, 69, 72

Gordonstoun School, Moray, Scotland, 7, 17, 50, 55-66, 131-133, 147-150, 166

Gray, James, 11, 49, 108, 110, 159

Gülen (Hoja Effendi), 1, 3, 5-25, 27-31, 33-43, 45, 47-57, 59-67, 69, 71-75, 77-81, 83-91, 93, 95-117, 119-121, 123, 125-134, 136-141, 143-144, 146-153, 155-158, 160-166, 172

Gülen Institute, Houston, Texas, 9, 161

Gülersoy, Çelik, 9

"guinea pigs", 21-22, 106, 140

H

Hahn, Kurt, 7, 9, 13-14, 17-19, 21, 26, 29, 34, 37, 41, 50, 55-66, 75-77, 80-82, 84, 87, 89, 102, 106-107, 109-110, 114-117, 123, 127-128, 131-136, 143, 147-150, 159, 164, 166

Harvard University, Cambridge, Massachusetts, 7, 17, 29, 45, 47-49, 59, 62-63, 72, 106-117, 119, 122-125, 128-129, 131-134, 158-161, 163-164, 172

Hayakawa, S. I., 107, 158

Head Start Program, 6, 81, 88

Heteroglossia, 125-126, 128-129, 164

Hitler, Adolf, 56-57, 63, 132

Hizmet Movement, 1, 9, 13, 17, 60, 66, 110, 136-137, 160, 166

Holy Qur'an, 9-10, 13, 15, 23, 25, 80, 85-86, 109, 134-135, 138, 152, 155, 157-158, 160-161, 163

Hutchins, Robert Maynard, 21

I

I/It, 23, 165

I/Thou, 7, 9, 13-14, 17-19, 21, 23, 25-26, 29, 34, 37, 41, 45, 47-48, 52, 55-56, 58-59, 62-63, 72, 75-77, 80-82, 84, 87, 89, 102, 106-117, 123, 127-129, 131-136, 143, 158-161, 163-166, 172

Ibn Rushd (Averroes), 7, 12-13, 15, 17, 135

Ibn Sena *****

Index, 13, 20, 22, 55, 57, 140, 142, 148, 150, 158

inner speech, 17, 42-54, 68, 72, 76-78, 93, 99, 110, 115-116, 119-122, 125, 132-133, 145-147, 151-153, 163

Interfaith Council, 10, 131

Istanbul, Turkey, 9, 13

J

James, William, 55, 68, 94-95

Johns Hopkins University, 20

K

Kant, Immanuel, 7, 12-13, 15, 17, 73, 77

Kohlberg, Lawrence, 30, 75, 79, 152

L

Lab School, Chicago, Illinois, 24-26

Lave, Jean, 17, 47

Locke, John, 72, 78

London Schools Council, 47, 146, 166

M

Maimonides, 7, 9-10, 17-23, 25-26, 28, 31-35, 37, 39-43, 45-47, 49-51, 53, 55-59, 61-63, 67-68, 72, 75-83, 86-87, 89-90, 93-98, 100-101, 103, 105-114, 116-117, 119-120, 122, 124-126, 128-131, 133-134, 136-137, 141-142, 145-146, 152-154, 157-158, 161-162, 164-165

mastery learning, 7, 16-17, 48, 52, 61, 80-91, 116-117, 121, 130-134, 153-156

Middle Ages, 10, 135

Mill, John Stuart, 13

millet (or dhimma in Arabic), 10

Moffett, James, 7, 14, 17, 19, 22, 25-26, 29-30, 32, 34, 37, 41, 43, 45, 47-48, 59, 62-63, 72, 78, 90, 93, 106-118, 122-123, 128-134, 136, 138, 148, 150-151, 158-161, 163-164, 172

Montessori, Maria (The "Montessori Method"), 7, 11, 16-19, 21, 23, 26, 28, 31-41, 45-47, 49-50, 55-57, 61-63, 76-80, 103, 107-111, 114, 126, 131, 133-134, 136, 142-144, 172

moral education, 13, 65

Moscow, Russia, 42

Muslim (Islam), 9-10, 13, 15, 23, 25, 80, 85, 109, 134-135, 138, 152, 157-158, 160-161, 163

N

National Council of Teachers of English (NCTE), 108-109, 146, 160-164

National Defense Education Act (NDEA), 107-108

National Writing Project, 11, 49, 108, 110, 159

nativism, 72
Neuchatel, University, Switzerland, 7, 11, 17, 39, 47, 50, 67-79,
94-95, 112, 120-121, 132, 151-153
No Child Left Behind, 6, 77, 81,
88
Novak, Dr. Bruce, 11, 17, 27, 47,
108-109, 138, 141, 146, 160-164,
166
orders of knowledge, 7, 17, 29,
45, 47-48, 59, 62-63, 72, 106-117,
128-129, 131, 133-134, 158-161,
163, 172

O
Outward Bound schools, 7, 17, 50,
55-66, 131-133, 147-150, 166

P
Paris, France, 8, 23, 68, 111, 151,
165
Philips Exeter Academy, 106
Piaget, Jean, 7, 11, 17, 23, 39, 47,
50, 67-79, 94-95, 112, 120-121,
125-126, 132, 151-153
preoperational stage (pre-moral),
7, 11, 17, 39, 47, 50, 67-79, 94-95,
112, 120-121, 132, 151-153
Progressive Education Association
(PEA), 21
Prophet Muhammad, 24
Psychological Institute of Moscow,
42

R
Renaissance, 76
Rome Sapienza, University of, 31
Rosenblatt, Dr. Louise, 27-29, 112,

141-142, 160
Round Square model, 7, 17, 50,
55-66, 131-133, 147-150, 161, 166
Rousseau, Jean-Jacque, 20, 68

S
Said, Edward, 9, 20, 75, 78, 112,
138, 160, 163
Salem School, Bavaria, Germany,
56, 61, 132, 161
San Francisco, California, 8, 10,
107, 152, 158, 160-161
Sartre, Jean-Paul, 10, 13
schools, 13, 65
self-efficacy theory, 7, 17, 93-101,
103-105, 119, 127, 129, 132, 134,
156-158
sensori-motor stage, 7, 11, 17, 39,
47, 50, 67-79, 94-95, 112, 120-
121, 132, 151-153
Seoul, Korea, 8
Skinner, B. F., 46, 72, 94-95, 99,
145, 152
social learning theory, 7, 17, 93-
101, 103-105, 119, 127, 129, 132,
134, 156-158
Squire, Dr. James R., 108
St. Thomas Aquinas, 135
Stanford University, 7, 17, 93-101,
103-105, 119, 123-125, 127-129,
131-132, 134, 156-158, 163-165
Steiner, Rudolph, 76
Sufi (Sufism), 10, 13, 18, 39, 52,
63, 78, 80, 85, 106
Sun Yat-Sen, 26

T
taxonomy of cognition and emo-

tion (cognitive and affective domains), 7, 16-17, 48, 52, 61, 80-91, 116-117, 121, 130-134, 153-156

Terman Study, 7, 17-18, 21-22, 40-43, 45, 47, 49, 51, 53, 58, 67-68, 76-77, 79-81, 89-90, 94-95, 97-98, 101, 106-111, 116-117, 119-120, 124-125, 128-129, 134, 137, 146, 154, 158, 161-162, 165

Transactional theory, 11, 27-29, 93, 96, 98, 104, 116, 132, 140-141

Treisman, Uri, 17, 47, 93-94, 123, 140, 156-157

Turkey, Republic of, 8, 12-14, 16, 27, 31, 39, 57, 84, 97, 103-104, 125, 132, 138, 140-141, 146-148, 153, 155-157, 165, 172

U

University of California at Berkeley, 8-9, 47, 108, 123, 159, 172

University of Texas, 123, 163

verbal thought, 17, 42-54, 68, 72, 76-78, 93, 99, 110, 115-116, 119-122, 125, 132-133, 145-147, 151-153, 163

V

von Baden, Prince Max, 7, 17, 50, 55-66, 131-133, 147-150, 166

Vygotsky, Lev (Vygotskian), 7, 17, 42-54, 68, 72, 76-78, 93, 99, 109-110, 113-116, 119-122, 125, 132-133, 145-147, 151-153, 160, 163

W

Willis, Margaret, 21-22, 106, 140, 153-154

World War I, 26, 55

World War II, 10, 56, 69

Y

yaqin , 16, 39, 52, 85, 132, 146-147, 155

Yildirim, Yetkin, 6, 69

Z

Zone of Proximal Development (ZPD), 17, 42-54, 68, 72, 76-78, 93, 99, 110, 115-116, 119-122, 125, 132-133, 145-147, 151-153, 163

Tom Gage

Professor Tom Gage has enjoyed a successful half-century career in education and taught graduate courses for over three decades at Humboldt State University. His interests range from John Steinbeck to Captain Bill Jones, a colorful figure from the life of Andrew Carnegie. Dr. Gage's book *Gülen's Dialogue on Education: A Caravanserai of Ideas* is a freewheeling exploration that connects the educational innovator James Moffett to the Turkish educator and inspirational figure Fethullah Gülen to John Dewey to Montessori and more.

Gage has been involved with the Middle East since the 1950s. Following a year of hitchhiking that landed him in Damascus in 1959, he returned to the University of California at Berkeley where earned BA, MA, and PhD degrees. He is a Fulbright scholar who taught in Aleppo, Syria for an academic year in 1983 and has also taught in China, Turkey, and Greece.

In the 1970s, Gage served as dean of three summer programs held in eight European nations. He has authored, co-authored, and edited / consulted on twenty books. In 2013, his e-book American Prometheus was recognized with two Silver awards from the Independent Book Publishers Association, one in history for "eLit Illuminating Digital Publishing Excellence" and the other for the "Best Regional E-Book" for the eastern region of the US. For more: www.gagepage.org

As Professor Emeritus of the California State University system, Gage continues to teach in the Osher Lifelong Learning Institute at the Humboldt campus. Over the last decades, he has interviewed academics and authors on TV and has initiated and participated in the development of software that won the "Best of the Best Award in Educational Software" of the Association of Supervision and Instruction for the year 2000.